The World Up Close

A Cyclist's Adventures on Five Continents

Kameel B. Nasr

Mills & Sanderson, Publishers
Bedford, Massachusetts

Copyright © 1990 by Kameel B. Nasr

All rights reserved. No part of this publication may be reproduced or transmitted in any form or by any means electronic or mechanical, including photocopy, recording or any information storage and retrieval system, without permission in writing from the publisher. First published in 1990 in a paperbound edition by Mills & Sanderson, Publishers, Box 665, Bedford, MA 01730.

LIBRARY OF CONGRESS
Library of Congress Cataloging-in-Publication Data

Nasr, Kameel B., 1949-
    The world up close : a cyclist's adventures on five continents / Kameel B. Nasr.
    p. cm.
    ISBN 0-938179-20-9 : $9.95
    1. Bicycle touring. 2. Voyages around the world. 3. Cognition and culture. I. Title.
GV1044.N37 1990
796.6'4--dc20   89-12539
                                                                      CIP

Printed and Bound in the United States of America

Cover photo and maps by Kameel Nasr.
Cover design by Lyrl Ahern.
Printed and manufactured by Thomson-Shore, Inc., Dexter, MI.

To those who helped me find my way, who fed me, filled my water bottles, told me about their country, gave me a bed, talked with me in sign language, and laughed with me.

Special thanks to Janet Boyter, Nancy Freehafer, Dina Lawrence, and Pamela Sourelis who read the manuscript and made penetrating comments. Dina worked on it twice.

Table of Contents

Novitiate: Stumbling Through Wyoming ... 1

First Journey

Appalachian Back Roads ... 15
A Jungle Rider Attacks Europe ... 29
Yugoslavia: Through the Dark Forest ... 39
Two Wheels Over the Sinai ... 49
Gods and Mortals in Southern India ... 65
Arkansas Accident ... 81

Second Journey

In and Out of Hades: Central America ... 89
Riding the Spine of the Andes ... 111
East African Swamps ... 137
Near the Lion's Roar ... 151
The Hashish Trail ... 161
Lines Written on a Ferry from Tunis to Palermo ... 179
Climbing the High Road ... 181
Chinese in a Bad Tone ... 197

Afterword: Seventy Words for Water ... 209

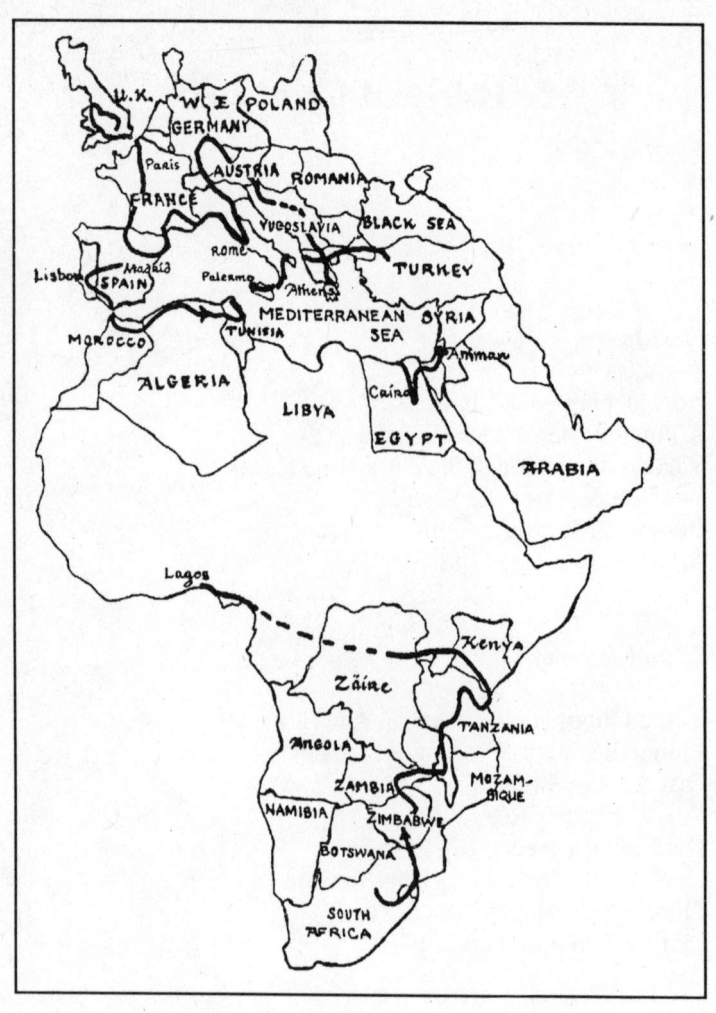

Routes through Europe, Africa and the Middle East

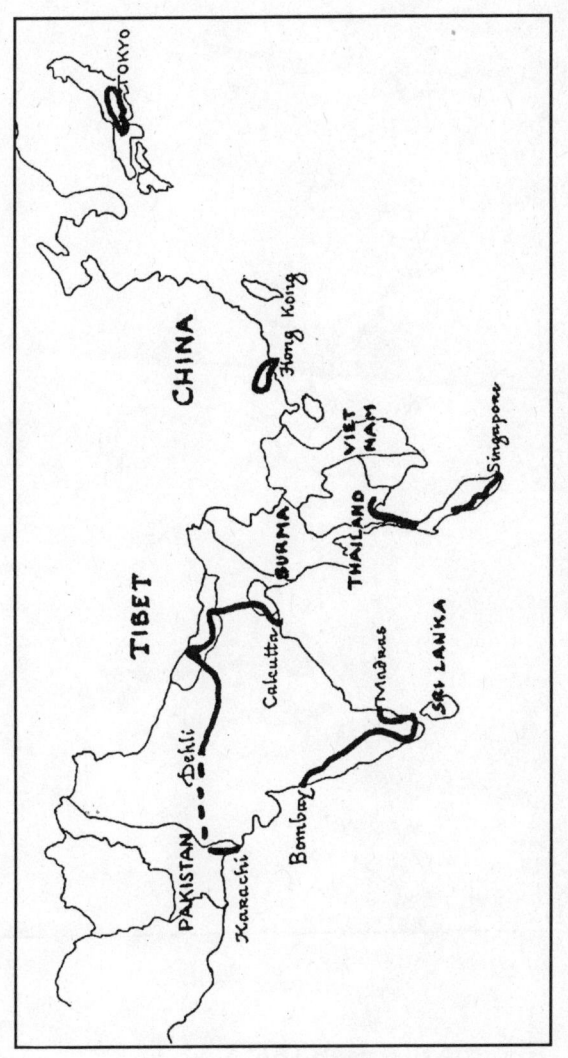

Routes in Asia

Routes through the Americas

Novitiate:
Stumbling Through Wyoming

On the empty shoulder of westbound I-80 I sensed the morning sun thawing my back as I perpetually pedaled into my solitary shadow. Tractor trailers four times my height rushed past, screamed past, each one throwing a wall of air that pushed me to the edge of the road followed by a momentary interval of quiet, a welcome relief from the constant wind I had to struggle against. I was fresh, green: a beginner intimidated by the wind and the mountains and the loneliness of the Wyoming wilderness.

My first long trip through America started in Chicago. After riding through Iowa and Nebraska I faced mountainous Wyoming on the shoulder of the interstate, the only road. A barren experience. Nothing around me was alive. The merciless sun sapped water out of my body. My lungs strained for the thin mountain air. My heart thumped forcefully in my thighs on upgrades. Salty sweat mingled with dust and dirt ran down my forehead and burned into my eyes. At night the air froze my hands and feet.

I fought an invisible brutal wind which forced me into my low gears, making me struggle over each inch of concrete road. It created an endless deafening drone in my ears, a roar more engulfing than the sound of a cathedral organ overpowering the singing of a community of believers. A person bicycling alone can do nothing but participate in sounds. Legs pedal themselves, lungs breathe on their own, the mind jumps from thought to thought and song to song, automatically. Mind and heart and sound fuse. I no longer know whether I think or I feel or I hear.

The interstate is an unpleasant bicycling experience. I was too impractical to bicycle properly, wearing clothes that flapped in the wind, carrying a bunch of inappropriate heavy equipment, having no detailed maps and only one water bottle, too inexperienced to know how to deal with this type of adversity, this type of loneliness.

Before reaching Wyoming I had bicycled through a delightful quiet on back roads in Iowa and Nebraska. I had heard the sound of tires turning on the road, the sound of the freewheel clicking when I stopped pedaling, sometimes a rattling in my handlebar bag: quiet sounds that mingled with the sound of tranquil thought. On quiet roads I could hear an approaching car a half mile away. It changes the countryside and drowns the sound of thought until it vanishes and the wind erases all evidence of its having been there, leaving a deeper and more profound silence.

Being alone becomes a state of mind. I know family people who live alone, school teachers and ministers and social workers who live as alone as hermits. I, too, had known many kinds of solitude and many kinds of silences: the desert, the forest, the abbey. I'd been alone all my life. I had seen other people with life-long friends, but at twenty-nine my only friend was my new bicycle, and it had no choice. I bought it two weeks before leaving Chicago, and we were both making our first long trip, together. I was full of the fanaticism of the newly converted: fresh and wild and ignorant. Somewhere in Iowa I called the bicycle Angel. I'm not sure what inspired the name; I certainly had no intention of giving a piece of metal an identity, but it's important to develop relationships. Most people have a relationship with another human. Some keep a dog or a cat.

It was a stock blue Fuji touring bicycle, a solid frame with standard Japanese parts. I spent all the money I had on it, but I couldn't afford pannier saddle bags, so I used cumbersome eight dollar metal shopping baskets from Sears. I bought a fluorescent yellow bag at the Maxwell Street flea market for two dollars, tied it to the handlebar with string, and stuffed it with equipment that I never did use. Except for gloves, I had no bicycling clothing. I knew nothing about the extra wind drag that T-shirts cause, but I appreciated the necessity of gloves; previously I had taken a short trip to Wisconsin without them, hurt the nerve in my hand, and lost the feeling in my fingers for a month. I used my running shoes and shorts and brought neither tent nor sleeping bag. Doing it the hard way, I thought, had to be part of the experience.

Angel shined then, and I treated it gently, leaned it gingerly on the wall and wiped off marks from the frame, never keeping it out of my sight when I had to go inside a store. Now it looks like an old work horse when I ride it next to bicycles of gleaming metal and bright paint. I've replaced every moving part many times since then, been through four or five clusters of gears on the rear wheel, and through countless tires. But on the first trip I knew little about its mechanics and had no tools to make basic adjustments. Foolish and serious Angel and I were then, with the enthusiasm of beginners, and we worked together for the next 80,000 miles, touring, training, and commuting.

I wanted to travel the world — that was my aim even then — but at that time I had no need for comfort or short cuts. I didn't need a radio for company or camera to prove to others that I'd been there: nothing extraneous for travel. I wanted not only to see the world, I wanted to feel it — the joy and the travail — bring myself close and touch it and have it touch me, engulf me. Eyes open, ears open, mind open, always listening, always seeing, always contemplating, always comparing, always working.

A few hours after I crossed into Iowa south of Dubuque I saw a man in overalls getting off a faded red tractor outside his farm house. I stopped and shouted "hello," asking if I could have water. The man had to quiet his German shepherd that was almost breaking its leash to jump on me. Dogs hate bicyclists. He signaled me to come over after giving stern words to the shepherd.

"You picked a hot day to be bicycling," he said seeing me empty the bottle.

"It's cooler riding a bike than standing still. The wind can feel like an ocean breeze."

The dog sniffed my shopping baskets. The farmer refilled my water bottle from the hose in his vegetable garden and asked me where I was going.

"San Francisco," I replied.

"That's mighty far, and across the Rockies. Can you go over the mountains on that thing?"

I had done no homework on my route, and this was the first time that I had to think about the Rockies. I didn't know how to respond. "Other people have crossed the country by bicycle, dozens of others. Only a hundred years ago people were walking across."

"What do you do, just get on any road and follow it?"

"I have maps. I pick the small roads, roads that were once pioneer trails, the Overland Express, the Mormon Trail."

He looked surprised that I could still stand and was smiling, got me more water, and paused. "Just what is it you're trying to do, go somewhere or get away from something else?"

"I'm just trying to find out how people live, the farmers and townspeople."

"Can't you do that by staying in the same place? It would be a lot easier."

Questions like those prove too deep for a novice to answer casually. It's possible to read about corn farming in Iowa and see pictures of ranchers. Or I could have taken an easier form of transportation to travel the world. A motorcycle would be faster and more convenient. A car would protect me from the elements. And if I were to tell you the truth, I would have to admit that many times when I'm struggling in deserts where my throat is cracked, through cold rain or hail or snow, through areas where I've picked up an unpleasant tropical disease, when I'm perspiring and dirty — God do I get dirty — in war torn areas or areas infamous for thievery, when I look down dirt or mud roads and up steep grades, then I too doubt if I should be on a bicycle instead of a more conventional and trouble-free form of transportation, or better yet, I wish I had never started. I often have fantasies of ending it: getting on a plane or a train, sleeping on a soft bed, drinking unquestionably clean water, and having someone carry my bags and serve me a decent meal.

But the day I entered Iowa I was frenzied with energy, hammering on the pedals, putting in a vigorous 130 miles on various farm roads by mid-afternoon, passing field after field of tasseled corn, groups of pigs, herds of cattle, and clusters of buildings that comprise a family farm: a frame house, barn, metal silo, sheds. Two hours before sundown I was spent. I sat under a tree and pulled out peanut butter and whole wheat bread from the metal baskets. A boy and girl about thirteen or fourteen years old, rode up the narrow asphalt road, stopped in front of me, looked me over, and politely asked me questions about where I was from and where I was going. The boy told me that that spring he had gone on a five-day bicycle tour with a church youth group.

"You look tired," the boy said. "Where you planning to sleep tonight?"

"Don't know. I usually don't think about that until near sundown. I can camp anywhere."

"I'll see if my father can help you," he said, and the two of them bicycled west, back the way they had come.

A few minutes later I got up and followed them, encountering the mother and father and their two children on bicycles on the other side of a bridge. The father asked me the same questions his son had, then invited me to stay with them for the night. I accepted eagerly. It was to be the first of hundreds of such invitations.

"We have a farm just a couple of miles from here. Do you think you can make it that far?" the mother asked.

"I'll give you a half mile head start and race you there," I replied.

The kids and I zig-zagged around each other down the road. After a stretch we hit dirt and turned left to a pig and corn farm. Before we got off the bicycles I said to the father, "I've been a city person. In Illinois farmers have been telling me about growing corn. I'd love to learn how you raise pigs."

The father, an upright, slender man in his mid-forties who sported a trimmed beard and spoke without emotion, looked at me directly and said, "I'll be glad to show you everything you need to know about pigs. We're Mennonites. We've been doing this for hundreds of years."

He took me to the pen where he showed me his stock, about 200 pigs in an area a quarter the size of a football field.

"That's the feed house," he said pointing to a metal structure that sat half in and half out of the pen. "We give them a mixture of corn and oats and vitamins: good feed. It costs us more, but we produce good pigs. The corn growing over there feeds the stock, though most years we have to buy more."

He took me to another enclosure where a large pig ran back and forth inside the wooden fence.

"He's the daddy. We just got him. Cost fifteen hundred."

My host climbed in the pen and began playing with the pig, making him run around in the dirt while pointing out to me the shape of his shoulders and legs and hind parts, qualities that make him a good breeder.

"We want to raise meat, not fat," he said. "A lot of other farmers give pig farming a bad name. To them it's a business, getting the most out of the least; to us it's our life's work."

Then he took me into a room about the size of a small hangar made out of galvanized metal.

"This is the breeding room," he said.

Clean cemented aisles separated four neat rows of stalls covered with hay. The screeches of pigs echoed off the metal walls, drowning out the sound of the air exchange fans. Troughs of water and feed ran through the room. My host and his son took me to a stall where a hefty sow lay exhausted after giving birth. The sow looked too weak to move or groan. The son counted the litter and exclaimed excitedly that the sow had sixteen little ones. A smile appeared on the father's otherwise expressionless face.

They carried three newborns from another stall into a room off to the side. Medicines and sterile products lined the shelves, making it look like a doctor's office. The father took out a syringe, filled it from a bottle, and gave each animal an injection. While the son held each pig upside down in his arms, the father took a surgical knife and cut each of their testicles and removed the two tiny organs, covering the wound with antiseptic. The pigs didn't seem to notice what happened.

"It's mostly to prevent disease," the father explained.

I wondered if it would make them sing better. "How long do they live before they're ready for market?" I asked.

"In six months they're about 220 pounds. That's the best weight."

"Only six months of life," I said astounded.

"We put them in that trailer and take them to town every couple of weeks," the son told me.

"Lots of folks are so removed from what they eat," the father said. "They think meat grows in the back of the supermarket and comes in plastic wrappers. I hope that you know more about pork now."

We went inside and found that the mother and daughter had laid out dinner. Everyone sat down, prayed, and took up fork and knife. I looked down on my plate and saw a large, thick slab of dark pink next to the white mashed potatoes and green peas.

"Everything on the table comes from the farm," the father said.

They explained to me that the Mennonites settled in that area last century, but since then the group had divided into reformed Mennonites such as themselves, and the more conservative group who live like the Amish.

"A Mennonite is a farmer," the father said.

None of us left anything on our plates.

Toward the end of dinner the father turned to me and asked, "What kind of meat do you eat in Chicago?"

I probably blushed. "I guess most people in Chicago eat beef." I didn't mention that I'm a vegetarian except when I stay on a pig farm.

The next morning, my energy regenerated, I pedaled robustly across the hot farmlands, stopping whenever I saw someone to ask about the roads and the crops. Although it was a month before harvest, everyone was predicting a near-record year for corn growers, but the farmers were complaining that that would drive the price of corn unacceptably low. After a couple of days I crossed into Nebraska, feeling the summer sun becoming more intense as I moved west. People began talking about the heat and drought.

"All the hay's been ruined this year," said one blond Polish farmer in a matter of fact tone. "Lots of folks going broke. People say that the drought's going to be worse in years to come."

But for cross-country bicycling Iowa and Nebraska were wonderful places: miles and miles of solitary open space. I got on one small farm road after another, over one rolling hill after another, where I pedaled, listened, and developed my relationship with Angel, encountering almost no traffic, perhaps a car an hour. I would see someone working the field, and we would exchange greetings, or a car would pass me, and we would wave to each other.

People in each part of the country have a way to wave and say hello. In some places you're supposed to lift the index finger above the handlebar or steering wheel and not look too interested. Other places require turning the wrist or nodding the head with eyes averted. Some places you just say "mornin'," while other places add a "good." You're supposed to smile in parts of the country, but that might mean you're peculiar in other parts. You can offend people by being friendly in some places.

The northern part of Nebraska requires a full-fledged wave, smile, and if you can, a hello. When I see another bicyclist in the city we don't even nod our heads or lift the index finger. But if we meet on the open road we don't just wave, we stop and talk, sometimes for a half hour or more, or we ride together if we're going the same way. On country roads other bicyclists become part of a common experience, but in less populated areas each person — old or young, male or female — is also part of that experience. We share something, our human condition or our need to talk, like dogs share their dogness. When you don't see many people, each human encounter becomes significant. We don't have to share the same political beliefs or share a similar hobby or pinpoint a common idiosyncrasy through which to approach each other: being human is enough.

I bicycled south to the North Platte River and began pedaling on a much busier road that paralleled I-80. The rolling hills of northern Nebraska ended, and the slow, imperceptible upward cycle toward the Rockies began. The quiet farm roads turned into a well-traveled one. I saw pairs of bicyclists coming from the west. Two by two they made their way on the Bicentennial Trail across the country. They would stop across the road for a chat, gazing in amazement at my metal shopping baskets and running shoes and the string holding my handlebar bag. I, in turn, would look at their clean panniers and unwrinkled clothing. They would ask me embarrassing questions, such as how I camp, what I would do if it rained, why I'm traveling alone. Eventually I would just say that I am from the area making a casual one-day trip. I didn't see any other lone bicyclist, or anyone with my type of equipment.

I didn't feel the uphill grade of the road until I looked over at a sign announcing a dirt runway airport that gave an elevation of over 4000 feet. Then the road turned a sharp left and fed into I-80, giving me no choice but to take to the shoulder. A half mile later I got excited when I saw a billboard cowboy riding a bucking bronco and waving his hat next to the words: "Welcome to Wyoming, the Cowboy State."

The thrill of coming to the fourth state of my trip made me begin cycling with tireless gusto, singing loudly to myself, and waving at drivers with unwarranted enthusiasm. I must have looked a little crazy. I suppose I was. I was so happy — joyous, ecstatic — about riding on an uninviting road with expressway litter, a dearth of scenery, and screaming trucks blasting wind that almost knocked me over.

In an hour an orange sun hung just above the interstate, and I rode uphill in front of my long, hazy shadow. Taking a turnoff before Cheyenne I found a place where the tall yellow grass would hide me from the road. I carefully set Angel down, foolishly drank my remaining water, and pulled out my two light blankets from those ridiculous metal baskets. I laid down on a plastic tarp that I had used for house painting and used a T-shirt on top of my shoes for a pillow.

While the sun gave its last light I brought out my maps and studied them, something I would do night after night for many nights to come, studying all the possible routes, putting the map down and picking it up again to re-study and stare at the same place with a mind full of different possibilities. Hours and hours of reading maps, of feeling the accomplishment of passing this city and this county that day, of having gone a tenth, a quarter, two-thirds of the way to my destination. I drifted off to sleep with a proud feeling, my satisfaction keeping me oblivious to the intense mountain cold that came with the darkness.

Dawn jolted me awake. The crop-destroying heat wave that had been pounding the Midwest all summer became a distant memory. I wrestled out of my tentless campsite and rode shivering to a truck stop. My legs could hardly turn the pedals, my fingers too numb to squeeze the brakes.

"We ain't seen this kind of cold this time of year," said the woman behind the counter who wore a peach-colored smock. "But don't you fret, it's going to heat up plenty soon."

She wasn't lying. When my toes thawed I started riding on a local road through Cheyenne. By the time I was on the other side of the city the sun became a blinding ball of heat; the cold air that came in the night vanished into the mountains, and my hard times began.

I stood straddling my bicycle looking at an isolated junction. The map I had picked up from the tourist office in Cheyenne told me I could either go straight back to the interstate or turn right to a secondary road that would take me part of the way through Wyoming, passing Medicine Bowl National Park. The small road looked longer, but I took it without hesitation and without asking anyone about it.

Hitting the Wyoming mountains after Cheyenne was like beginning to run by entering a marathon. I had trained in Chicago, riding my bicycle everywhere during every season, cycling twenty-five or fifty miles every day. But Chicago is sea level flat; to train on hills you have to go to a street that goes under a train tunnel and then climbs a two percent grade over an expressway. You have to pedal up, turn around when the traffic is clear, coast down, and again wait for the traffic, back and forth over the quarter-mile hill until you're sick of it. There's nothing better for a hundred miles, but the hills that faced me made that overpass seem like walking up to the first floor of a skyscraper.

The road wound around the clay mountains, passing vistas of open land scattered with scrub brush and tumbleweed which sat on the surface of the hard earth and looked as if it was ready to blow away. A few gaunt herds of cattle grazed on the austere vegetation. By mid-morning the wind whipped around the hills, searching me out and hitting me in the face with its total ferocity. I emptied my water bottle in the first few miles, having to stop several times along the way to give my lungs a chance to grab the thin air.

Two hours after noon I couldn't go any further. I wasn't sure if it was because of the heat, the altitude, my parched throat, the wind, or the loneliness. Quiet roads, dry roads are wonderful cycling experiences. Desert trips are often the most rewarding. But what do you do in the middle of Wyoming on a deserted road when you can't go farther, when you have to beat the pedals for every inch of road, where a pleasant trip turns into an agony? You have to continue.

I had no idea how many miles I had gone; the road seemed never to end — just wind and mountains and my baked throat. When the road turned into dirt, something my map didn't show me, I clenched my teeth and loosened my toe straps and cursed Wyoming.

By late afternoon the drone of the wind quieted slightly, and I felt relieved to hear the roar of expressway trucks. I promised myself that never again would I leave the safety and convenience and smoothness of the paved road to be alone in the mountains. I stopped at a gas station at the edge of the expressway, drank two liters of foul-tasting water, and spent well over my three dollar a day budget on plastic food.

"Doesn't the wind ever come out of the east?" I asked the attendant.

"When it does you don't want to be here," he said. "Ain't often that I see bicyclists, but when I do they come the other way. I don't understand why you guys wouldn't be afraid to ride on the expressway."

"I never have been afraid. But I have an entire lane. I have to be careful at turnoffs and avoid pieces of truck tires, dead animals, and beer bottles."

Wind is the biggest obstacle to bicyclists. Energy is lost to friction between the wheels and the pavement, to friction in the moving parts, and to the bending of the frame. Except on dirt roads, friction is insignificant compared to the energy lost from the wind. It takes eight times as much energy to go against a ten mph wind as with it. If the wind is twenty mph it is like the difference between going up and down a steep hill. The constant noise in the ears, created by the wind, eventually wears the rider down, and the wind wouldn't give up in Wyoming. I had to pedal in low gear to go downhill.

Bicycling during the coming days became a hell I couldn't find a way out of. The wind required a reserve of energy, and when that reserve was exhausted, the wind sapped my will like a relentless demon, leaving my body empty, a distasteful shell void of rationality. Several times I quit, got off my bike and screamed, "Fuck you, you son-of-a-bitching ass hole place. Fuck this road, and fuck you truck." I cursed Wyoming, I-80, life, and the stupid silly idea of traveling by bicycle.

No one heard: wasted obscenities lost to the wind. I understood ranters and ravers that roam city streets, those who had been treated unkindly by this harsh life, those who society had gratuitously thrown condemnation and humiliation like the wind had thrown dirt in my face, drowning me like a cigarette butt in a urinal while alternately drying the sweat from my forehead, leaving a layer of grimy salt. Sometimes physical aloneness brings happiness; sometimes it brings despair.

When an unchecked wind blows against a defenseless face, everything is wrong: the legs can't pedal, the lungs don't breathe, and the mind stops. Wyoming lasted 400 miles, through Laramie and Rawlings and Rock Springs. My body and mind matched the desolate mountain wilderness around me.

Curses escaped from both sides of my mouth, making my throat even drier. No matter how much my mind suggested it should, no matter how much I hoped it would, the wind never let up. What's a few days of agony in a lifetime, a few days of riding from morning till dusk on the interstate without shade from the sun or shelter from the wind? What was it for?

By the time I arrived at the old railroad town of Evanston I was too tired to notice it was near the border of the state. Soon after another billboard announced the beginning of Utah, I stopped on top of a long hill and looked down, expecting more of the same.

Somewhere down that hill the wind seemed to quiet. I looked around and saw trees and plants. Green life. The desert experience was coming to an end. What excitement pioneers must have felt knowing that the specter of death had passed and life was beginning.

Signs warned trucks to use caution; songs came to my mouth and relief to my soul. I stopped and listened. Nothing. Four hundred miles of drone had ended. The Mormons declared that green Salt Lake Valley the land God gave them, and I remembered a Bret Harte comment that Californians owe their existence to the Mormons for providing an oasis for those going west. I too made the crossing. Turning off the interstate I started cycling through the valley, feeling the sun behind me and seeing my solitary shadow pulling me, my mind filled with a deeper quiet, ready for more bicycling challenges.

I returned to Chicago and took other shorter bicycling trips around the Midwest until I felt ready to undertake the first around-the-world bicycling tour a year and a half later.

First

Journey

Appalachian Back Roads

He couldn't have been over five feet two inches tall, standing at a slant, leaning to the side like Pisa's tower, greasy right hand holding his chin like a gnome. He eyed my bicycle up and down, front and back, appraising the idea of cross-country bicycling. I stood nearby taking a drink out of my freshly filled water bottle, my eyes never leaving his tilted form. Without moving his feet he stretched his unevenly shaven face over my map and looked at it as if he had never seen the name of his town on a piece of paper before. His mouth crunched to the right, and sounds came out of it, like "gollie" or "oowie." Finally he turned and looked at me: "Boy," he said. "You ain't got a lick of sense."

His words caught me off guard, like hearing flamenco dancers actually shouting "ole" or Italians saying "mama mia." I thought he was putting me on.

"Don't you know enough to go places by car?" he added. "Bicycle's for kids."

A small fat back truck drove into the station. The short man greeted the driver by his first name, and he walked away to fill the customer's gas tank with regular, leaving me in front of his disorganized garage, next to the water hose that fed the tire pan. I took the map of southeastern Ohio out of the map case and threw it in the garbage, then began examining the new West Virginia map.

"Look like we gettin' a heap more rain," said the attendant when he returned. It had stopped raining two hours earlier, but the road was still wet, and the pavement near the gas pumps had puddles deeper than people's shoes.

I looked up at the sky and agreed with him. He turned to Angel and put his hands on his hips. I could see he hadn't washed them after working in the garage on an old red pickup.

"Don't it get cold ridin' a bicycle in the rain? Well, least you ain't gotta worry none 'bout water; you can just go down the road real fast with your mouth open." His body shook with laughter at his own humor, making me laugh watching him.

"Where you been on that gizmo?" he asked, pointing to Angel.

"A week ago I rode from Chicago through Indiana and Kentucky and Ohio." His mouth opened but nothing came out. "I'm planning to take it around the world, riding east."

"They're crazy everywhere else. Ain't no place like America. Too scary to go to them strange places." He got interrupted by the sound of a car. Two of his buddies were driving down the road in a patched-up car with either an old muffler or one that someone had deliberately punched a hole in. The short attendant waved them in.

"You gotta get ahold of this guy," he said, as if I came from a circus.

They swerved into the driveway at top speed, keeping the noisy engine running as they got out. The driver asked me where I was from, then opened the trunk and offered me a beer while he began talking about how cool it was that I came from the big city of Chicago, for they too went regularly into the cities, Parkersburg and Morgantown.

"Nothing doin' here in Winnet," he said. "Town packs up at six. We got to have us some fun."

"What kind of fun are you talkin' 'bout?" I asked. "Winnet's the first town I hit since the sign on the river tellin' me I'm in West Virginia." I realized that I was speaking in their dialect.

"We go drivin' around, go to bars. A lot to do in the city."

"Tell me," I said. "I'm fixin' to head into the hills, then go over the Potomac and ride down Pennsylvania Avenue. Which is the best way to go?"

"You can't go into the hills like that," said the young driver. "Shucks, why'd you want to anyhow?"

They saw that I wouldn't change my mind, then walked over and looked at my map. The two who had been in the car joined the attendant in an argument about the roads, their voices exceeding the noise of their running engine. Finally they came to a consensus.

"There ain't no sense on going on K because it got too many hills and all the people on it are simple folk," said the driver. "Best make tracks on forty-seven."

County Road K was the one that struck my fancy when I looked at the map since it was a small winding road. Highway 47 looked like it might have a lot of traffic.

"K's full of nothin' but hicks," the attendant added.

I thanked them, saying that I enjoyed their company. They told me to be cool. I began bicycling east on Highway 47, taking the turn-off to Route K a mile out of town. It turned out to be an ideal road for bicycling: smooth and hardly used, curving through unspoiled green country.

After my trip through Wyoming I began making trips to other states in order to train on mountains. Piece by piece I bought good equipment and always studied my route and read about the places where I would be cycling. A week after I finished my undergraduate degree, I felt ready for a world trip: from Chicago to the east coast and up to Boston, then up and down Europe, the Middle East, India, and east Asia.

Packing my bicycle became a precise science. Everything I carry has to justify its weight and size. I put aluminum racks over the front and rear wheels, attach large pannier saddlebags on the back and a roomy handlebar bag on the front where I load the heavy items — tools, replacement parts, camera equipment — as well as my important documents. In my rear panniers I stuff a minimum amount of clothing, a medical kit, vitamin pills and water purification pills, maps (these take a lot of space) and a compass, a tube repair kit and two extra tubes, rain coat and plastic bags, bar soap and razor, a paring knife, spoon, and tin cup, nothing more to cook with, for I can't be bothered to prepare food on the road. I bring a flashlight, a journal, and a fly swatter (flies and mosquitoes can make camping miserable), and I wear bicycling shoes without cleats so I can walk around. The panniers have room for a two day food supply.

Over the racks I tie a sleeping bag, tent, camp mattress, and spare tires. I often dry a piece of clothing over the sleeping bag while cycling. I wash it the night before, and next morning the sun and wind dry it quickly. Inside the handlebar I roll up an emergency $50.

Shortly after taking the turnoff for Route K, I began feeling a spring drizzle, but the heavy rain that other people were talking about had not yet made its debut. I bicycled quietly contented in the drizzle until mid-afternoon when a group of four beer drinking boys in a fired-up purple Dodge drove up beside me, squeezing me to the side of the narrow road.

The fellow in the front passenger seat stuck his head half out the window and said, "Get off the fuckin' road, boy."

The others laughed in the style of the country, making hehaw noises between open-mouthed guttural sounds. The guy in the back seat close to me said through the open window: "Hey faggot," and began unzipping his pants to show his vital organ. "You suck dick, boy?" The others responded with guffaws.

The driver squeezed me closer to the edge of the road, dangerously close to the soft dirt. They raised their beer cans and howled again. I stopped.

"Ain't you gonna offer me no fuckin' beer," I said caricaturing them.

"Hey, man." said the driver as he jumped on the brake and brought the car to a stop. "He's fuckin' all right, man." The fellow who called me a faggot reached into the cooler at his feet and handed me an iced Budweiser. His cheeks were pitted with acne. I put the can to my mouth and took a long draught.

"What the fuck do you guys do in this shit heap of a place?" I asked, putting them on the defensive.

A pig-eyed overgrown teenager in the backseat yelled out, "We head down to fuckin' Charleston, get fuckin' loaded, and pick up some fuckin' broads."

They laughed. I joined in. The guy in the front seat described the wonderfully rowdy time they have in the big city, "shit," "bitch," and similar adjectives forming the basis of his dialogue.

They asked me where I was going. "D.C.," I replied. "Bicycle's the best way to go."

They said, "Yea, man," then wished me a good one, man. The driver put the Dodge in gear and popped the clutch, burning rubber as he slithered on the wet road, out of sight and into silence. I emptied the rest of the beer in the weeds and was off again.

The next day involved a lot of changing gears, turning the levers down for low gears to go up hills, then slowly opening the gears as I gained downhill speed until my wheels outran the pedals. I lowered my head against the wind and the rain to gain downhill momentum for the upgrade which began at the bottom of the hill, then repeatedly downshifted up the hill until I had to stand, breathe deep, and push myself over the peak. These mountains were tough to ride, the toughest area I had ridden in North America.

The mountains were not tall — the tallest is not much over 3000 feet according to my map — but the roads were a constant up and down, making the overall altitude change tremendous. I would climb for two or three miles, reach the peak, go down hill, have to climb another mile, go down again, then climb for three or four miles, and so on. Such roads train a cyclist. It takes little effort to bicycle briskly over flats, but to take a bicycle loaded with camping equipment, clothes, tools, and a dozen other pieces of equipment, to pedal the rider's weight plus 70 pounds over mountain after mountain, that requires many hours of training, building the muscles and expanding the lung and heart capacity.

The rain changed from a drizzle to a downpour, making the curvy road treacherous. Bicycling downhill in the rain, building up speed along the way until I was going over forty miles an hour, sometimes reaching fifty, the brakes became useless. Even without the extra momentum that the weight of the equipment creates, stopping or slowing down would have been impossible. The wheels threw out a spray of water two feet above them, spraying water over my head; the rims became dangerously lubricated.

Once that day I was coasting down hill and let myself go too fast. I squeezed the brakes to slow for a curve and got no response. My knuckles turned white trying to slow the bicycle to make the turn so I wouldn't throw myself off the mountain. Helplessly I watched the curve come closer, unable to do anything to slow down. I tucked my head and shoulders below the handlebar, stuck out my left knee, shifted my weight, and saw my wet front wheel come to the edge of the road, a millimeter this side of eternity. If I had gone over into the dense wild vegetation at the bottom of the hill, no one would ever have known. I would have been erased and forgotten.

By afternoon I was so drenched it no longer mattered if it continued to rain. After a few hours of riding in hard rain my raingear became useless; even the most breathable raincoat closes off the body, building moisture under it, especially while pedaling energetically. The road crossed a town, and I went into a supermarket, spending a long time inside to stay out of the rain, trying in vain to dry off. While I stood inside the supermarket door, two long-haired men in their twenties and a woman with many strands of bead necklaces saw me and began a conversation. "We got a house a spell down the road," said a fellow with muscles bulging from his plaid long sleeve wool shirt. "Looks like you need a dry place for the night."

I put my bicycle into the back of their four-wheel drive Travelall, and we went on a different road for twenty miles then turned to a small dirt road at the bottom of a hill. I never understood why people bought flashy four-wheel drives with oversize balloon tires that make a car stand three feet off the ground until I saw that road. The rain made it look like a battlefield, with pot holes that could have been made from cannon balls. Mike, the driver, put it in low gear and forced his way through deep mud, finally arriving at a clearing where stood two wood buildings: a run-down farmhouse, and a barn which had one wall caved in, the front sliding door off its rollers, and water pouring down the center onto a rusty tractor. A six-year-old boy ran out of the house to greet us. Mike picked him up and playfully threw him over his head.

"We like to have elbow room," said Bob, a dark-haired man who wore a camouflage jacket with the sleeves cut off. "Ain't nobody else around for a good bit." He curved his hand over his mouth to make a horn and let out a loud scream to the mountains.

"We rent this place for $65 a month," Mike added. "It got 150 acres around it. An old lady, a widow, owns it. If anybody wants to go hunting or anything round here, they got to see us first."

The house used to have a farm around it but now suffered from obvious neglect. A flat uncultivated area the size of a football field had been taken over by weeds. The house sat at the corner of the farm; lush green mountains surrounded it. Two mutt dogs, a half dozen chickens, and too many cats ran between the dilapidated barn and the horseless stable. The mountains began abruptly as soon as the flat space of the farm ended.

Mike's wife came out of the house with a baby in her arms and casually said hi to me. She and Bob's wife took groceries into the kitchen and began putting them away while preparing a meal. I went into the bathroom and changed out of my wet clothes, then joined the men who sat on a stained couch in the living room. Overflowing ashtrays were scattered around us. Beer cans with cigarette butts smashed on the lids lay on the floor. The couch, a couple of odd chairs, a coffee table, and a television comprised the furniture. Bob started a fire from the wood near the fireplace.

"We're rough-necks," Mike said through the side of his mouth while lighting up a cigarette. I felt embarrassed that he called himself that; it sounded like calling himself a goon.

"We work oil rigs," Bob said when he saw that I didn't understand. "Least when they got work. Ain't nobody hirin' now: everybody layin' off." He went into the kitchen and came back with three beers, passing two to Mike and me.

"There's oil here?" I asked.

"Nooo," Mike replied. "Ain't nothin' here but coal, and that's runnin' out. We go to Ohia to work."

"That's a hell of a long way," I said. "I cycled through the Ohio oil area a few days ago."

"Six hours going and six hours coming, driving fast. We go for a week and come back on Friday night."

"They pay us good cause they got plenty of accidents," Bob said without an inflection in his voice, "twenty an hour." He lit up a joint and passed it around. I took a drag, but didn't inhale.

The six-year-old turned on the television and the radio, listening to both. The local news came on and competed with rock music. Like almost everyone I met in West Virginia, the disk jockey spoke in a local accent, but the television local news, the national news that followed, and the other inane television programs that the child switched to, had people speaking the standard Midwest dialect.

I was a student of linguistics and was interested in the various American dialects. I turned to Mike and asked, "Does my accent sound strange to you?"

"You talk like everyone else who's not from these here parts," said Mike. "Nothin' strange about that."

"Your boy listens to people on radio and television who speak like me. Yet he speaks like you, not like me."

"Course," responded Mike. "He's a West Virginian. He's always been speaking like his ma and pa."

"Maybe television ain't as important as folks say," added Bob.

We ate dinner on paper plates while sitting on the sofa and scattered chairs. I put more wood on the fire, oiled the child's tricycle chain, and we started a game of Monopoly which lasted past midnight. My hosts went upstairs to bed, leaving me the couch. I brushed off the crumbs and lay on my sleeping bag.

The next morning it drizzled quietly, and in the north I saw a break in the dark clouds. I took down my clothes which were hanging on a line in an unused room. The household went outside to see me off with a warm country good-bye, then Mike took me back to the blacktop in the four-wheel drive. I began making my way deeper into the mountains, climbing hill roads surrounded by run-down farms with junk lying around them, an antique collector's paradise. Mist covered the heavily wooded mountains, giving them an aura of mystery. Branches of large trees drooped over the road. I traveled through several small towns whose streets were deserted, stopping in a grocery store or gas station to dry my face and discuss with self-assured experts what the weather might be like tomorrow.

Toward the end of the day the drizzle stopped. I saw an old man sitting on his porch with a heavy hunting jacket and a black hat pulled low over his forehead, staring reflectively into space. His eyes met mine when I stopped in front of his wooden fence.

"Howdy," I said. "Mind if I pitch my tent in your front yard?"

With an expressionless face he said, "Sure, go ahead," turned around and walked into his house. When darkness fell a half hour later, he came out again with a full dinner on a tray: two heaping plates of potatoes and spinach and roast and pie, and a glass of lemonade.

"Thought you might be hungry," he said as his strong large hands placed the tray at the mouth of the tent. He crouched on his hams to be able to talk to me. "Lost the wife last year; the children work far away, and their's nobody to talk to 'cept at church on Wednesday and Sunday. Folks now don't have the time."

He got up and brought over two chairs from the porch. We sat on them in our jackets, talking and looking at the stars which began to appear wherever there was a break in the clouds.

"We been mightily lucky," he said. "People on the other side of the hill had it rough when coal weren't no good. We don't see them much. They speak so strange no one can hardly understand them."

His reflective voice solicited trust. "This side of the mountain is farmland," he said; "here we don't have to mess with working for someone else."

"The young people don't seem interested in staying," I said.

"I suppose they're like you, want to see more. We never had the chance. I don't fault them; I wanted to see more when I was their age too."

"So you live alone now?" I asked.

"Don't want to. People are made to talk. What's life about if you're alone? You got a wife?"

I shook my head.

"You'll get one soon."

There was a short silence. "I've been having a lot of rain all the way through the state." I said. "Hope I'll have a few days to dry off."

"Yea," he said. "You got a lot of days to get wet and dry off. Getting wet is good. Let me teach you something, young man. I've been on God's earth a good bit. I can tell that you're a decent fellow looking to do good. I've seen so many people turn out to be my age and be unhappy. They missed something in life, and I don't mean missed seeing something. They missed getting wet. They always looked for a way to keep out of the rain. Now, there ain't no way to make them happy. You can give them anything, and they'd still be miserable."

After this piece of advice he wished me a good night. I got into my dry tent and immediately went to sleep. The next morning the old man and I had a conversation about the countryside. He put a couple of apples in my panniers as I was taking down my tent and said that he would pray that I would have a safe trip around the world. It began drizzling as we shook hands. He returned to his chair for more reflection while I rode off.

Several hills later I pulled up under an empty wooden shelter on the side of the road that probably served as a fruit stand.

A small red car was parked next to it, but I saw no one. I got off, unfastened my yellow rain suit, and began making a sandwich. The brush behind rustled, and I turned to see a middle-aged man dressed in black zipping up his suspendered pants while walking to his car. He saw me, moved his head to the side, and spit out a wad of brown saliva.

He looked at my bicycle then turned his eyes to heaven, either to look at the rain clouds or to receive divine inspiration. "Ain't it the wrong day to be ridin'," he said to begin a conversation.

"Sure enough," I said, looking at his disheveled hair and unshaven gray whiskers. I realized that I, too, hadn't shaved for two days.

"It's a might better than yesterday," I added.

"Reckon you right." He looked closer at my bicycle, not focusing on anything. "Where do you say you ridin' from?"

"Illinois."

He paused. His pants barely reached the top of his wrinkled socks. "Last time I was in Illinois was in nineteen hundred and thirty-four." He took a deep breath, as if winding up. "My pappy, bless his soul, took me when I was barely nine years old. Went by train. Took three days and two nights. Train broke down outside Muncie, Indiana, and we had to walk five miles. Man told my pappy it was cause the depression. Pappy tried to get work. Got to Illinois to see corn tasseling."

"Ain't changed much I don't reckon," I said, interrupting him.

"The only thing that changes is that things get worse. There's more sin in the world today." Another wad of tobacco was building in his mouth. "You too young to know the Great Depression, but that ain't nothin' like what's comin'."

"Why," I said to his eyes set inside rays of wrinkles, "seems to me you a preacher."

"Spent seventeen years in the pulpit tellin' 'em to turn away from their wicked ways. Preached Christ crucified all the way." He paused and looked at me for the first time. "I believe you an edacated man."

I took off my glasses. "I'm always learning something new," I said.

"But you edacated with the fear of God," he said. "All a body got to do is read the Bible." He spit another stream, wiped his mouth with his unbuttoned sleeve, and continued. "Yes, sir, ain't nothin' worth readin' but the Bible. I done all my learnin' from the Bible. If it ain't writ' there, it wrong."

"Amen," I said, for I could tell he was on the brink of beginning a sermon. He tightened his lips, looked around, then turned to me as if he was telling me a secret. "You know the sixth seal has been broken?"

I wasn't sure if I was supposed to know or have him tell me. "This here's the end time," I said, knowing that's been a safe answer for 2000 years.

"Yes sir," he said without listening to my response. "Soon the beast of the north be a fightin' the beast of the south. Them communists and them homosexuals will have their day before they tossed into the lake of fire. It's all writ' in the book. Soon the rich and the strong will hide in caves and among the rocks of these very mountains."

"Tell me, where shall we seek shelter?" I asked.

"I believe you a God-fearing young man. You know that the Anti-Christ is already loosed on the earth?" He didn't look at me or allow me to answer. "Homosexuals and communists will rule." He pronounced "communists" as J. Edgar Hoover had. "Sin and corruption are gonna be everywhere. You know that Russia is the beast of the north and the Pope is the scarlet whore?" Again, he didn't wait for a response. I took another bite out of my sandwich. "The chosen will gather in hills, here and in other places, but before we do they gonna have their reign; you mark my word."

"I know your words are inspired," I said, offering him bread and cheese. He took a piece of cheese in one hand and bread in the other, but he didn't put them together and continued speaking.

"I preached 'em with the holy spirit seventeen years, yes sir. I give 'em the wrath of God, telling 'em about their sins, I did. They came back every week. They wanted it harder and stronger. I tell 'em about the time of the end and what the Word of God says. I tell 'em that when Albania became communist, they fulfilled the fifth seal. You know that?"

He looked at me for a response. "Ain't communism bringin' 'bout the end of the world?" I asked, thinking that would be the right thing to say.

"Communism and homosexuality. It says it in the Bible. When you can't tell a man from a woman. They ain't no difference 'tween communists and homosexualists. They all the same in the eye of God. They all perverted. It ain't what I say; it's writ' in the book. What do I know? I don't know nothin' from myself. I only know what the Bible says. I started working when I was eleven. My pappy was too poor. I work the mines for five years before I ever shaved. Had to support the family. I don't know nothing but what the Bible says." His mouth was getting ready for another salivation.

"I can tell that your inspiration didn't come easily," I said, unaware that I lost my fake dialect until after the words came out of my mouth. He didn't notice.

"I was pullin' coal out of mines before I even knew about the commies and the homos destroying God's world. Used to like workin' down there. It be cold or hot up here, but you go down and it always nice. Didn't get the callin' til I was twenty-nine. I'm alone now."

He spit again, and finally ate a piece of bread, almost unaware of what he was doing. He thought for a minute, then looked me in the eye. "You know, I believe that God has called the two of us together, two believers, to share the good news of his return. You believe God works that way?"

"I believe what you say to be genuine." It was the first time that he listened to me.

"Here you come down the road all the way from Illinois, meeting me on this here small road with nothin' around excepting trees. What could be more the hand of God than that?"

He took out a can of Skool and put a pinch in his mouth.

"Where's your church?" I asked.

"Don't preach no more, not for the last ten years." He spit, then talked more about Daniel and Revelation. He was happy and satisfied to have an audience again. We exchanged good-byes — he cautioned me to watch out for the subtleness of Satan — then he got in his car and drove off.

Not many miles farther, the mountains became hills, then rolling earth. A sign welcomed me to Virginia. I stopped in a store and asked for directions: "You got a mountain to cross before you get to Washington," said the man behind the counter. "It's pretty tough. I don't know if you can make it on a bicycle."

"Is it tougher than the mountains in West Virginia?"

"This isn't anything like that. If you've been in West Virginia you'll have no problem with this. Two hundred years ago we cut the state in half and gave the mountains to West Virginia. Only kept one or two. A lot of strange folks live over there, didn't you think?"

"Perhaps," I said.

I packed my raincoat in the panniers, stopped at a coin operated laundry to dry my clothes, then with little effort climbed on a wide road over the last peak. After two days of postcard scenery, I bicycled into Washington's traffic between the grand and pretentious buildings of the city. After three days I began the ride to Boston. From Boston I took my flight over the Atlantic.

A Jungle Rider Attacks Europe

I arrived in London in the morning, put my bicycle together at the airport, rode to the other side of the city, and headed north on a local road. I had wanted to travel across the country to the Lake District and take a ferry to Ireland. As it turned out, I never made it: the cold and damp discouraged me. Even when it didn't actually rain, it always threatened.

On the first evening I found myself near Cambridge. A woman directed me to an empty patch of grass surrounded by trees, and away from road noise, where I could pitch my tent and go to sleep. The next day I took small roads across the island toward Wales, riding from dawn until the sun touched the horizon. Twenty or thirty miles from Stratford-on-Avon I spotted a rugby field, thought it would be a good place to camp, and was about to stake my tent next to the clubhouse when I noticed that the door to the clubhouse had a padlock and latch held on the door with two loose screws, terrible security. Thinking that it would be nicer to sleep inside out of the cold and rain, I took out my screwdriver, and within fifteen seconds I was inside the clubhouse, which contained a bar, showers, and locker room. This happened in the days before I knew how to ask for accommodation.

After I was comfortably inside, I saw two teenagers around the field. I didn't bother to think much of them since I was tired from a full cycling day. A few minutes later a police car rushed up. I knew they had come for me, especially when the policemen hurried in and handcuffed me.

"Is this necessary?" I asked. "I've just come in for a night's sleep."

The policemen insisted, and I had to go with them in the back of the car. I asked about my bicycle, but they told me not to worry, and I didn't worry, not only because I had no choice, but because one of the policemen, a thin person in his early twenties, rolled up his trousers and began to ride Angel back to the station. I could see that he was proficient at riding bicycles, but he had trouble balancing mine since it was loaded with so much gear.

"Have you ever been in trouble before?" asked the middle-aged driver in a slow professional voice.

"Am I in trouble now?"

"You most certainly are. Breaking and entering, and I don't know what else."

"I'm sorry. I was only trying to get out of the rain."

"There's liquor in there."

"I was too tired to notice. I'm suffering from jet lag. I don't drink. The door was almost open. It looked empty inside."

He looked at me in the rearview mirror. "Well, you shouldn't have gone inside," he said excitedly, fatherly, shedding his policeman tone.

When we got to the station the driver and another officer in the station put me in a cell, but when they saw I was harmless and benign, they took me out and treated me civilly. Twenty minutes later we saw the young policeman come up on my bicycle, puffing from the three mile ride to the station. The sight gave us all a chuckle.

He sensed that we had become friendly, so he asked, "How do you pedal such a heavy thing?" The others made English jokes about him being out of shape.

The man in charge of the clubhouse lived nearby. He had gone to examine it and told them that nothing was touched except the latch. I told them my complete story, apologized to them and the owner, and then we began a lively discussion about the differences between the U.S. and England. The young policeman was also interested in colloquial linguistics, and we struck up a lively conversation about the dissimilarity between American English and British English, giving many examples of our uncommon language. The officer who had driven me to the station talked about the differences between the English and American law enforcement.

"You should be glad you're here," he said. "What would the cops have done to you in America?"

"I don't know. Probably told me to go somewhere else."

"Come on," said another. "They'd have been ten times rougher, grabbed you by the cuff, slapped you in jail, and thrown away the key."

He began naming several American television cop shows that I've never seen.

"Do you believe that stuff." I asked.

No one knew what to say, as if they had been caught in their naivete. I decided to delve further.

"I've lived in the U.S. many years — in the big cities — and I've never seen a car chase or a gun fight. Most American cops are overweight and have boring jobs. They certainly wouldn't have ridden my bicycle to the station."

"Their jobs are probably more interesting than ours," one said. "You're the most excitement we've had here in months."

Amid laughter they examined all my things, more out of curiosity than necessity — "sun block, you'll not need that here." They filled out a form, and wished me well, but by this time darkness had fallen, and I had nowhere to stay. If a moon was out, the rain clouds hid it. The policemen worried about my sleep more than I did. They didn't want to be inhospitable and let me out alone in the middle of the night, so they tried to find me a place to stay.

"I can put up my tent in the dark," I said.

"We won't have you do that."

"Can't I stay in the cell?"

"It would take too much form filling. We close at night."

Each of them wanted to help me personally, but I felt bad about causing them trouble and felt embarrassed to impose further, so they took me to a bed and breakfast house where I destroyed my budget and laid in too comfortable a bed contemplating my renegade American judgments as excess baggage that I'd brought with me.

American cites had made me a jungle rider, fighting my way through traffic, untamed, a non-believer in politeness, a lawless athlete struggling against equally lawless drivers, curses loaded in my mouth, battling man-eating dogs and bullies behind the wheel. Too many Americans are obsessed with their cars, big and fast, bullying bicyclists with their steering wheels like so many transformed cowboys.

On my first bicycling trip outside the U.S. and Canada, it took me a few days to learn to stop at red lights and ride in the bicycle lane. Much of Europe has an excellent variety of bicycling roads. Riding in the Alps is a fairy tale experience. I saw men wearing short pants, wide suspenders, and knapsacks walking over breath-taking hills; I passed hillside resorts where men and women moved their ornate beer mugs to and fro in unison, to the sound of fiddles and accordions. I saw castles until I was tired of seeing castles. I passed an assortment of loaded fruit trees, and when I stopped to pick fruit and people saw me, they usually called me over and gave me tomatoes or cucumbers. Once when I was resting in the shade, an Italian rushed out of his house and gave me handfuls of almonds and figs.

I crossed the English Channel to France, which holds the reputation as the cycling mecca: every distance bicyclist picks up a green Michelin map and explores the variegated country roads that pass one farm village after another, crossing between pear or cherry orchards, spans of golden wheat, varieties of beans, alfalfa, barley, rows of potatoes, carrots, or strawberries, acres of fat sunflowers, and hill after hill of grapes. From a good map you can find the quiet, well-surfaced roads, roads so narrow that when two small Renaults come face to face, one of them has to move off the pavement to allow the other to pass.

I was bicycling on one of those small quiet roads in the Loire valley, singing at high volume, when I happened to see on the ground in front of me a round object reflecting the sun. I often see that, and it's usually a smashed bottle top, but as I got closer I saw that it was a one franc coin. I stopped, picked it up, and put it in the pocket on the back of my cycling jersey without interrupting my song. At that time the franc was worth about twenty-two cents. Thirty or forty yards later I saw another, and again I stopped and put another franc coin in my pocket.

The next coin was closer, about twenty yards past the last, and the fourth coin was still closer. One by one I added them to my bounty. By the time I came to the fifth coin, I was actively looking for a treasure chest of one franc pieces. I looked around to see if anyone was playing a joke on me. Not a soul. Every few yards I spotted another shiny coin. I got the knack of slowing down, bending all the way over, and reaching them without having to stop and take my foot out of the straps.

Most coins were on the right edge of the pavement, but several were closer to the center of the road, and these were nicked and scratched from being run over by cars. Considering the negligible number of cars on the road, they must have been there a long time. Some coins were off the road surface in the weeds, and many of these I missed, but I ruled out the idea of going back for a closer look. I hadn't come to a foreign country to spend time looking for money on the street.

In a mile the pockets on my jersey and shorts were so heavy with metal that I was stuffing francs into my handlebar bag. This couldn't actually be happening; there must be some hitch. I looked around. Nothing but the sound of the wind over the open fields. The coins kept coming, each sparkling in the summer sunlight.

About two miles from the start of this silver trail, the number of franc pieces began thinning and finally ended. By that time I had over 150 one franc pieces on me. I felt guilty. I looked around again. Nothing. Guilt changed to a snicker. It must be heaven's gift, I thought, and rode off laughing to the nearby town where I handed a bunch of coins to the grocer to pay for a bag of celebration food: creamy cheeses, chocolate, and apricots. He felt the coins and asked me why some were damaged. I started to tell him what happened. Excitement filled me, but my French failed, and I had to relate it to him mostly in sign language. He smiled and called over a couple of men wearing short brim caps who were talking in the center square. He showed them the coins. I enthusiastically showed them my full pockets. They loved the story. One fellow patted me on the back, and two others took me to the cafe, bought me a beer, and talked about the times long since past when they rode their bicycles to Nice and Lyon and Belgium.

"The money allows me to spend an extra week here," I said.

"Maybe they fell out of a car little by little," said one man. "A slow moving car."

"It's God's blessing," said another as he finished his beer. "God's blessing, our hospitality, and your good fortune."

I agreed.

***

I was too tired to ride the extra twenty miles to the small town near Stuttgart to meet a friend, so I stopped where I was and asked directions to the local youth hostel, an ornate edifice used as a private school most of the year. The town's name escaped my notice, but its charm and cleanliness typified southern Germany. A stone church with a single high steeple stood opposite a manicured square. Park benches placed next to neat circles of soil filled with symmetrical patterns of blooming flowers lined the smooth streets. There seemed to be no garbage and no graffiti. The lights and fountains worked; the houses were neatly painted; the cars shined. So clean and orderly was the cemetery that I took a picture of it: polished marble tombs and vaults topped with fresh flowers surrounded by square hedges and golf course grass carefully trimmed at the edges. Germans pay regular visits to the cemetery, I learned.

The woman who ran the hostel wouldn't let me enter the building with Angel, so I took off everything that could be taken off, removed the front wheel, and put my Kryptonite lock between the frame, the two wheels, and a post. The action was automatic and without thought; I do it every time I stop somewhere in the United States. People who don't do that lose their bicycles or their front wheels.

The next morning, a bright Sunday, I woke to the sound of children playing in the yard and shared breakfast and stories with various international travelers staying at the hostel. When I was ready to leave, I took all my possessions and went downstairs to the statue-filled lobby and stepped through the carved wood doors. Boys and girls filled the yard. I looked to the side, and in a wave of embarrassment realized that dozens of shiny bicycles paralleled mine, lined up one after another on both sides, and none of them had a lock. My blue bicycle stood in the middle, the front wheel off and a fat lock holding it to a post, a lock that you'd need an acetylene torch to take off if you lost the key, a lock that would defy a hardened criminal.

A twelve-year-old blond kid in shorts ran toward me, stopped ten yards away, and yelled over in English. "No man is going to take what doesn't belong to him." Then he ran off playing while two of his small friends stared in disdain at me from across the yard.

I put my panniers on my bicycle as fast as possible and rode off.

***

Bicycle tourists flock to Western Europe not only because of their familiarity with the continent but because bicycles are a respectable form of sport and transportation. When the Tour de France comes around, for example, it causes mass hysteria. A bicycle on the road is treated as a legitimate vehicle. In most places I wouldn't have to fight through traffic, get cut off by turning cars, or listen to cars honking impatiently at me to get out of the way. When I found the less traveled European roads a cycling paradise unfolded for me.

I rode down to Rome and played tourist for several days. The chaotic Roman traffic was exciting riding, but the cobble streets in the old city can give a bicyclist a vigorous rattling. Impulsively, I decided to go to Assisi to be part of the 800th anniversary celebration of St. Francis' birth. Being on a bicycle granted me the freedom to hop on the saddle and leave anytime and go anywhere. Following my compass and taking the curvy main roads, I reached the suburbs of the city, then I started asking people for directions. It took three hours to reach the country roads.

Mountains, which I learned to love riding, cover the middle of Italy. Thin roads wind back and forth like tossed strands of fettuccini on the sides of green mountains. Away from the industrial regions, hamlets of a half dozen 200-year-old stone houses are nestled among the forests. Crossing a flat stretch between hills, five team racers riding in a straight line passed me, glancing at me condescendingly as they passed, like a Ferrari passing a Fiat. Their clothes fit like spray paint on their slim bodies. Their bicycles gleamed. They wore bright green and red jerseys, black shorts, and white socks, perfectly white, all identical. Their wheels turned precisely true, and they had exactly the right amount of oil on their chains. Their club name was written in script on the backs of their jerseys and on the front lip of their traditional white caps that had a colored stripe running down the center. One had shaved legs.

I had been cycling leisurely, but after they passed me I got on the handlebar drops, forced out a few hard strokes until I could change to a higher gear, then maintained a crisp pace. It's hard to catch up on your own; you have to apply a lot of energy, and you can only do that for a short while. Once I caught up with the racers, pedaling behind their broken wind was easier, although still requiring force to keep my heavy bicycle behind the pack.

The last person saw my shadow and looked behind at my smiling face. He didn't know how to respond, so he shouted at the others, and they all turned and looked at me.

"Buon Giorno. Nice day to bicycle," I said in poor Italian, pretending that their pace was relaxed by not showing any strain in my voice.

Their eyes inspected me as they tried to make up their minds whether they should like me or not. First they looked at my bicycle and didn't recognize the Japanese make, but they saw all Italian moving parts, and that made them happy. Their eyes went up. They saw a standard pair of racing shorts, but that day I wore a tight T-shirt instead of a proper cycling jersey. But finally they saw a hat with the name of a bicycling club from a small city north of Genoa, and I could see that it won them over.

"Buon Giorno," they said. "Where are you going?"

"Assisi."

They liked that as well. A lot of pious Catholics were converging on Assisi for the festivities, and they must have assumed that I too was devout. Most young Italians do not practice their religion, and even though these racers may not have seen the inside of a church since being brought by their mothers for baptism, even though they probably philosophized against every religious tenet, they gained a lump-in-the-throat respect for me. One of them broke their tight formation, and they started riding in pairs, riding alongside to give me an easier time by breaking more wind.

Without slowing the pace we began to talk in a mixture of broken languages, about prices of bicycles in America, about Italian roads and mountains, about races, talking and keeping a training pace, changing over the lead positions periodically. Cars had to wait until it was clear to pass, for we took half the road. Someone honked at us; one of the cyclists flipped his wrist at him.

The group suddenly got excited and started pointing at another racing team going the opposite direction on the other side of the road. The other group looked over, and I could see that they were puzzled about me, wondering what I was doing training with a rival club. When both teams were even, everyone started shouting a series of harsh sounding words that I didn't understand and making obscene arm gestures that were too easy to understand, then my group broke out in spontaneous laughter, inviting me to laugh with them, and I understood that the two clubs had a heavy competition.

"They ride dirty," said one in I can't remember what language. Racers always make that comment about other clubs.

After ten or fifteen miles of bicycling at that pace we arrived in a modern town full of young people milling around the open central square. A bright movie house and fashionable boutiques stood on all sides of the square. The expressions on the faces of my group completely changed as soon as we reached the square. No longer were they smiling or being friendly; instead, they put on stern, professional faces, riding like proud heroes, pretending not to notice everyone looking admiringly at them.

When we stopped my legs felt like two strips of rubber. I bought the group ice cream, shook hands with friends of theirs who came over to talk, and was soon ready to hit the road again. Taking my cue from the racers, I mounted my bicycle with dignity, sat high and looked straight ahead while riding out of the square without showing that my legs were still trembling from the brisk ride into town.

Yugoslavia:
Through the Dark Forest

"Caution, 18% Grade Ahead," read the sign in German, a few miles before the Yugoslavian border. I stopped and rested well under one of the hundreds of tall trees at the base of the hill, but before I got to the steep part I had to take four more rest stops. The lower part of the mountain, before the 18% grade, was so hard I could only climb a couple hundred yards between rests. My heart raced, my lungs inhaled vigorously, sweat poured down my face and back. I could feel the veins in my neck and legs bulging out of my skin. The heat of the day made it even harder. When I turned the last corner I saw cars straining to make the long steep grade. Several came to a halt, put their cars in first gear, raced their engines and began burning their clutches. The Mercedes and the BMWs made it, but the modest Renaults and Volkswagons didn't have a chance.

A tractor worked the road, towing stalled cars up the hill. Other cars came down the hill slowly, backfiring, their drivers sitting close to the windshield clutching the steering wheel tightly as if that would help slow the car on the downgrade.

I tried to bicycle up the hill, stood over the handlebar in my lowest gear, applying all the force my legs were capable of, but I couldn't push the pedals. I tried to zig-zag up the road. Every time I stopped it became increasingly difficult to start again. By the time I brought my second foot to the pedals I was at a standstill and had to quickly return it to the ground to avoid falling over.

A farm tractor came up the road behind me. I looked back and exchanged glances with the driver. He came alongside me and slowed down. I grabbed a piece of metal sticking out of the rear with my left hand and yelled out, "OK." He gradually stepped on the accelerator while I pedaled hard to take the strain off my pulling arm. We passed the stalled cars which were waiting for the tow line of the other tractor. When we arrived at the top, I let go and pedaled up to the driver to thank him. He nodded and waved good-bye.

Wurzen Pass. A sign on the side of the road indicated an elevation of less than a 1000 meters, much less than it felt, but most of that almost 1000 meters came in one steep grade.

A camper waving a large Swedish flag came up alongside me. The half dozen young people inside asked me where I was from and where I was going.

"I'm taking a trip to Athens," I said.

They offered me something cool to drink, which I readily accepted.

One young man said in perfect English, "I think you'll be tired when you're through."

"I think you're right," I said. "I'm tired already."

I commented on the number of tourists going into Yugoslavia, saying that it must be a popular place.

"All these cars are going to Greece," said the driver. "They will just pass through Yugoslavia, usually as fast as they can."

The border facilities were located a mile after the top of the hill. The Austrian officials waved me on without looking at my passport. On the Yugoslavian side a guard stood in the street with his hand out ready to receive passports. He took mine without speaking, quickly found the visa to his country which I had gotten in Chicago, and while holding the passport in his left hand, he produced a rubber stamp from his side, stamped an empty square, handed the passport back to me, then motioned the car behind me forward. Other guards sat on chairs nearby, I nodded to them; they looked me in the eye but they didn't respond. I walked to the bank to change a little money. The clerk took my bills and, without saying a word, handed me Yugoslavian bills.

"How's the road to Zagreb," I asked.

He looked up, but didn't answer. Perhaps officials here have a habit of not talking, I thought.

The Yugoslavian side of the mountain was as densely forested as the Austrian side. Both sides of the road were thick with pine, maple, and oak. I coasted down and came to a town and stopped, seeing a factory at the bottom of the hill, a large brick building surrounded by a cyclone fence. Three brick smoke stacks four stories high billowed thick orange-yellow smoke. I felt asphyxiated just looking at it from the distance. The brilliant color of the smoke horrified me: it left the stacks and dissipated into the atmosphere over the town, turning the sky a bright orange.

I found a grocery store. The owner asked me in German what I wanted as soon as I entered.

"This bread and a bit of this cheese," I said while holding the bread in my hand.

Without responding he took the bread out of my hand and cut a piece of cheese, wrapping it in white paper.

"How much does it cost?" I asked.

"200 dinar."

I began looking at my money trying to figure out how much each bill was. Impatiently, he reached over and grabbed a bill and gave me change, then began waiting on another customer, not saying another word.

Outside the store I stood next to my bicycle and took out the sheet of Serbo-Croatian words and practiced pronouncing "Where is the road to Zagreb?" The words contained clusters of consonants that made it hard for an unpracticed tongue. I approached the first man who was walking toward the store and tried the phrase on him. He stopped for a second, looked at me, then walked right past into the store. I tried the next man, he listened to my phrase but couldn't understand what I was asking. I said it again, looking at the words and pronouncing slowly. He took the paper from me. I pointed to the phrase, adding the word "Zagreb" for the three dots. He pointed down the road, and vanished.

I bicycled through small and large towns, farmlands, keeping to myself. At the tourist office in Zagreb a friendly young woman who spoke a plethora of languages told me the best roads to take.

I confided in her: "People have not been very friendly to me so far."

She blushed. "They're not used to foreigners. Most visitors go to the Adriatic coast. The people that come into the center of the country come with a camping trailer and only pass to Greece."

"I was told that the Adriatic is full of tourists. That's why I wanted to bicycle through the center of the country."

"I believe you will find the people in the interior a bit more closed than you have been used to in Western Europe. Many people stay to themselves and are suspicious of foreigners."

I was surprised at her frankness. Most tourist offices just dispense public relations. She walked outside with me and pointed me to the road south. For the next couple of days I spent almost all the daylight hours pedaling, making good time despite the mountainous roads. At night I stayed at campgrounds that are scattered near all European roads. Except for brief stops for food and water, I found no avenue that would allow me to mix with the local people.

Halfway through the country, on a road with a moderate amount of traffic, a young blond policeman got out of his car and waved me to a stop. He came over to me and held my arm in a steel grip. Perhaps he thought I would try to outrun his car. He tried to get the attention of his superior who was leaning on the door of a car talking to a young woman through her open window. The fellow holding my arm didn't want to interrupt him. He shook his finger at my bicycle and pointed to the road, making me understand that I couldn't bicycle there.

When the woman drove away, the superior came over and, I could see, felt uneasy about seeing his cohort's hand gripping my arm. I pulled out my phrase sheet and asked, "What's wrong?" They didn't understand. I asked in German. Still no understanding. The superior's lip quivered, and English words came out slowly:

"Prohibit to drive on road." He pointed to a sandy path running alongside. "Drive here." His face had an expression of apology, sorry to have to give me this news.

"I can't ride in the sand," I said. The other fellow let go of my arm, leaving a white imprint where his hand had been.

"This is auto road." He pointed to the blacktop.

I looked down the two lane road which seemed like a casual country lane. How can he equate it to the slick cars-only motorways in the north? Cars passed at regular intervals, but it didn't compare with many secondary European roads I had just come from.

"You ride here." He pointed to the sandy path: "For bicycles."

The superior was decent but firm about it. I could see no way to continue on the pavement. I carried Angel over to the sandy path. The two watched me begin bicycling. But I could hardly get any traction, and at the first turn I almost fell over.

I wasn't quite halfway down the country. My map showed a railway paralleling the road. When I reached the next town, I pulled out my phrase sheet and stopped four men in their early twenties.

"Where is the railroad station?" I asked, trying to pronounce the words as they were written on the page.

They began laughing at me. I showed them my sheet. One grabbed it out of my hand to read it. Another began clowning:

"Hello, Mr. Brown," he said, pronouncing each word distinctly, imitating a school text book that they must have been subjected to in grammar school. "How are you?" The other three laughed.

"Come in, Mr. Brown," said another in staccato, "Please write your name on chalk."

The first person corrected him: "Write your name on blackboard."

They buffooned all the more. I said distinctly in English, "The train," then made the sound of a train whistle. This turned out to be a mistake, for it sent them howling and reeling all over the sidewalk. They obviously had a private joke. They continued down the street without telling me anything about the train.

I tried my phrase on an old man. He looked puzzled. I made the train sound. He pointed his finger around the corner and walked away. I followed the direction but got nowhere, so I returned to where I saw train tracks cross the road and followed them to the station, a warehouse type of building where grains were stored and shipped. A man saw me riding toward the main building and ran up to me speaking fluent English.

"Good to see you," he said out of breath. "I lived five years in Australia."

"Really?" I said. "When did you get back?"

"Last year. My family's here. They couldn't go. People here don't like me because I left them and worked somewhere else. They don't trust me. What do you think of Yugoslavia?"

Before I had time to answer he said, "I bet you don't like it. The people aren't friendly. Where do you want to go?"

"The police wouldn't let me ride on the road, and I don't feel so well, as if I drank some bad water. Can I take a train to Skopje?"

"You're lucky. There's a train coming through in a half hour, the Athens Express. I'll flag it down so it will stop here. We'll put your bicycle in the baggage car. I'll tell them to be careful with it. There's so much theft, you know."

He took me to the ticket window and fetched a rounded woman in standard blue workers' dress who wrote me a ticket. We went out to sit on the dock near several other blue-clad railroad employees. He began talking about Tito:

"The country has changed a lot since the old man died. I don't want to say his name in front of these people or they'll think I'm up to no good, but you know who I mean. They're already suspicious of me. I don't talk about anything political with them. Everyone around here is afraid. No one wants to do or say anything unusual, anything that can get them in trouble."

"People don't seem happy here," I said.

"You noticed. Everyone notices. It's not a good place to ride a bicycle."

We talked for over an hour until the train came. My friend helped me put Angel in baggage then escorted me to the next car.

"Thank you for your help," I said as the train began moving.

"No. Thank you," he said, as if I had done him a favor.

I found a compartment with a Greek fruit exporter who was drinking wine and eating olives and cheese. Enthusiastically, he welcomed me in English and offered me food and drink.

"Thanks," I said, "but my stomach isn't feeling well."

"Ah, yes. It's hard in Yugoslavia," he said.

During the next stops, many more people boarded the train. Six entered our compartment at various stops and silently filled the seats. By sundown the aisle overflowed with an active, noisy group, a hefty share of which were military men. The cabin doors remained open while people talked loudly and smoked endlessly. Those who could not find a seat were relegated to a space in the aisle where they sat cramped between walls and doors. If a person stood up, someone else took his place. Two people saw a few millimeters of space between the people sitting opposite me on the Greek's side and tried to force themselves in, but the people sitting pushed them off with their hands and their sharp language.

The smoke turned everyone's eyes red. The person sitting next to me, a former guest-worker in Germany, said to me, "I'm sorry for the way these people behave. They are uneducated country folk."

"You don't have to apologize," I said. "Country folk are fine with me."

"Yes, but they're gruff and have no sensitivity," he said.

The noise, the choking smoke, and the loud conversation added to the discomfort and made it impossible for anyone to sleep until dawn when we were beside ourselves with fatigue. Among the cigarette butts on the floor lay clumps of uncomfortable bodies, arms twisted over and under necks, legs squeezed or coiled around corners and under baggage.

Suddenly the whistle blew and the brakes squeaked loudly. All of us were thrown into other people's laps as the train came to a dead stop. I lowered the window to look out, seeing only a line of heads doing the same thing. On the other side of the train came a rumble of excitement. People were talking. The guest-worker told me that the train had killed someone.

I was able to make my way to the other window and saw a woman in a blue workers' uniform lying five feet from the locomotive. No one was around her. Her legs were exposed, the blue dress laying ruffled above her knees, but her head was buried in the weeds.

"How do you know she's dead?" I asked the guest-worker who joined me at the window.

"They say she's dead," he said, his eyes on the woman in the grass.

I started walking out the door to see the poor woman, but two military men stopped me, wagging their fingers at me, telling me in sign language that I had no business outside the train.

I said to the Greek in English, "There's no telling if she really is dead. No one has gone out to see her."

"In this country you mind your own affairs," said the Greek.

I returned to the window. The woman got hit by the train at a level crossing on the periphery of a village. Many local people, all dressed in blue, walked back and forth near the train. They turned to look at the woman, then continued walking.

I said to the Greek, "Surely in this small village people know each other, but no one makes the slightest gesture toward the woman."

He acknowledged what I said with a shrug. Someone had taken my seat opposite him. The guest-worker told me that we were waiting for the authorities to arrive. I looked out the window: villagers passed, looked over, and continued on their way. An hour passed. People on the train were standing around smoking, probably complaining about the delay. The soldiers who had stopped me from leaving had gone somewhere else, so I got off the train quietly with my camera on the pretext of taking a picture. I walked over to the woman. I couldn't see any breathing. One of the soldiers on the train yelled over. I took a picture. In an instant, a dozen voices began shouting at me, waving me to leave the area and get back on the train. I looked at their threatening gestures and complied, returning to the window.

Not long after, two police cars with sirens pulled up to the train. The engineer got out and shook hands with the six policemen. They glanced over at the woman, then talked for a couple of minutes. One of the policemen went to his car, brought out a camera, and took three pictures of the woman. Another policeman came close to her and, bending from the waist, looked down at her with his hands in his pockets. They signaled to the conductor to move the train. As we were leaving I saw another policeman bring out a white sheet. The villagers ignored the scene.

We arrived at Skopje four hours behind schedule. Two men handed Angel down to me from the baggage car. I walked out of the station and was struck by the historic beauty of the city. Heavy stone buildings, old and ornate, lined the streets, a definite contrast to the grotesque post Bauhaus modern apartment buildings that seem to be destroying every other city.

As I rode into the countryside, I was also struck by the country's natural beauty, its open green hills, rolling country where large farms were harvesting, bundling stacks of hay at regular intervals over the brown and yellow ground. A few tractors worked the land, but much of the labor was done by groups of women who hand bundled the large cubes of hay.

An hour later I arrived at a town. A procession was coming down the main street toward me. I took off my bicycling cap and stood with Angel on the side of the road. An Orthodox priest swinging incense and reading from a small black Bible lead the group. A bass drum and two trumpets played a simple dirge. A horse pulled a cart which carried a wood casket without flowers. About ten mourners walked behind, talking quietly among themselves.

No one else in the town seemed to pay attention to the funeral. A couple of children came over to me and said a few words, then walked away when they realized that I couldn't understand them.

When I arrived at the border of Greece a short time later, a German couple who had passed me on the road in their car and were waiting in line for border formalities came up to me to wish me well. As it turned out they had a house in Greece and traveled through Yugoslavia a couple of times a year.

"It seems here that one is supposed to be detached and unemotional," I said.

"Things are different on the coast," said the man. "But most tourists pass through quickly."

"It's a beautiful country," I said.

"Yes, you have to find the beauty," he said. "It isn't in the society."

Two Wheels Over the Sinai

Two women sitting in the shade under a canvas tarp saw me in the distance bicycling down the sandy road toward their solitary house. They were startled for a second, then quickly crossed their faces with white veils. Everything else they wore was black — not just black, but a thick black, a dense, choking black that defied both the sun and reason, making their white veils appear too progressive. Like other Bedouin women I had seen, they sat, cooked, and farmed in their weighty woolen gowns, as if they were doing penance for the sins of the world.

Custom wouldn't allow me, a male stranger, to approach them. I got off Angel and walked to the pile of watermelons under the canvas awning that hung from four wooden posts staked in the sand. The women automatically moved to the shady side of their flimsy wooden house where they could be alone, away from intrusive eyes, and without veils.

"Which one would the bicyclist like?" asked the man in a friendly tone while giving the melons a gentle tap. He was small with a straight back, kind face, and docile manner. He wore dark baggy trousers, a long shirt with sleeves that came down to his thumbs, and a white triangular *hatta* headdress. All the while I was with him under the awning he spoke only a little, his voice always gentle and caring.

Another middle-aged man and a boy about fourteen appeared suddenly from nowhere, inspected my bicycle with smiles of curiosity, and came over jovially to socialize. As the vendor helped me choose a crisp, sweet, deep red watermelon, the others brought out a heavy linen bag of inch thick pita bread and cubes of salty white cheese from a deep hole in the sand. The white summer sun beat mercilessly on the canvas tarp. It was the middle of Ramadan, the Islamic holy month, when devout Moslems don't eat or drink during the daytime, but these people of the Sinai were more practical than devout. The watermelon vendor laid a blanket on the sand under the tarp. The four of us sat down on the edges of it, exchanged customary niceties, insisting that each other start first, then enjoyed the refreshing feast before us.

"Where are you from?" the boy asked, after listening to my English-accented Arabic.

I told them my father's name and his town of origin.

"Our hearts welcome you here," said the watermelon vendor.

"Thanks be to God you arrived safely," said the other.

"I have been traveling on bicycle since Cairo," I said. They didn't restrain their amazement. I didn't tell them that Cairo was just my last stop after riding through Europe and taking a ferry to Alexandria.

"Khalif here has been to the other side of the Suez several times," the watermelon vendor said. "To me it's another world. It's enough for me to know the Sinai."

Khalif and the watermelon vendor exhorted me to eat more, saying that I hardly touched anything.

"We're *falah*," said the boy. Almost everyone in the desert calls himself a *falah*, a peasant, a commoner whose life has changed little since the time of Christ.

"We make things work," said Khalif while eating a slice of watermelon in his hands. "Sometimes we sell wood or the parts of army vehicles that have been left behind. We sell fruits and now and then a camel."

"It all works out, thank God," added the watermelon vendor.

"I have water," I said triumphantly.

"We're happy for you," said Khalif, his smile showing a mouth of teeth.

Here, as in other areas of the Sinai, water was surprisingly not a problem. Nile water was brought in by truck to most towns and was being piped to the coastal communities. Each household put an oil drum with a lid on it near the street in front of their house, and a water truck came regularly to fill it. Women or children scooped the water out of the oil drum with a pail and carried it into their homes.

Foolishly, I hauled a lot of water all the way from Cairo in an expandable plastic container. My friends in Cairo told me I wouldn't need that much, but I'll be damned if after lugging that empty container half way around the world, through fourteen states and ten European countries, I was not going to use it. Empty, the container took up too much room in my panniers, so I had to carry it on the rear rack with my sleeping bag. When filled, it was so heavy it eventually broke two spokes on the freewheel side of my rear wheel, and I had to yank off the freewheel and change those spokes under the midday desert sun.

Desert people are used to long travel, albeit not on a packed bicycle.

"If we don't like it here we go somewhere else," said the boy who ate with us, echoing my own philosophy."

"Why do you travel this way?" asked Khalif.

"With a bicycle I go slowly and see the land and the people. I travel quietly, without disturbing anyone, so I can see how people live."

"But we live like everyone else," he said. "We eat bread and cheese and watermelon. We don't have as many cars and not as much noise, but plenty of light to give you deep vision."

"Yes," I said. "Here a person feels at peace."

"By the grace of God," added the watermelon vendor, slipping another slice of melon into my hand.

Sitting in the quietness of the desert, sometimes talking sometimes passing through long periods of silence when words seemed superfluous, a land where women wore veils and scurried away as soon as a male arrived, it was difficult for me to realize that only a few days before I had bicycled along the Nile and through the chaotic capital. I hadn't experienced insane traffic until I bicycled in the hectic pace of Cairo's streets. The streets were crowded with people, animals, ox carts, push carts, heavy single-speed bicycles, motorcycles, cars, busses, trucks — every person, every animal, every vehicle propelled by a kind of frenzy. There were few sidewalks, and drivers paid little attention to traffic laws or rational driving. If a car were to stop at a red light in Cairo people would think that the car had stalled and would go around it. I plunged into the madness, riding all around the city, flinging up my arms when a car cut in front of me, telling taxi drivers what I thought of their maneuvers.

Egyptian drivers love their horns. It took me a bit of time to get used to this. Not only did drivers honk at me for no good reason, occasionally sticking their heads out the window to comment, but cars and trucks continuously honked while there was absolutely nothing around. Ready to capitalize on the Egyptians' mania, the Japanese came up with more and more elaborate horn sounds — bird calls, whistles, a few bars of a popular song, animal calls, even a horn that simulated an automobile accident. The government finally put an end to the revelry, and now one can only hear innocent beeps and honks; most of them are drivers saying hello to each other.

After leaving the numerous dusty, heavily-populated suburbs of Cairo, I came up the desert roads to Ismailia. I could have drawn a line where the green Nile Valley ended and the desert began. Suddenly, the world became much hotter and drier. The sand reflected the raw heat of the sun across the handlebar and slammed it into my face. It was like opening an oven door. I followed the example of the natives and wore a white *hatta* to shield my head. I was told that thick wool clothing protects the body from the heat of the sun, but I didn't test the theory. I kept my chain oiled and cleaned sand and dirt from the moving parts often: a desert like this, I thought, is not the place for trouble.

I bicycled along the Suez — one of the most scenic rides of my trip — passing villages and farmlands and sand dunes and too many military checkpoints. All along the way people treated me to generous hospitality, offering me coffee or complete meals or shelter for the night, and a continuous offer of cigarettes. When I first arrived in Egypt I declined the cigarettes, saying that I didn't smoke, but no one ever believed me. As soon as I finished one cigarette, another person was eagerly flashing another pack under my nose, their way of being generous. I accepted, thanking them.

The Egyptians, a spirited and gregarious people, would have been insulted if I refused their hospitality. It also wouldn't be fun, for the Egyptians love foreigners, and all my encounters with them were lively: they may be used to tourists, but they rightly regarded bicycle touring as an entirely different activity. They also have an odd custom about giving directions. Signs are not plentiful, and whenever I asked someone the route to a town, he would tell me, even if he didn't know. A crazy custom: he doesn't want to show either ignorance or unfriendliness. After going the wrong way several times, I became adept at figuring out who actually knew and who was courteously bluffing, yet I would never insult people by not making at least a show of following their directions.

A group of young men directed me to a metal flatbed ferry which was just returning from the other side of the Suez. I bicycled aboard with a lively crowd of about fifty soldiers. The officer of the group approached me and bought me a Coca Cola from a ten-year-old who carried a portable cooler full of ice and little bottles. I tried to buy them a bottle or two as well, but they wouldn't allow it. Our cigarettes had burned down by the time we reached the other shore, but as I was getting off a soldier on the shore stopped me, saying that the road I wanted to take was a closed military area. This news came as a surprise to everyone on the ferry who crowded around me to discuss the matter among themselves. I felt sure that the soldier had made up this regulation on a whim. Out of politeness, the officer and three of the others who had been talking to me accompanied me back to the southern shore — smoking more cigarettes and talking more about life in the West — then they told me to go a few miles up the coast where another ferry would take me across.

This second ferry turned out to be a small boat for eight passengers. I had to tie Angel on top of the bow and hope for no jerky movements. The ferry pilot got a lot of mileage out of making jokes to others about my trepidation at seeing Angel loosely tied like a masthead to the bow. One of the young men on the ferry who helped me with Angel proclaimed to the other passengers every part of our conversation on the shore: where I was from and what I was doing. The group nodded their heads in approval.

When we got off on the opposite shore, the young man took me by the elbow and stopped me. "I only want to know one thing," he said. "Why does America support Israel as it does?"

"I really don't know. I'm going to Israel for the first time. Perhaps I'll find out then," I answered.

"But Palestine is your country."

"No," I said. "I've been living in America since I was six years old. I'm as American as you're Egyptian."

"When you find the answer to my question, come back and tell us. No one here understands."

When I crossed over the Suez I crossed into another civilization. The cigarettes stopped, thank God, the people seemed more traditional, and the quiet of a non-Western world caught hold of me.

A newly paved road runs straight to the Gaza Strip near the Mediterranean; other paved roads branch through the Sinai. Traffic is scarce, a few trucks and the occasional car. The sand blows in on all roads. Many times I had to walk my bicycle over short stretches, even with the fat tires that I brought for the trip. I explored, taking a few roads that weren't paved, traveling on them slowly. I found that they led to desert villages of ten to 100 inhabitants.

At the end of one sandy road only a few miles from the Mediterranean, I came upon a tented community with camels hobbled in front, women in dark full-length garments were beating grain with mallets under the shade trees, and men in long robes were playing backgammon on a blanket: a romantic setting out of a Biblical movie. The leader of the group was a plump jolly man who stayed in his tent watching color television run off a generator. I had Arabic coffee with him, served by a young boy.

"Your tongue is heavy," he remarked at my halting speech.

"I haven't spoken Arabic for twenty-five years."

"Are you married?" he asked.

"Yes," I said, lying, not wanting to hear about his wonderful daughter.

"How many children?"

"Two." I answered, thinking fast.

"God keep them and give you more. I have seven."

This community seemed to be an exception; most others lived in more humble circumstances. I would be riding with nothing but mountains of sand in view and suddenly see a few trees in the distance, a sure sign of a place with people and, probably, watermelons. Around the trees would be a half dozen Bedouin tents, or a single dwelling such as the one where I'd eaten bread and cheese. A few people found a place in the sand and made that their home, but most lived at an oasis. Occasionally a traveling mystic would pass me on the road, a wise man locked in his own thoughts who hardly notices the stranger on a bicycle riding past him.

The evening after I met the sheikh with the color television, I saw a lone house in the desert with an old car in front. A man saw me coming, went up to the road and waved me in to spend the night. There was neither well nor trees around his house. He wore the typical white gown and headdress and had two children who played with my cycle computer and other New World toys I brought out. The man wasn't an ordinary Bedouin; he had a car and worked as a migrant laborer in several Arab countries, leaving for a year or two at a time and returning with money to support his family. I never saw his wife; she prepared dinner and handed it through the kitchen door to the children, and they brought it to us as we ate on the sand watching the setting sun turn the desert a rich amber.

It's a myth that deserts are cold at night. In high altitudes and during cold seasons deserts lose their heat, but most deserts remain warm through the night. Without using my tent, I lay on my sleeping bag and wrapped myself in the solitude of a desert that has been the mentor for countless seekers. The clean quiet of the desert for only one night is worth all the trouble of getting there.

The peace treaty between Israel and Egypt opened a border near the town of Al-Arish a couple of months before I arrived. After I had bicycled back to the Sinai's Mediterranean coast, I came through Al-Arish, a crowded community of Palestinian refugees, then cycled north over a newly paved road surrounded by more sand dunes. A mile north of the city a red stained wooden building standing among desert vegetation served as the Egyptian border station. A bureaucratic exit procedure lasted until a guard who looked no older than sixteen raised the yellow barrier and let me pass along with a native family of five who were on foot. The family came to the border before I arrived. I couldn't imagine how they got there, but when the guard let us go, they began walking to the Israeli side. They told me that they were going to see relatives, and we wished each other well as I bicycled past them.

Halfway between the two borders I changed from long pants to bicycling shorts, from desert headgear to a bicycling cap, and continued along the half mile no-man's-land until I came to a pair of Israeli soldiers who sat in the shade of a corrugated metal shack talking on a two-way radio. The shack stood incongruously among sand dunes containing only the occasional desert brush. The young soldiers stationed at this remote outpost wore grenades on their sides and had their guns ready on their laps. They gave the feeling that they belonged to a special group, a feeling of camaraderie among themselves.

Another half mile of bicycling brought me to the customs and immigration building, a large temporary structure that obliged a dozen Sinai and Palestinian families to sit in the sun on the sandy ground surrounded by bags and sacks, like abandoned wagon train pioneers. From my handlebar bag I pulled out my American passport and flashed it to the guards. They ushered me into the shady porch in front of the immigration office window. A soldier with a New York accent was amazed that I crossed the Sinai by bicycle and asked me excitedly where I was from. I told him Chicago.

"Great. I always wanted to travel by bicycle, too."

He looked at the equipment on my bicycle, then took my passport. I saw his eyes drop down to the line "Place of Birth: Lebanon." His buoyant spirit plummeted, setting in motion a cycle of well-orchestrated events.

"Wait here. Someone will come out to talk to you," he said in a somber tone without looking at me.

He took my passport inside, and five minutes later a soldier in his mid-30s came out with it in his hand.

"Why do you want to come to Israel?" he said in a Hebrew-accented English, making no pretense of being polite.

"I want to see what it's like," I said.

A string of accusatory questions followed: Who packed your bags? What did you do in Egypt? Who did you stay with? Where are you going after this? What do you do in America? What are you going to do here? How are you going to leave? Do you have any family here? If we allow you to enter, how long are you going to stay? Do you have anything on you that anyone gave you in Egypt?

He didn't seem that interested in my responses. He too told me to wait while he went back inside. I sensed people watching me.

A few minutes later an attractive young woman about twenty-four, wearing make-up and a pressed uniform, came out and said in perfect English, "Hi, how you doin'?"

I looked at her and sensed a shallow level of sincerity. "Real good," I answered, mimicking her, thinking how out of place she seemed in the Sinai.

She held her shoulders way back so that I could see her large breasts. "You're from Lebanon, right?"

"No. I'm from the United States."

"Where have you been travelin'?" She kept a cool, informal style, clichéd and transparent, leaning on the wall with me like talking to an old friend.

"I'm on a world trip, starting from America to Europe to the Middle East and going to Asia."

"That's great. Where do you stay at night?"

"In a hotel, or else I camp."

"Where did you stay last night?"

"Some Bedouins let me stay with them."

"How do you communicate with the Arabs?"

"I know some Arabic. What I don't know I communicate with sign language."

"But how can you stand it in Egypt? Aren't the people dirty?"

I shrugged off the question. She then asked the same string of questions that the first fellow asked, again hardly listening to my responses.

Finally, she asked, "Do you know why I have to ask all these questions?"

"You can ask any question you like."

This must have impressed her, for she walked me through the customs room where the local people where being subjected to minute searches amid an atmosphere of haggling and wailing. No one looked at anything I had.

"Please don't stamp my passport," I asked the person in a make-shift booth who stamps passports. "I'm planning to go on to other Arab..."

"Don't worry, don't worry," he said, waving me off and giving me a slip of paper.

The money-changer, thinking that I was a Jew, exhorted me to keep away from those "dirty Arabs — you can never trust them, the little thieves." Another border guard warned me to stay on the road because there were still land mines intact, a warning that was confirmed by several road signs. I looked back and saw the same group of Arabs sitting on the ground in the sun in front of the building.

Bicycling north I passed a few more tented communities with camels and laundry spread out on bushes to dry. Gradually the area became more populated, and the nomadic people became fewer. Men no longer rode camels, and few women wore veils. Twenty miles after the Al-Arish border I came to the first military roadblock. I couldn't tell, but I thought it must have been the beginning of the Gaza, where, eventually, the new border between Egypt and Israel might be placed.

One of the soldiers took my passport, and upon seeing my name said, "Nasr. You are Arab man."

"I'm an American," I said.

He and the other two soldiers became brusque and made me take out everything in my panniers.

Gaza was a sad sight. I bicycled in front of a couple of refugee camps where barefoot children played in the narrow, sand-filled alleys between the cement-block houses. The inhabitants' vivacious spirit didn't match their condition. People, especially young people, freely came up to me and asked me where I was from and what I was doing. They gave me a piece of what they were eating and offered me the hospitality of their homes. One young man insisted so much that I had to follow him to his modest house in the middle of a refugee camp. Men and women greeted us as we passed the narrow alleys of the camp. He told them that I was a Palestinian.

"No," I thought to myself, "I'm an American."

We walked through the metal door of the young man's house, entered a small courtyard, and walked up four stairs to the cement-block sitting room. Carpets covered the floor of the front room. Family pictures and framed diplomas hung high on the walls, well above eye level.

Young men and women came from neighboring homes to sit on the carpets with me and talk. Each person shook my hand and said welcome. The mother brought coffee and pastries for everyone. We had a jovial time, talking, giggling, and laughing like old family friends.

"Do you go to school?" I asked the group.

"When it's open," one girl responded.

"The Israelis don't want us to learn, so they close the schools," said a young man.

"If you had the chance to move to another country," I asked, "would you?"

"The Israelis want us to go, but we won't," one of them said.
"Why should we go? Palestine is our home," replied someone else.
"It's your home as well," added a young woman. "Wouldn't you want to return?"

The question puzzled me. My link to this land disturbed me. I grew up as an American. I speak like an American. I studied American literature. Going to Palestine was like going to a foreign country. Their ways were a novelty to me. But a home? I didn't have one. Since I was eighteen I never lived in the same place for over a year. I gave up my apartment when I had started the trip. The few things I owned, clothes and books and dishes, were in four cardboard boxes in a friend's basement in Chicago. In that way I was like these Palestinians who live in a temporary home in the refugee camp, only they had a strong sense of national identity. They came from a village near what is now Tel Aviv, a village that was erased from the map twenty-five years before they were born, yet they called it home.

I don't know what I answered. The idea of belonging to Palestine was something to contemplate while bicycling. When it was time to leave, I thanked the group.

"Don't thank us," said one teenager. "It's our pleasure to talk about our country, ours and yours."

Bicycling on the main road into Gaza City, I met my second military roadblock. A group of five armed soldiers checked cars selectively, creating a long line of vehicles. Instead of passing, I took my place in line like a car, and watched what the soldiers were doing. First they looked at the car's license plate. Sometimes they waved the car on; sometimes they told the men to get out and examined their identity cards and searched their bodies, rudely, gruffly. The Palestinians were docilely abject.

As we were waiting in line, a couple of cars with yellow Israeli license plates passed the whole line and drove through. I held myself back from yelling at them for cutting the line which was made up of cars with silver plates, signifying an Arab car.

My turn at the queue came. A twenty-year-old soldier looked at my face, was puzzled, then looked at my passport.

"You vere born Levanon." I didn't answer. "Move," he said pointing to the side, coming with me. "Take all out," indicating my panniers.

"They just checked me five kilometers ago." He didn't understand. I tried Arabic. No understanding.

It takes a lot of time to pack the panniers properly, and I didn't want to take everything out again. I opened one pannier, took out a jersey that was on top, and pointed at him to look at the rest.

"Take all out," he demanded. I could see that his rifle on his chest made him slightly immobile.

I took out another piece of clothing.

"All out." He growled.

He motioned with his gun. I took out one other piece of clothing and started refolding the jersey so I could put it back. He got angry, repeating "All out." I took out a bit more, making it clear to him that he would have a hard time getting to the bottom of both panniers. Finally he grew tired and rudely told me to go.

In Gaza city I spotted a tray of pistachio nut sweets in a shop window and wasted no time getting inside to taste them. In my opinion the pastries of the Levant can only be rivaled by Vienna's, although they are very different from each other. When the husband and wife that owned the store heard my heavily accented Arabic they remained friendly but guarded, presenting me a honey-drenched, nut-filled sweet on a plate and returning behind the counter. I realized that I had forgotten to change out of my shorts into long pants, making them suspicious of me.

"My family is from Palestine," I said to clear the air.

The husband looked delighted and responded, "From where? What family?"

"From Nazareth. Nasr family. They became refugees to Lebanon in '48 and went to America in '56."

"Thank God that you came back safely." He asked his wife to serve tea with mint. "I'll bring my son. He talks about America and wants to meet people from there." He stopped, turned to me, and said, "It's wonderful that you came back."

The son soon appeared from a room behind the store. He looked about eighteen. I stood up to shake hands, and we began speaking in English since, as he said, it would be easier for me. His cousin had been to Duke University to study, and he wanted to do the same.

"But if you go, will they allow you back?" I asked.

He looked at me and smiled. "There are no jobs here," he replied. "We can only work stupid jobs, jobs no one else would want. It's not good here for us." He talked without a negative tone in his voice.

"What about your family?"

"They understand that I have to go away to support them. We all have to make this sacrifice. But Palestine will be ours again, and you and I will be able to come back."

There was a pause. "Tell me," I said, "is there a special problem today? I had to pass two checkpoints."

"Two is light. When there's a problem there can be ten, even more. They're not looking for anything; they just want to make life difficult."

The mother saw how much I liked the sweet and gave me two more, telling me that I needed to eat them because I was too thin. The young man gave me a *kafeyah*, a Palestinian head scarf, and wanted me to stay with them for the night. It was early, and I told them that I wanted to ride more that day. Honestly, I didn't accept his offer because I felt intimidated by the Israeli military presence which I was unused to. The military gave me a feeling of fear, and I didn't want to stay in a Palestinian house. I think that the boy's father intuitively understood this. I almost insulted him when I pulled out money to pay for the sweets. He put his hands on both my arms and kissed me on each cheek, wishing God's protection on me during my travel and telling me to return to them.

After bicycling another ten miles I passed a checkpoint signaling the beginning of Israel's 1967 boundaries, and soon after entered Askelon, a modern ugly city along the Mediterranean. The high rises were a contrast to the modest buildings I had been seeing since Cairo. Every place I went — into two grocery stores to buy food, a bank to change money, a gas station to fill up water — people seemed to treat me rudely, without knowing my name or place of birth, so I left, bicycled farther, and camped. The next morning a bearded American was bicycling in the opposite direction. He came over and befriended me, and I discovered he was from Berkeley.

"I'm working on a kibbutz," he said. "Would you like to come over to see?"

I accepted. It was a farming kibbutz filled with other genial young Americans. The sound of a screaming jet dominated life every five minutes.

"It's an air base," said my host. "After three months here I don't even hear them any more."

He took me all around the farm, showing me the harvesting equipment, the common library and dining room, the apartments, and the fields.

"It's a hard time for the kibbutzim," he said. "Most are losing operations and have to be supported by the government. Now only about three percent of Israelis live on a kibbutz."

"How many people are here?" I asked.

"About fifty. Most are leftists from America who came to Israel for an experience in communal living."

Jets continued to take off and land, their sound destroying the otherwise peaceful atmosphere. I guessed by the sound that they must be sophisticated fighters and bombers: skyhawks, spitfires, phantoms.

"Could I join the kibbutz?" I asked. "I was a member of a religious order and know what community living is like."

"You can work on the kibbutz for a month or so," he said.

"But if I wanted to move here and live, like you?"

"There's a law of return. Any Jew can return to Israel."

"I'm not a Jew. I just don't understand why everyone here comes from America and is supported by the government while the people in Gaza whose families have lived here for thousands of years are considered stateless. And why can't I live here if I want to? My family were forced to leave their home. It's only a few miles away. It isn't right."

"The people on the kibbutz don't necessarily like Israel's politics," he said. "It's not a happy situation, but there's nothing you and I can do."

"The people in Gaza were telling me that things are becoming worse all the time. It looks to me like the Israelis have laid the foundation for a civil war."

I adjusted the derailleurs on two of the community's ten-speed bicycles, paid for a cafeteria-style meal, and listened to people telling me about the Israeli-Palestinian political situation between the intermittent roar of jets. Although they voiced opposition to the way the Israeli government treated the

Palestinians, they had never been inside Palestinian villages and refugee camps and had no contact with what they called "non-Jews." It seemed strange to me that Americans who considered themselves leftists should accept such ethnic or racial divisions.

The next few days I rode up and down the country. It's relatively easy to bicycle up to the Lebanese border from the Tel Aviv area in less than a day. I found nothing exceptionally interesting, and I noticed that the people didn't know the rules of hospitality of the Middle East. The presence of the military was overwhelming. I made my way up the hills to Jerusalem, saw the buildings one usually sees, then began riding into the semi-arid West Bank. New constructions were beginning, constructions of entire towns for Israeli settlers: colorless, fortresses behind walls of barbed wire. They seemed more like tombs than houses.

The enthusiasm of the Palestinian community made the trip worthwhile. In village after village young men would come up to me and want to converse. They saw that although I had a Palestinian name, I belonged to another world, that I spoke faulty Arabic and had no experience in traditional Arab customs. But they would take me to their homes for tea or coffee and proudly introduce me to their parents and brothers and sisters.

I always asked questions about the relation between Jew and Palestinian, and got a steady stream of horror stories, tales of abuse and brutality at the hands of the military occupation. The new Jewish settlers took away the land and the trees and the water of Palestinians. The military raided villages at night and took away young boys to prison. Each story attacked my sense of justice.

One young man I met in a grocery store took me around the corner to his house for coffee. "Right now there aren't many checkpoints, and you won't see many military patrols," he said. "School is out, and things are quiet. But when something happens, the military are everywhere."

Chairs and coffee tables stood at the sides of the room. The walls were white and the floor was tile. Pictures and diplomas, which were too high for reading, hung one after another on the walls, separated by large windows looking out on ancient olive trees deeply rooted in the rocky brown earth. The whole family had gathered around to talk to me, to insist that I stay for lunch, dinner, the night.

"Why don't you come back here to live?" asked his mother.

"I can only stay here as a tourist," I answered.

"It's too bad you went to America," said her youngest son. "You could have joined us in liberating Palestine."

Gods and Mortals in Southern India

I bicycled down the paved road into the center of the village, a cluster of twenty or so straw-thatched mud huts that lined both sides of the street. No one noticed me except the mustached little man who ran the teahouse. The rest of the town slept; nothing moved the midday tropical air but the sound of the plodding hooves of four lead-black water buffalo lazily walking down the middle of the street. The man in the bamboo hut that served as the village teahouse took his eyes off the pile of twigs under the large pot of water and looked in silent amazement at the sight in front of him. I stopped at the edge of the road, loosened the straps on my toe clips and got off my bicycle to walk across the broad patch of empty dirt to the teahouse. As soon as I leaned Angel on the side of the bamboo counter, a crowd of men and boys surrounded me.

No one called them; they gathered like birds suddenly gather at a spot, coming from nowhere, running from every direction, breaking the still, silent air to appear in front of the teahouse and form a crescent of astonished faces around me. After a minute of staring, one person ventured to disturb the soundlessness of the afternoon and began speaking to me in Tamil. I responded with a greeting from the handful of Tamil words I had learned. He turned to look at the others who wore vacant faces, shrugged his shoulders, and asked me if I knew any words of Tamil. I laughed from my belly.

All at once the crowd changed from a solemn group of observers to a lively band of fun-lovers. They started joking with each other, laughing, jesting, putting their arms around each other's shoulders while pointing at me and Angel. A few children touched my legs and arms to see if I was made out of the same stuff as they. An English-speaking man came forward, breaking the group's formation as he began the cycle of questions: "What is your native country?" That's always the first question, not where do you come from, or what country are you from, but what is your native country. The second question varies. This time it was, "And what is your final destination?" I answered, "Madras," and he exclaimed, "What? On cycle?" — that's always the exclaimed response — he told the crowd which stirred with excitement.

I must be insane, obviously. But since I was a foreigner who looked happy, another English-speaking man in creased trousers stepped forward and invited me inside for tea. The crowd divided itself naturally into three groups. The first consisted of eight distinguished villagers wearing faded polyester trousers and short-sleeved white or off-white shirts, form fitting, who accompanied me into the hut and ordered tea. The second group, twenty lively barefoot children wearing dirty shorts and torn T-shirts, took their position outside the teahouse, standing still, leaning into the hut, anchored to the light brown earth by very thin dark brown legs, staring at the scene inside with large unblinking eyes, not daring to ask the owner to let them pass the invisible line which separated the road's shoulder from the dirt-floored business establishment.

The third group, men dressed in nothing but white dhoti (loincloths), some wearing white caps, the others wearing oil in their thick black hair, gathered around Angel. They inspected the handlebar, the gearing system, the metal pedals with the toe clips and red leather straps, moving every lever back and forth and watching its effect. They discussed and argued about the function of each part, speculating that the dusty red plastic bottles mounted on the frame were motors. They felt the material of the panniers, the sleeping bag casing, the narrow seat. They played with the digital watch strapped around the handlebar and examined the map on the top of the handlebar bag, pointing to each road and city as if it was the first map they had ever seen. Finally, everyone, every single person near the bicycle, would squeeze the skinny tires and comment on the air pressure.

The group inside the teahouse crowded around me on three benches which were placed around a wood picnic table. "Are you making an all-India tour?" asked the spokesman, a school teacher who spoke four Indian languages as well as English.

I gave them a brief description of my time in India: "I arrived in Bombay a few weeks ago, in the middle of the rains. I've cycled through hundreds of villages, coming through Bangalore, then crossed into Tamil Nadu province."

The owner carried a hard plastic tray with nine glass cups of creamed and sugared tea and put a glass on a stainless steel saucer in front of each man, then stood behind listening intently to the translator repeating what I had said.

"We hear about people of other countries but never see them," said the school teacher. "Lorries do not pass this way. One Englishman came by foot many years ago, and of course Ghandi passed the villages. Isn't it very difficult on cycle?"

"The mountains were hard," I said.

"The Ghats." The picnic table shook as the group turned to each other in excited exchanges. I could only listen to their melodic language and imagine what they were saying. "You crossed the Ghats by cycle?" the teacher asked. I nodded. "For thousands of years the Ghats have been our protection against invaders. No one crossed the Ghats until the British came."

"You call them Ghats. When I was crossing them I called them a lot of other names." The school teacher turned his head from side to side to acknowledge what I said, but I don't think he understood my humor.

"This man would like to know if you like our country?" he asked, pointing to a man with a clean-shaven wrinkled face who wore a red cap with the name of an American Midwest fertilizer on the visor. That question is always part of the pattern of questions.

"I don't like your country," I said to their open mouths, blowing on my tea to cool it. Several of the men poured a bit of tea over the sides of their cups into their saucers and sipped it, trying not to show their emotion. "No," I said to heighten the drama, "I don't like your country. I love it." Everyone laughed a laugh of relief. I continued. "Not one day has gone by when people have not treated me to hospitality. They've offered me food, tea, places to stay for the night, even insisted to pay the postage for letters I was sending abroad."

"Are you not afraid? There are bad people in India."

"I have yet to meet them."

"But what made you come to our country?"

"I studied Hinduism and Buddhism, under several gurus. I came to learn more."

"Where are you going next, to the temples along the Cauvery?"

"Yes, then to Ramnad in order to take a ferry to Sri Lanka."

Finishing our tea, it came time to leave. The people outside were still debating about the function of Angel's front and rear derailleurs. The children were waiting for me to come out so they could again touch my hairy sun-baked skin and black shorts. I put down five rupees for the tea which usually costs half a rupee each, but each man insisted on paying.

"Please give the money to the poor," I said, a precept they had been fulfilling for centuries without my encouragement; the poor are not forgotten in the villages of southern India.

"Your cycle carries a big load," said the translator, speaking for one of the men looking at the bicycle.

"I've seen many others here carrying much more on their cycles," I replied, thinking about the young Indian men who carry twenty gallons of water in an assortment of metal and plastic containers while pedaling with bare feet, or those who bicycle with a passenger on the rear rack and another passenger on the top strut. I once saw a cycle-rickshaw driver pedal twelve children crammed into the carriage. "I would break every spoke if I carried as much as these young men on their cycles," I said. All the men that I had been talking to inside the teahouse came over to squeeze Angel's tires.

In India the usual bicycle is a standard black single speed clunker. They weigh as much as mine does when it's fully loaded.

I took my camera from the handlebar bag, and the children went wild, pushing each other playfully out of the way to be in the center of the picture. One of the respected men told them to calm down, and the school teacher told everyone to stand in front of the teahouse for a picture. When they gathered their smiling faces were suddenly transformed to stoney statue expressions, their agile bodies assumed a military parade posture.

I snapped the picture, promised to send them a copy, then took Angel, my cycle, and walked it to the road, waving and thanking everyone. A half dozen young men on clunkers escorted me out of the village with great merriment, each trying to keep up with me until the last young man faded away and left me to a narrow road surrounded by green and brown hills sitting still under the midday sun.

Tamil Nadu, the province that sits at the bottom of India, was the place to which I had bicycled to escape the heavy northern rain. I had landed in Bombay — much more chaotic than Cairo — and rode through its dilapidated, crammed outskirts, riding over mud roads, crossing ravines of soaked earth and flowing mud, ditches of brown water so high that when I crossed my feet only got out of the water on the top of the up stroke. It was a warm rain that didn't inhibit anyone from being outside, but it was useless to try to keep myself or my equipment dry: water eventually found its way through plastic bags and air tight containers.

I traveled south, finding myself in Poona two days later. I didn't know what it meant to be in Poona because I wasn't planning to go south from Bombay. Once I got to the city people kept directing me to a certain part of the city, and when I finally arrived there, a stocky young Indian wearing a saffron robe, beads, a 60s peace button, and a hippie-type ponytail looked at me and said in English with a heavy Indian accent, "Groovy man. You come all the way from America on cycle. Far out, man." He pronounced each word distinctly, pausing slightly, comically, between words. "Dynamite, man," he added as he squeezed my tire.

It threw me back ten years. "Come, man. You can crash in my pad." He continued using stilted, vintage slang while leading me down a muddy path through a maze of bamboo huts, passing two blond women in bright red robes drifting between huts. "Come in, man," he said as he stopped in front of his hut and unlocked the padlock. "My spiritual name is Bacharia. We smoke and talk." He threw himself on a bare mattress that was slightly raised off the wet dirt floor. "When do you want to see Bhagwan?"

"Who?" I asked.

A baby cried in the next hut, and I heard a woman speaking English with a German accent say to the crying child, "Stop this shit."

"Bhagwan, man. You come to see Bhagwan."

"Who's Bhagwan? I'm on a cycling trip."

He stopped, looked up at me, and laughed the laugh of a mad man. "It's Bhagwan's idea. He brings you here, and you don't know what's going on. Far out man." From his cryptic remarks I realized that this must be the home of Bhagwan Rajneesh, a pop guru figure in Europe and the United States who was, at that time, making plans to live in the U.S. I had been a guru connoisseur, studied under two of them and escorted others around Miami and New York, taking them to radio and TV shows. I knew little of Bhagwan because his immature spirituality had never appealed to me.

My ludicrous friend lit up a joint and passed it to me. It tasted as moldy as his language.

"We go to meditation soon," said Bacharia. "Do you want to come?"

"I didn't know you practiced meditation. I thought you were a bhakti yoga group, following the spiritual path by following Bhagwan."

"We meditate. Come, man, let's get a rickshaw."

I left my bicycle and let him lead me to a three-wheel motorcycle-rickshaw taxi which joined the procession of similar vehicles heading in the same direction. A mile later we arrived at a large stone structure where hundreds of Europeans and Americans dressed in scarlet or yellow robes gathered in clusters like giant marigolds. Bacharia seemed to be the only Indian in the group of light-skinned Westerners.

The temple was a large open hall with straw mats on the floor. A multitude of young followers sat cross-legged, looking mystical, spiritual. Flute music began; everyone's face became tight and serious: mouths opened, eyes looked to heaven, palms unfolded to the sky. Young men and women arose when the spirit inspired them and began sensually moving their arms and bodies to the dulcet music as in a Dionysian rite. This session of what Bacharia called meditation lasted about a half hour, after which the devotees gathered in groups for hugs and conversation then scattered to the hundred waiting motorcycle-rickshaw taxis.

Bacharia took me to the house of four of his male friends who had not been at the meditation. We entered the bamboo structure and walked into a cloud of marijuana and incense floating in the air, hovering over the four, two who were from London and the other two from California. They wore little or no clothing, played Grateful Dead and Jefferson Airplane cassettes, and spoke a language sprinkled with phrases which fell out of use when George McGovern lost his bid for the presidency. Their voices were slow and quiet, tranquilized, sounding like the drone of a Wyoming wind. They philosophized on the inane, wondered where they were going to get money for more dope, talked in reverent tones of their bearded spiritual leader whose picture was hung all around the untidy room.

"Bhagwan says that one day we'll get tired of drugs and sex, and that will be our spiritual awakening," one of the group said, when I asked him if marijuana helped his spiritual search. "He doesn't try to restrict us."

"Just being with him is a spiritual experience," said another. "You don't have to do anything; he does it for you."

I kept my thoughts to myself. Out of curiosity I waited to see this spiritual leader, but after two days of his non-appearance, I could no longer endure being in their mock ashram and in the midst of a lifeless, directionless, opiated existence. I jumped on my bicycle, agitated, hot to escape their euphoric banality, tearing at the pedals, pumping with my thighs, my back, my shoulders, keeping a sweating cadence as I traveled south out of the wetness of the monsoon rains. A couple of hours later, invigorated by non-stop bicycling I arrived at a village where another crowd gathered around Angel and me, laughing, asking questions, jesting, squeezing the tires. What a relief.

After several days of light bicycling I crossed into the Tamil state. I came upon an outdoor market where dozens of men and women laid out light-colored cloths on the street and sold everything from fresh vegetables to a handful of electrical parts. Most of the vendors sat on the ground next to their goods. The men wore a variety of clothes: mid-length shorts or long pants, dhotis, short-sleeved shirts. The women wore saris of every brilliant color like scattered zinnias on the ground. I gave coins to the beggars who approached and bought a couple of pieces of sugar cane from an old woman who sat behind twenty pieces of cut cane.

Three young men came up to me and directed me to the house of a merchant who ran the town and lived in its center. A group formed and accompanied me to the merchant's house. The other people who sold their goods along the side of the street looked on while children and young men joined the procession. By the time we turned the corner and faced the bright blue two-story house, a crowd of fifty thin, carob-colored people walked around and behind me. Some wore shoes; most didn't. The merchant's wife or a servant — I never discovered which — let me in, but the crowd remained huddled together outside as if they were awaiting spectacular news. Before the woman closed the door behind us, I looked back and saw people gathered around Angel, putting their feet in the pedals, moving the levers and squeezing the tires.

The merchant was, predictably, a heavy man, the only man his size among a town of delicately-framed people. He walked into the room carrying his stomach in his long fingered hands as if cradling a melon. He took me in cordially, indicating that my presence as a foreigner was an honor to his house, then sat me down by a long table that stood in the middle of the large empty room. The room was so big that if there had been another eight people we could have started a basketball game. Brilliantly colored unframed posters of Shiva mythology decorated the walls, and an altar with a god I didn't recognize stood in the corner. Speaking in perfect English, he said he felt it his duty to show me different Indian foods and explain to me about Indian life.

I thanked him, expressing appreciation for his kindness.

"Do you pray in front of the statue," I asked, pointing to a clay figure which was painted in bright blue and red and yellow and had bowls of food and fresh-cut flowers in front of it.

"Parjamante?" he said as he began to tell me about his god. "Every morning and every evening my wife petitions its good graces. She makes an offering and anoints her forehead. I don't believe in it anymore. Modern people are moving away from such ideas."

"Many gurus have come to America to teach the Hindu religion," I said. "They speak about living free from material comfort."

"It is very good that our people have gone to your country to teach, but Hindu religion is an integral part of the culture. You cannot take the religion and leave the culture. Gurus that talk about doing away with money are not popular among the people."

"What about inward spiritual development?" I asked.

He looked at me, then he said, "These people want something simple, making an offering in front of a god, or as you call it, a statue."

"But the gurus in America teach various forms of meditation, sitting quietly alone."

"No one does that here. The people believe in gods. Each person has his own god, a cow or an elephant or something else. They make an image of the god and worship it. This is their religion, not meditation or philosophy."

The woman silently brought out dish after dish of multi-spiced food and laid them in front of us. The businessman told her something, and she went back and got us each a spoon, a tool I had not used since arriving in India. She returned to the back room leaving us to feast like raja lords in a palaced room with heaping plates of entrees. I could hear the crowd, which now sounded like a small army, gathering outside waiting for me to emerge, the street vendors and the beggars and the children.

My host described in minute detail every dish in front of us. After I took my first spoonful, my mouth was so aflame that I couldn't taste anything else. I acknowledged his explanation with tears of gratitude.

"How does the caste system work?" I asked, trying to forget my scorched mouth.

"Originally it was intended to put the right person in the right occupation and to stabilize people, but now it has become troublesome. Many lower caste Hindus are converting to Islam for social reasons. This is becoming a very big problem in our country. The caste system is old and obsolete."

"What keeps it alive?"

"My friend, you cannot change 5000 years of tradition in a few years. These things take time. Americans are always in a hurry. The lower castes have to be slowly incorporated into the mainstream. You cannot rush these things. We do everything we can to help everyone in the town, but many people don't want help; they want to continue sweeping the streets and stay on their own level."

Before I had a chance to respond, he changed the subject, talking about business. He wanted to begin an import/export enterprise in the U.S. with me, but he had a hard time believing that I'm not a businessman — "everyone in America is wealthy: you all must be businessmen."

When dinner was over we got up and washed our mouths from a pitcher and bowl in one corner of the room. I excused myself and went out to rejoin the crowd waiting for another look at the stranger. The group talked and joked. Some wanted to correspond with me; we exchanged addresses. The merchant followed me and rudely brushed people away like crumbs from his table. He squeezed Angel's front tire, then, overriding my protests, took me to an upstairs room for the night. I slept on a metal spring bed with a two-inch mattress in an empty room with a twelve-foot ceiling but, typically, it had no netting on the windows to keep the thirsty mosquitoes from draining my blood.

The next day I took leave of my host and bicycled thirty or forty miles until I approached another large town. I saw women in bright saris — scarlet and ocher and sulfur and emerald and orange — stooped over working the land. Men and boys herded animals, walked, bicycled, or pushed loaded carts. All eyes turned to me as I bicycled down the left side of the road. One or two young men shouted jubilant greetings, and I responded enthusiastically. Everyone else stood still and looked at me, returning my wave. The density of the population increased as I approached the center of town, Keelapalar. I could have ridden to it in two hours, but because I accepted many invitations to stay for meals, tea, and conversation, it took me an entire day.

I saw a government guest house standing isolated, a semi-modern bungalow run by the provincial government. I had stayed at another such house a week before and enjoyed two large airy rooms, so I rode my bicycle through the metal gate and gave the caretaker three rupees for the night's stay. At that time about ten rupees made a dollar.

Two young men saw me carrying Angel over the two stairs to the doorway. They came up the gravel walkway and stepped into my room. After the usual questions, Amitava, a spirited young man who wore a Western-style short-sleeved red shirt over his slender body, said in fluent English, "We could not leave you alone at night. It is our duty to stay with you."

"That's very kind of you," I said as we sat on straight-backed chairs around a small table. "India has the reputation of being a place where one is left alone to meditate, but since I've been here I haven't spent a minute alone."

"None of us can stand being alone," said his friend Rajeshwari. "It is a grave insult, especially to a guest; no one would want to be alone."

"What about the sanyasis?" I asked, referring to the holy men who renounce natural life and live secluded.

Amitava lit a cigarette and answered, "There are a few fanatics everywhere."

"Aren't they respected?"

"The older people tolerate them. Both of us have taken our degrees from the Madras University; we have a different vision of life."

"What did you study?"

"Engineering," said Rajeshwari.

"International economics," said Amitava. "Neither of us have jobs yet. It is very difficult. We have put in applications to the government and several companies. It will take at least another two years before anyone will hire us, so we live with our families."

They invited me to see the town, starting with the temple. I accepted readily. We walked, arriving at the temple with an entourage of boys. A delicate old man with dry, tanned skin the color of pecans greeted us with clasped hands and an affectionate smile. Humbly, he invited us to enter and worship. I stepped over the stone threshold respectfully, bowing with hands clasped, then stood in front of the gods that were enshrined in small stone monuments. The children followed my every move but did not enter the temple.

"We don't believe these things," said Amitava in the middle of the temple. The caretaker smiled, thinking that Amitava had explained something to me about the temple. "It is superstition, mythology," he went on. "Only old people believe in this."

The temple was a relatively small structure with about a half dozen shrines. I stopped in front of each shrine. Believers opened the gate in front of each god, made an offering of fruit or flowers, then clasped their hands and bowed their heads in front of it for a few moments of prayer. No philosophy, no meditation, just faith.

I thanked the old man as we left the temple grounds. The two young men led me to the center of town, a two minute walk from the temple. We entered a restaurant housed in the bottom of a two-story wooden building. Inside were about ten large tables. The kitchen area was in the corner where a fire burned under several five gallon pots. On one side was a sink for washing. Like most similar establishments, the customers were only men. My friends ordered a round of dosa, vegetables wrapped inside a pancake with a variety of spices that once again made my mouth breathe fire.

"The town is in the middle of a feast," said Rajeshwari, "the fifth day in an eight-day festival. It will start at seven. We have to go home now. We will bring you from your bungalow at nine."

"I don't want you to miss the beginning of the festivities."

"In India if something starts at seven, it will take two hours before it actually begins."

Once back at the guest bungalow I had a chance to wash, do laundry, and clean Angel's moving parts before the fellows returned and took me to the festival. An outdoor speaker set at a ridiculously high volume blared out recorded music so distorted it was unrecognizable. Half the town was there, and most were talking among themselves; few people were watching the stage where, my friends told me, the stories of the Indian classical religious epic the *Mahabarata* was being re-enacted. The event was full of color, smoke, drama, and exaggerated dance movements. The men on stage wore multi-colored costumes and hats, and made slow, pronounced gestures almost like the Japanese Kabuki. Apart from the discomfort caused by the tyrannical sound system, it looked like a festival of happiness. Our presence created a big stir as soon as we walked onto the open field where the audience sat on the ground. The entire town knew everything there was to know about me as if I had told each one of them personally. Many said hello and smiled.

We found a place and sat cross-legged on the dirt. The children stopped paying attention to the Brahmins who were using this occasion to teach the public the Hindu heritage, playing out the scenes of gods who walked the earth before barbarians walked on European soil. All the children flocked around and surrounded us. They took turns feeling my arms and examining the size of my cycling shoes, exceptionally large by their standards. My presence in the audience created such a commotion that the Brahmins came over and told my two friends to get me to leave so the festivities could continue. The two explained to me the difficulty, and we left.

They took me to their home where their family greeted me as an honored guest. Their three sisters stood up so we men could sit down, then the sisters served us tea and sat on the floor listening to the conversation. The father asked many questions about life in the West. Later, he turned on the black and white television for my benefit, and we saw a traditional dance by a woman with large painted eyes who dressed in a sari and wore many necklaces and bracelets. She made graceful arm and hand movements to the sitar and taba music. The young men told me that she was telling a story of a woman's love for a Hindu god.

The next day a young school master who introduced himself as Parauthy came to the travelers bungalow and persuaded me to talk to his English class. A group of thirty-five students as young as twelve and as old as forty crowded around the floor of the small room. They stood up as we entered. Parauthy made a fuss, and half the class rushed out the door, coming back a couple of minutes later with chairs for everyone. They must have grabbed every chair in the town.

I laughed to myself and said to the class, "When an Indian guru comes to the West, spiritual seekers make him feel at home by sitting on the floor with him. Thank you for making me feel at home."

"Please tell the class why it's important to speak English," Parauthy said, putting me on the spot.

"English has become the language for business and technology," I said. "But more than that, it is the language that you and I can communicate in. Our world is coming closer together. If people from Sweden and Japan and Nigeria come together, they need a common language."

"This is true," one of the older students said. "The government wants us to speak Hindi. But it is the language of the north and we have no use for it."

"The people in south India want to keep English as the official language since it is the international language," explained the teacher. "India has sixteen main languages; none should dominate."

The class loudly agreed. I didn't realize how sensitive a nerve I had hit. The language controversy has been a deeply emotional issue, leading to demonstrations and riots in the southern part of India.

We talked about pronunciation and grammar, about spelling and reading. After class I prepared to leave. The people in the town wished me a warm farewell. Even the Brahmins who had asked me to leave the drama the night before came to send me off. I waited until everyone squeezed the bicycle tires; then in the midst of ten other cyclists, my escort out of town, I waved back to those who stood and watched me ride away.

Bicycling along the Cauvery, the sacred river of the south, I encountered hundreds of temples. Many of these places of worship were very small, some no larger than a closet. They sat near the river and each one housed a god. Other temples were the size of cities. Guides took me around, showed me the statues, halls, and rituals.

Out of curiosity I asked one man if there was a place to meditate in the half mile structure. He showed me twenty stone steps near a pool of pale green water where people wash. Many people walked up and down to bathe. An elephant whose trunk had white diamond shaped decorations ate straw nearby. It certainly wasn't a private or quiet place.

"Meditation is done in a group," he told me in the most matter of fact way. "People come together and sing chants and make offerings and receive blessings. That is true meditation."

While I was bicycling along a road that paralleled the Cauvery River I saw a small sign for an ashram. Its name looked familiar. I bicycled in and discovered that it was the ashram run by a British Benedictine priest, Father Griffith Bede. Amazingly enough I had met him two years before when he was at a Trappist monastery in Iowa talking about the links between Hinduism and Christianity, but I didn't exactly know where in India his ashram was located. Dressed in a long peach robe, he greeted me with clasped hands and gave me a small room where I stayed a week.

Father Bede tried to integrate Eastern and Western religion. Hindu chants were sung during Mass. While someone read from the Bible or the Baghavad Gita, we ate a simple meal with our hands while sitting on mats in the dining room. The library stocked books about Christian saints as well as translations of Hindu and Buddhist texts. Guests and residents lived a monastic life. Father Bede was a kind old man who loved philosophical discussions. He and I sat in front of his bamboo hut in the center of the ashram talking about the similarity between Christian and Hindu mythology. He and his followers ate and slept like Indians, bathing in the river and observing regional customs.

The land around the Cauvery River was rich and fertile; every inch of it was being farmed. The area abounded in green vegetation. Monkeys swung from banyan trees. The wind came strongly from the west, so I rode with it to the hot eastern coast to visit the old French town Pondichery, home of the Sri Arobindo Ashram. I had been a semi-devoted reader of the spiritual philosophy of this contemporary political and religious leader. He had married a European woman whom his disciples referred to as "the Mother." Both were dead.

The city's level of sophistication became conspicuous as soon as I bicycled into the center. No one gathered in a crowd around me when I stopped and looked at the impressive white colonial buildings. A few Europeans walked the streets, mixing freely with the Indians.

The Sri Arobindo Ashram dominated the city center and gave the town a feeling of affluence, something I had not seen in India. I took a room at one of the retreat houses located a few yards from the gentle waves of the Indian Ocean, then went into the Ashram where someone directed me to the Mother's bed which was placed in the courtyard behind vases of flowers. People came — Indians and Europeans — and knelt on the marble floor in front of the bed for a few minutes of devotion. A tomb covered with flowers stood on the other side of the courtyard, and the devoted came to offer prayers and more flowers in front of it as well. I thought of Sri Arobindo as a profound man. The idea of him now being semi-deified made me shrink from the site feeling dejected.

I left and toured the city. The town's gardens contained plants with leaves the size of elephant ears and red and peach flowers with a yellow stamen. Among palm trees on the street in front of the beach stood a large Catholic church which held Mass in French. It had fewer statues than the Hindu temples I had seen, and they weren't half so imaginative. I told the priest that I thought he was lucky to be in such beautiful surroundings, referring to the beach and the trees.

"Yes," he said. "But near here there are many poor. We can't be happy when others suffer."

I asked no more questions about gods or temples. When I had arrived in India I had a mind full of ideas and $100 in my pocket. After six weeks of bicycling around the south, I arrived in Madras with $15 left, ready to take a pre-paid flight to Malaysia for as much riding as possible with $15. I arrived at Singapore hungry. Shortly after I landed in California, I discovered that I had hepatitis. By the time I recovered it was too cold to ride back to Chicago, so I had to start on the last leg of the journey a year later.

Arkansas Accident

I'm not sure why I'm lying on the pavement. There is the sound of car doors slamming shut followed by the shuffling of feet. Everything is blue, a big band of bright blue. People talk, and I talk back. I think I talk back. It's the space between light and dark; sometimes it turns dark, and the blackness eliminates the blue. A pink face with a fat red smile interrupts the blue, a pink head with a clump of yellow hair on top. The red mouth moves, and words come out very fast. He tells me how lucky I am, but my head hurts trying to understand why I'm lucky to be lying on the pavement. It turns dark.

There is the sound of a car door followed by the shuffling of feet. People talk in wobbling voices. The man's voice tells me again that I was sure lucky and how good and fine everything is. Perhaps I won something. He tells me that he's going to take care of me and that I shouldn't worry. Why should I worry if I'm lucky? There is more talk about how he got hit. I'm not sure who they're talking about. Other voices tell me that everything is going to be all right. The man tells them that he's going to do me a big favor. Darkness falls.

Light pours through the windshield, blinding light. There's the loud roar of the engine and the thunder of the wind coming in the open windows. Who is this woman? She's driving fast, looking straight ahead. A small boy is squeezed next to her looking at me, staring at me. His feet reach the edge of the seat. I have to figure this out, why I'm in a shiny red pickup. The road is surrounded by tall trees and green grass. A truck passes from the other side, making a lot of noise. The woman is not distracted. She looks straight ahead; the boy continues staring at me. The woman is thin, with light hair on a thin, handsome head. I must know her.

The white light blinds me. We're speeding down the road. There are no road signs telling me where I am. It wouldn't be right to ask a stupid question like, where am I? I have to act like I know. I must be in America: the road is smooth and the land is fertile. It's a big new American pickup. There are no towns or buildings or people around. The hot air pours through the open windows. The engine roars. I need a clue, a reference, to erase this confusion.

But looking around I see nothing familiar. Wait, there's Angel in the back, loaded for touring. It looks like Angel. I must be on a trip. Of course, I'm taking a trip through America, and for some reason that I must pretend to know, I'm in the shiny red pickup with the woman who sits straight and the boy who stares at me. I need more information. My head hurts, but I have to take myself in hand and analyze the situation.

I know I'm on a trip in America. The woman and boy can't be anything but American. I must have a map in the case on top of the handlebar bag. I look back. Angel is at a forty-five degree angle, resting on the side of the rear bed. The bright red handlebar bag has a map case on top. The map will clarify everything. It's the fragment of knowledge, the missing link, that will make sense of a senseless situation. Meanwhile, my head floats between light and dark, between noise and quiet.

The woman twists her head and looks at me. The look in her eyes is alarming. She turns away quickly. I put on a smile, say gosh, I guess I'm tired. She doesn't laugh, but looks in the rearview mirror for a long time. I look back and see a green pickup close behind. The woman wiggles around trying to get comfortable.

I remember: I'm going to Chicago and will later begin another long bicycle trip to other countries. Or am I. Maybe I'm leaving Chicago. Maybe I'm in Oregon. There's a map on the dash board. It might tell me what state I'm in. I'll just reach over and take it in my hand as if it were a newspaper. My hand goes out. The woman abruptly turns her head to look at me, then she turns and looks straight down the road. The son looks at his mother. My hand brings the map to me, and I unfold it. It could be anywhere in America. I try to analyze it, but it hurts my head to figure out the roads and the towns and the dividing lines and all those names. I have to put it down again to keep out the confusion. I fold it and return it as I found it. When we stop I'll get out and look at the handlebar bag. I look back. The bicycle and the green pickup are still there.

We keep moving through tall grass, bushes, trees. No towns. The sun is less bright. The woman looks straight ahead or in the mirror.

The truck slows down and starts moving across the center line, turning into a large dirt parking lot in front of a liquor store. The pickup stops. The green truck pulls up next to us. The woman gets out. I hear her talking in a low and rushed voice through the open windows about a hospital. The man gets out and starts talking loudly. Everything is mighty fine, he says. His voice, his fat pink face, his yellow hair spark a tinge of memory to the left side of my aching head. I climb out. He tells me about how they done me a big favor, yes siree, a mighty big favor.

Something is clicking in my brain; my stomach doesn't like it. The man tells the woman to be quiet. She puts her fingers in her mouth and squeezes her forehead so that it wrinkles. He turns to me and says that everything is fine and wonderful. They're going to take this road, and I'm going on that one, and isn't it good to meet, and have a good ride now. Ride? Oh yes, I say, my bicycle. Of course. Ha, ha, he says. I echo him: Ha, ha.

I look at the two pickups and remember that I'm going north. He's carrying Angel off the back of the truck, telling me, ha, ha, how heavy it is. But don't you worry, he says, everything is going to be mighty fine. I don't like his fat smile and his fat face and his fat body. The man is in a hurry. The woman looks at me with her fingers in her mouth. He motions to her, says something to her, goes and pushes her into the red truck.

He's in a hurry. I need to say something quickly, but I'm not sure what. The ground is moving. He gets into his truck, and they both go off, spitting dust and dirt off their back tires. They hit asphalt and vanish over the hill. It turns hazy, and I have to put my hand out to stop the ground from hitting me.

The bicycle is resting on top of me, but the left pedal is near my hand. A piece of metal is sticking out of the left crank arm. I remember something about a couple of pickups, but there isn't anything around except a liquor store and two cars. I have to try to put the bits of information together and remember. That's the problem: I can't remember. My forehead is sore and swelling.

I go into the liquor store and ask the man for a cold Coke. Sure thing, he says, looking at me. I'm tired, I say, bicycling you know, it's tiring. Sure thing, he says. He speaks in a Southern accent. I just got hit by a car, I say. I think I need help. He's silent. He gets me a can of Coke from a cooler. Is there anything nearby, I ask. He asks me which way I'm going. I point. He says there's a town called Hoxie that's got a motel, and it's twenty something miles down the road. I don't hear the exact number. Where you coming from, he asks. There's a pause. I take a drink and feel a rush of energy from the sugar. Long way away, I say, and we drop it. He goes to unpack boxes. Oh, the map. I forgot about the map. That will tell me where I am.

I go outside and see Angel lying on the dirt. I remember having smashed into the pickup's bumper. I can't stay in the middle of nowhere with my head becoming hazy every so often. Twenty and something miles, that's what he said. I look up: there's forty-five minutes of sun left. What's the name of that town? Here it is on the map. It's coming back to me. I was aiming to get to Newport by six o'clock. That's over here on the map. I remember. Hoxie, the town the guy inside mentioned, is here. I see on the map the fork in the road where I'm standing.

The woman's bumper must have plowed into my head a few miles from Newport on the top end of Arkansas. Now I'm on a different road but still going north. In forty-five minutes the sun will be lost under the earth, maybe fifty minutes. I have to get serious and apply my mind to get to the town.

I pick the broken pedal off the ground, tie the toe strap around my foot, and stick the pedal through the spindle, but it doesn't work. I can only use the spindle, hitting my left foot on it while pulling up with the right foot. I begin, get back on the road, and work up to a strong cadence. I have to keep eighty strokes a minute. I count the strokes every ten seconds: thirteen strokes every period. On a high gear that will be twenty-four miles an hour. It's flat without a wind; I can use a high gear. That will bring me to town in an hour: forty-five minutes while the sun is above the earth and another fifteen minutes of twilight, enough light to travel in. Nothing more; I can't be caught on the road after dark.

My mind feels clearer as I concentrate on cadence. Now I know where I am. I came from Los Angeles and went south into the Mexican desert, then crossed the Rio Grande at Juarez, rode through Texas, and now I'm going north to Chicago to finish my trip from where I started. Since leaving Los Angeles it's been a high daily mileage trip until this.

He'll say that it was the fault of the guy in front of her who ran me off the road, some guy who didn't even stop. The other guy made me fall into the shoulder. See, he'll say to her, we stopped and took that guy ten miles down the road. It wasn't our fault, he'll say to her. He fell over into you. We can't afford more insurance.

My head hurts. I'll stop and sleep. Wait! I'm in the dirt. I have to get back on the road. By focusing I'll drive out the darkness inside me before night overtakes me. Thirteen beats every ten seconds. Begin another ten second period, one-two-three. What's the name of that town? Here it is on the map: Hoxie. Perhaps a small wind is behind me, helping me. I hear a car coming up behind. Give me plenty of room — I'm not sure whether I yell that or think it — I keep my head down as it passes. I only wear a helmet in cities.

The loss of the left pedal makes it hard, but I hit hard on the spindle while my right ankle pulls up. About fifteen minutes of sun remaining, another thirty minutes of usable light. Count thirteen beats in my highest gear, fifty-three teeth on the front sprocket, fourteen on the back. Every time I turn the pedal the rear wheel turns 3.8 times, bringing me 8.9 yards closer to Hoxie. For twenty miles that's 4000 strokes in that high gear. It would require less force to push the pedals in a lower gear, to move to my forty-two gear in the front, but I'd have to spin more strokes a minute. Over this short distance a lower cadence in a higher gear is better for me.

The sun is hitting the horizon. Another truck passes. Its noise frightens me. At the time of the accident I must have bicycled 125 miles that day. My head and my legs are painful, but I have to keep a steady pace. If I let up the pace, it would take too much energy to work back up to it.

Fifteen minutes after sundown, after the last patch of red leaves the horizon on my left, there's still no town. It's getting dangerous to ride. Around a curve and after a clearing I see lights; only a few more minutes and I'll be in the safety of the city street lights.

The weeds on the side of the road end, and a sidewalk begins. The street lights cast a moving shadow of me on the street. The shadow starts behind me on my left side and quickly moves in front of me until it fades and another shadow on the right overpowers it. The street is lined with buildings, but there are no people. In the central area, I see a twenty-foot flashing arrow for a 24-hour donut shop. It flashes red and competes with the light of the street lamp. A second later it goes off and allows the pale light of the street lamp to have its moment, then it flashes on again: light and dark, endlessly oscillating. Next door is a large sign for a motel and restaurant. Other stores on the street are closed. I go to the motel office and pay a young woman $18 for a room. That's neat, she says, traveling by bicycle, must be a lot of fun. My head turns to look at the bicycle leaning on the wall, and I get an idea about how to temporarily repair the pedal.

I put Angel in the nondescript room, and walked to the donut house. A couple of policemen in an unmarked car pass me, stop, and back up. We saw you holding a towel on your head, the large one on the passenger side says. He gets out and asks why. I tell him that I'm a bicyclist and a pickup ran me off the road into another pickup's bumper. The driver dumped me in front of a liquor store twenty-five miles back.

Ain't that too bad, he says and asks for identification. I ask what for, and he says it's just routine, boy. We gotta be careful about anyone not from these here parts, boy. I give him a California driver's license and tell him that my head hurts. He hands the license through the window to a clean-cut driver who gets on his two-way and begins talking in the microphone. I start telling them about the accident, but they're not interested. In two minutes noise comes over their radio. He gives me back my license and says just routine, then gets in, and they drive off. I buy three spongy donuts and return to the motel room.

I set my watch to wake up every two hours to make sure I still have my faculties. In the morning I wait until the grocery store opens and buy a heavy carbohydrate breakfast to eat on the way. I poke a hole in the pedal's dust cover and keep it in place with a washer and a nut. It works as long as I don't move my foot left or right.

The swelling on my forehead has gone down, and my mind is much clearer. I keep a conservative pace the first day, eighty miles, and pick up to a hundred the second. The third day I cross Missouri and am in southern Illinois. I work up to a 150 miles a day pace until I pass suburbs and reach Chicago's South Side. I look around and see beat-up cars, run-down houses, streets full of litter, and children wearing cheap clothes. I'm home.

Second

Journey

In and Out of Hades: Central America

I was furious by the time the gun-carrying boy lifted the barrier and let me pass from Guatemala into El Salvador. His sinister smile flashed an incisor with a gold star embedded in it. I'd done everything wrong at the entry border, everything that put me on the wrong footing with all the border guards. I told them I wouldn't pay bribes, and they laughed at me. I told them I was in a hurry, and they went slower. I told them I didn't have a license plate on my bicycle when I should have made up a number so they could fill in their bureaucratic forms. I told them I wanted to see the boss, and they ignored me. I got angry, and they became more belligerent. And I almost slugged the star-toothed soldier when he sent me back to get yet another rubber stamp from an unattended office. I felt as if my body had been taken over by a demon.

Times must have been hard for them. Fewer and fewer foreigners were coming into El Salvador since the war, so they had to extract as many bribes as possible from the little business they had. But it wasn't enough for them to collect one bribe, as in other countries where foreigners are supposed to hand over their passports with a bill folded inside which the immigration officer casually pockets. Instead they had six different departments: customs, police, immigration, quarantine, transit, and military. Each wanted palm grease to rubber stamp a poorly printed scrap of paper that I was given upon arrival, and each greased palm made my temper tremble. The police officer wrote a line of useless information about me in an equally useless ledger; the immigration officer filled out a long form with five carbons.

Taking money wasn't enough satisfaction for them; they also needed to exercise their power by giving me ridiculously bad directions and mocking advice, by laughing in my face because

I traveled by bicycle, and by wasting my precious daylight hours. My anger increased each hour I was detained. Finally, the man who filled out the long form wanted a five-colon bribe instead of the usual two; I began to fume. Indignation overtook me as I began venting my rage.

Nothing was going to stop me from seeing the boss, a small man who sat in a revolving wooden armchair and wore a white shirt with a dirty brown collar. He was too afraid to deal with the wall of crazed fury I had become. Without taking his eyes off the paper in front of him, he gestured me away with his hairless arm like he was waving away flies, telling the man filling out the long form behind the black Royal typewriter to reduce my final bribe to two colon in order to keep me on the inner fringes of sanity.

For the third time I went out to see if star-tooth would let me pass. His uniform was as crisp and bright as his gold star. His white-gloved hand took a corner of my paper delicately, as if it carried a disease. In mock humor he waved the piece of paper at the people standing near him, laughing at me, encouraging the others to join in the laugh. I exploded like a volcano. My body erupted: I began yelling and waving my arms and spewing curses from my foaming mouth. I didn't know how to curse in Spanish. I cursed in Arabic. I cursed with my hands; I spat on the ground in front of him. The others had to stop him from taking his shiny automatic from his chest and shooting me.

He let me through.

I was in fact in a hurry. I felt the brutal heat and sweltering humidity already eating up my energy. The cooler morning was the only good time for brisk bicycling, and December gave me few hours of daylight. I wanted to make it to the capital, San Salvador, that evening because I had heard repeated warnings from Guatemalans about the level of danger to foreigners in Salvador. A bicyclist, as an old man near the border told me, would make an easy target.

This second long international bicycling tour began in Mexico City. I had planned to ride through Central America, then down the Andean countries and across to Rio de Janeiro. I had a plane ticket to South Africa where I was going to ride up to the Sahara, across North Africa to Turkey, then fly to India. I spent months planning the journey.

From Mexico City I bicycled south to Guatemala. Mexico and Central America gave me two choices for routes; riding inland up and down scores of mountains where the temperature is ideal for bicycling, or riding flat on the hot coast. I did both, and when I was on the coast in the middle of the afternoon, I wanted to return to the cool mountains as soon as I could. But cycling inland was rough, not only because the mountains are high, but because there was mountain after mountain to cross, and after two days of it I would be overcome with a "get me to the flat lands" desire, and I would descend to the coast and the insufferable heat, only to want to return to the hills to escape the mugginess.

I felt a strangeness in a few Guatemalan villages that I can't quite describe. Perhaps the Christmas season accented this, or the amount of alcoholism I saw. The people were friendly enough, as poor people generally are, but I couldn't figure out what half the people did. Too many people stood around, wearing blank expressions, their body language expressing a feeling of defeat.

On Christmas Eve I slept in the central building of a poor village, next to a funeral parlor that had a twenty-four-hour walk-up window. Drunks slept on the cracked concrete around the room I was sharing with a dozen other men. Others who were also intoxicated slept in the open courtyard, Outside, older people prayed avidly to Jesus and the Virgin at candle-lit shrines next door to cafes with outdoor speakers blaring rock music at a distortion level. An American 1940s bus meant to seat twelve shook through the bumpy streets with forty small, round-faced Indians and mestizos inside, on top, and hanging on the side. Dozens of barefoot children roamed the disrepaired cobblestone streets. Groups of young men, older men, and women huddled together at corners, talking or sitting idly.

In the middle of Guatemala I went off the main road, the Pan American Highway, affectionately known as the "Gringo Trail," and used the road that skirted the Pacific. I came down from the central mountains and sank into a pool of liquifying coastal heat and wilting humidity. It was the type of climate that fogs up watches and causes green fungus to grow on eyeglasses. I had to wash my water bottles constantly in order to stop the green moss from growing inside them. The place was certainly alive, an ever-growing jungle of vegetation nurtured by a complex network of rivers. Groups of men and boys worked both sides of the road, cutting the tall grass with machetes to prevent it from overrunning the pavement.

I reached the Guatemala-El Salvador border late in the afternoon, just after the border closed. Across the open plain I looked out and saw a few houses scattered near the road. One large adobe building with a Spanish facade had a small sign identifying it as a hotel. I went there to get a good night's sleep and psyche myself up to ride through El Salvador quickly and avoid trouble.

The only other person in the hotel was a traveling merchant with a beefy face. He wore a brim hat with a dent on the side and an open white shirt that showed his smooth chest as well as the top of his round stomach. He spotted me taking Angel into my room and came over to size me up while striking a conversation, talking so fast that I only caught every third word. I understood that he knew a good place to eat.

We went out to the main road and walked past the border post toward a river that separated Guatemala from El Salvador. Down from the road close to the river stood a small wooden building that looked like a typical peasant's house. We walked into the smoke-filled kitchen where two women, probably a sixty-year-old mother and her daughter, were talking. The daughter stood up and directed us to one of the three tables in the next room, then she went back to the kitchen and began preparing a meal for us.

"Where did you learn Spanish?" the merchant asked.

"I studied it in the United States," I said. "I only know a little."

"Yes, but you know the basics. You have to know what people are saying to keep out of trouble."

He said that he traveled back and forth between countries. I asked him if he thought it would be safe to bicycle in El Salvador.

"If you have money," he said after the women brought us each a plate of beans and rice, "no one will dare to bother you."

"I don't have money," I said.

"Ah, that's a problem," he replied with a jovial smile. "You have to stay away from officials." He looked around to see if anyone was watching, then said to me in a whisper, "If you want

something done you have to give them something." He rubbed his fingers together to indicate money.
After he quickly shoveled down his food with a spoon, he yelled over to the woman in the next room for another plate. I tried to ask what type of merchandise he was going to sell in Salvador, but he began talking incoherently.
"Do you think it's safe to bicycle there?" I asked.
"The fighting changes," he replied. "Right now there is no problem from here to the capital. South of the capital, ah, that's a problem."
"Who should I be more afraid of, the soldiers or the revolutionaries?"
He looked around again, as if someone cared about the conversation in an old shack in no-man's-land. "The person you should be afraid of is the one who points a gun at you. Just mind your own business."
"But if I want to find out what's going on there?"
"Ah, that's a problem," he said. "If you're interested in money," he said, rubbing his fingers again, "that's healthy. If you're interested in anything else..."
"I know," I said. "That's a problem."
We walked back to the hotel in the darkness. I got a good night's sleep, thinking that I would need the whole day to ride to the capital. After the guards wasted three hours of the best riding time and star-tooth let me into the country, I pedaled furiously for five or ten miles to dissipate my anger and to try to disengage my mind from the border experience. I pumped aggressively, lashing out at the pedals, not letting up until I saw a fellow selling watermelon under a tarp supported by four pieces of sugarcane stuck in the ground. I couldn't tell how old he was, twenty or forty. The top of his triangular head stood five feet from the ground, and he weighed less than ninety pounds. His wide nose curved slightly to the left, and was set between vacant black eyes.
"Is it dangerous to ride to the capital?" I asked as he gave me a slice of melon.
He didn't look at me as he spoke. "Yes, at night it's dangerous."
"Does the FMLN operate here?"
His eyes looked up into mine, two pairs of dark eyes denying the sun's brightness over a table of red watermelon. He ignored

what I had said, looked down, and began cutting another wedge of watermelon, leaving my eyes hanging over the empty horizon.

I looked to the side and asked, "Is there fighting here?" asking in the same tone as I had asked about the sweetness of the watermelon.

He clammed up. I changed the subject and talked about watermelon, but he said nothing more to me. After the same experience with two other people, I realized that I shouldn't ask any questions about political or military matters. I ate the slice of watermelon and threw the rind onto the garbage pile next to the stand. The fellow raised his eyes and looked at the pile, and I immediately saw that my rind looked out of place. Every other rind, I noticed, was eaten to the green outside skin; mine showed a thick section of white.

I kept to the sugarcane-lined coastal road and bicycled south. Star-tooth had been the last military man I saw for many miles. I had heard that not long before major battles had been fought in Santa Anna, a town slightly inland from where I was cycling, but I could not see a single sign that a war was ravaging the country. I guessed that the intensity of the war must have been exaggerated.

I pedaled past endless rows of sugarcane, past clusters of outdoor vendors selling fruit and Coca Cola, past flocks of anonymous barefoot children playing with an imaginary ball, past unpainted wood and dirt houses, past piles of watermelon rind eaten to the outside green skin, past lifeless towns and poverty-stricken settlements, past cutters clearing the weeds with machetes, past slow-moving trucks carrying stacks of cane twenty feet high.

With an element of either bravado, stupidity, or a desire for excitement that I had been deprived of while riding in Guatemala, I drafted these swaying cane trucks, getting six inches behind them and facing a moving mass of sugarcane of different lengths pointing at me. They used rickety 1930s trucks that tilted from side to side like boats in turbulent waters. Their outside wheels looked as if they alternately left the ground as they littered the road with cane. One bad move would have wiped me out. The truck drivers seemed to enjoy seeing a foreigner dressed in cycling shorts, colorful shirt, strange hat, and long shoes, pedaling an odd-looking bicycle with an impractical handlebar, carrying a household in two bags, yet managing to keep up with them. I did it with a disarming smile and lots of boisterous arm waving.

By noon the ground began to steam. People continued working in their fields. They would see me coming, and they would stop, look up, and stare; sometimes they would wave; sometimes they would shout for their friends to come quickly and see the spectacle. I stopped often to drink water or semicold drinks and to eat watermelon and other fruits. Cane was good to chew while riding.

At one stop two friendly but staid young men came out of the tall cane onto the clearing where I was sitting on a tree stump facing a fruit stand. They stood in front of me without talking. I stood up and shook hands. They were both about the size of the watermelon vendor; one was eighteen, although he looked like he hadn't begun shaving; the other, fifteen, had his hair cut as if a bowl were placed over his head. Both wore dirty T-shirts with English writing on them; one advertising a pizza parlor in New York, and the other saying he liked getting stoned.

"Where does such a bicycle come from?" the eighteen-year-old asked. Inside their reserved faces they had quiet smiles.

"It's from Japan, but I brought it from the United States."

"We've heard a lot about the United States," the older one boasted. "How far is it from here?"

"Four or five thousand kilometers," I replied.

They wrung their wrists. The younger asked: "Do they speak Spanish there?"

"Only in cities where there are a lot of people from Latin America," I answered.

"Everyone is rich in the United States," proclaimed the older one.

"Not everyone," I replied. "But the country is big, and most people can find work that pays well."

"People get rich here too," said the younger. "When they join the army they get new clothes and eat meat."

"I see," I said, then pulled out colorful elastic hair bands for their sisters. I bought them two soft drinks, telling them that I was sorry to run off, but I had to make it to the capital before night. They agreed that at night it could be dangerous and stood watching while I rode off.

The country changed when I approached the capital. As the traces of Western influence intensified, the smiles on people's faces faded. The military, which I had not seen since I left star tooth that morning, became omnipresent. As I reached the suburbs of the city I began to see vast military compounds with watchtowers and guards in front. The soldiers wore impressive uniforms; each carried a forty-cartridge automatic. There were no bombed stores or burnt buildings, but the signs of a nation under siege were unmistakable.

In the city itself troops stood in front of every bank, and at least one automatic-carrying soldier guarded each intersection. They were young boys who stood on the corner or else directed traffic from the middle of the street. The Salvadorans are generally small framed, rarely over five foot seven, with lean, agile bodies, and it looked awkward and incongruous for a small fellow to carry a rifle as big as he was on his chest while directing traffic. They had weapon power, and they exercised their power openly: they blew their whistles angrily at jay-walkers and ran over and shouted at them; they told cars when to move and rudely gestured some to pull over and show papers.

The military dominated all aspects of daily life in San Salvador: they were everywhere. When I pedaled into the capital I asked various soldiers for directions, such as how I could reach the center of town and find a hotel, but they impatiently told me to move on, as if it was part of their duty to be rude.

I checked into a dingy downtown hotel that charged by the hour or by the day. No other foreigners were in the city. Since I wanted to take a ferry across the Gulf of Fonseca into Nicaragua, I went to the Nicaraguan consulate to get a visa. I wanted a visa to avoid problems that my American passport might present, but the Nicaraguans told me not to worry and just to arrive at the border. Along the way I passed the U.S. embassy complex. I didn't need a sign to tell me what it was. Around the small-windowed fortress-like building stood a thick wall of concrete topped with barbed wire, metal turnstile gates, security cameras, and several "we mean business"-type guards with machine guns who, unlike the hapless kids who bullied old ladies, wore plain-clothes and looked like professional thugs.

More disturbing than the presence of the military was the cheap imitation of U.S. consumerism to be seen everywhere, taking the worst aspects of decadent commercialism and amplifying them to their most grotesque. People sold goods on the street with bull horns; not just sold, but pushed: "This way, this way, only four for a dollar." You got the feeling that life was reduced to nickel and dime merchandise.

At night the capital changed. The street sweepers were gone; the bargain-sale vendors vanished; the military deserted the streets; the chaotic din that had dominated the day turned into silence, leaving not a peaceful, but a tense quiet. The woman who ran the hotel told me not to go out at night, but when all seemed still I walked the empty streets trying to uncover the reason for my anxiety, but found instead a growing feeling of loneliness. I wanted to talk to someone, but I couldn't bring myself to go to the night club district.

I returned to my hotel room and turned on the bare light bulb over the iron bed, the only piece of furniture in the room. I could see the imprints of the lumpy mattress's protruding springs through the well-used sheet. Angel stood in the corner amid crumbled candy and cigarette wrappers from previous guests. I turned on my radio and discovered that I could pick up stations from all over Central America including Nicaragua. The local stations imitated American rock stations, with even faster talk and more hype, playing the same songs that U.S. top forty stations were playing. I turned off the radio and rested on my sleeping bag. Thinking about the way people with power — military power or financial power or rubber stamp power — treated others produced in me a feeling of dread; I could not quiet my mind or calm my misgivings enough to sleep.

When the gray light of dawn filtered through the dirt of my window I was anxious to get on my way. I found the southbound continuation of the Pan American Highway at the edge of town near the bus terminal. After riding into the terminal to buy something to eat, I was surrounded by youths who wanted me to take their overcrowded busses. It didn't matter which direction I was headed; each person made a pitch for his bus's destination. They tried everything to entice me to buy a ticket: they begged, they promised, they pretended to be my friend, and they didn't want to take no for an answer. With difficulty, I got away from them and began bicycling south, watching the sun rising over the mountains on my left.

The absence of the military in the north of El Salvador was more than amply offset by their presence in the countryside south of the capital. Soldiers wearing grim faces carried out military exercises: driving tanks and armored carriers, talking on field radios, standing near the road and guarding empty spaces with automatics. I didn't know if they were training or fighting. They traveled in packs and took their tasks seriously. One guard on the road who checked the papers of cars — and my bicycle — was not only dressed in camouflage, his face was painted green and brown as well. He too had a gold tooth with a star, which made his appearance ludicrous.

"Papers," he demanded.

I gave him my passport and he opened it, feigning competence, but he had no idea how to read a passport.

"Where are you going?"

"Nicaragua." I said it for effect.

He wasn't sure what to do. He turned to a page in the passport that had an Indian visa on one side of the page and a Zambian visa on the other side and studied the information.

"This place is not for foreigners," he said.

I remained quiet. He looked harder at my Zambia visa.

"You'll have to see the boss."

"Look," I said. "It says right here that I can pass."

I pointed to the Indian visa which he read carefully. He reluctantly nodded his head, then threw the passport back to me, gruffly telling me to go, which I did.

Danger is a matter of perception. Many people would say that New York is too dangerous; others would say that a remote U.S. suburb is also dangerous. Both would back their claims with stories and statistics. The U.S. is a dangerous country in which to travel, certainly the most dangerous for women and old people, but there's an entirely different element of danger when sixteen- or eighteen-year-old boys run around with automatics, a danger you can't escape from by hiding behind a locked door.

Twice I stopped to eat and drink, and both times the people warned me that it would be too dangerous to bicycle further south. I didn't want to submit to fear, but my mind was becoming uneasy, so when I got near the rebel-active town of San Vicente, I opted for safety in numbers and began looking for one of those busses I had to work to avoid in San Salvador. Two bus conductors doing a good imitation of Chicago gangsters tried to hustle me onto their bus, but I saw another bus where the conductor didn't act like an ass, and I took off my panniers, carried Angel on top of that bus, and laid it on bags of fruit and crates of live chickens. The second I stepped inside I sensed a relaxed atmosphere, and by the time the bus left San Vicente everyone aboard knew who I was and where I was going.

The driver gave us a wild ride as he drove recklessly, tossing the passengers from one side of the bus to the other. At each curve I felt people poking elbows and knees into me. Others played radios, and everyone talked.

I wasn't sure precisely how dangerous the situation was. Even though my head was twisted to fit under the low ceiling, I was able to see a strong military presence: well-uniformed and handsomely equipped troops marching in squads over the countryside. An endless line of troop-carrying trucks went back and forth on the road. One group hauled a large cannon; another stood around two helicopters. Every piece of equipment looked clean and modern.

In the middle of an active military area six army troopers stopped the bus and squeezed on in order to go a few miles down the road. The spontaneous chatter that had been part of the bus ride died. One boy soldier was operating an army radio, and they were impatient to get to their new location, telling the driver to hurry. He, however, began driving cautiously.

"Here, here. Stop here," they ordered the driver.

He stopped and let them jump off, and the radios and chatter gradually resumed.

As we approached a bridge, the bus stopped at an improvised checkpoint. After the soldiers looked inside, they told everyone to get out, and began searching people selectively, taking special delight in harassing young men, calling them bad names and pretending to strike them with their rifles so they could watch them cower as they covered their faces with their arms. One soldier threw a teenager to the ground and made a gesture of hitting him in the groin. I quietly moved to the side of the road, hoping that they wouldn't notice me, and they didn't until they ordered everyone back on the bus. Suddenly, the leader, a soldier in his mid-thirties wearing pressed camouflage, came over and exclaimed, "Where did you come from?" As if I'd materialized from the air.

"I'm a Nordamericano."

"What are you doing here?"

"Vacationing."
He started walking around me, looking up and down my body disapprovingly. I had on my black bicycling shorts and orange cycling jersey and stood a head and a half shoulder above him. He looked at the handlebar bag which I carried over my shoulder and saw that it contained maps and a compass in the clear map case on top. That made him excited out of proportion.
"What are you doing with that?" he demanded.
The other three boy-soldiers came over and surrounded me with their guns. I looked at the leader's agitated expression. A V-shaped vein was protruding from the center of his forehead.
"I travel by bicycle, capo. I need maps." I had little to say to people with guns. I held off telling him that I needed maps to get out of his country as fast as possible.
He became more suspicious and kept eyeing me up and down. By this time everyone was back on the bus waiting for me, but that didn't bother the head soldier. In fact it enabled him to show them that he had power to control their lives. I began to worry that he would order the bus to leave without me, or do something more drastic. I didn't take my eyes off him, but I felt everyone looking intently through the bus windows at the scene. Capo didn't know what to do with me. I could see his mind working, worrying about possibly doing the wrong thing. He made a cursory check of my handlebar bag, saw my Nikon camera, and stopped.
"You can't take the maps," he said.
The automatics began to point in my direction. I kept the bag over my shoulder with my right arm over it.
"I need maps to travel."
"Fine, but you don't need this camera," he said with a peculiar twist of logic.
I said nothing. My eyes never left him, and my face gave him no satisfaction. There was a long pause.
"Which do you need more, maps or a camera?" he asked, as if giving me a choice.
I remained stern and silent with unblinking eyes looking straight down at him.
One of the boys surrounding me began nudging me with his gun, gesturing me to give my camera. I stood like a statue, my eyes locked into the soldier's.
He waited, but he couldn't overcome my obstinate stare. Finally, he shouted a series of curses — I guessed at their

meaning — then told me to get on the bus. As I was getting on I couldn't help cracking a victorious smile. He saw it from the side, but the driver quickly released the clutch and started rolling across the bridge before the soldier could think of a way to punish me.

One fellow on the bus humbled me by saying, "You were lucky with the maps. If you had boots on he wouldn't have asked you any questions. He would have shot you on the spot."

We passed a couple of blown-up bridges. The bus had to cross the streams by driving down to the river bed. Signs of war covered the countryside. When the bus stopped at San Miguel I eagerly climbed up to the top of the bus, carried down my bicycle, then rode the short distance to the port city of La Union where I expected to take a ferry the next morning across the Gulf of Fonseca to Nicaragua. I had read about this daily ferry from two guidebooks before I left the U.S., but when I arrived at the port I discovered that the ferry was out of service. The tourist office in San Salvador was closed for the Christmas-New Year holiday, so I hadn't been able to double-check this information beforehand.

"It hasn't been running for two years," said one man. He stood with a group of fishermen; all could see that I was anxious to leave the country.

"Can I pay someone to take me across?" I asked looking at the fishing boats.

It was forbidden, and they rightly balked at the risk. I felt bad that desperation had prompted me to ask them. They told me that I had to go through Honduras to get to Nicaragua, a detour that I had not planned. It was getting late; I got on the bicycle and hammered vigorously for twenty-five miles until I reached the Honduran border. The area south of San Miguel was peaceful, and like the north, it had no military presence. I didn't know whether it was because the rebels or the government controlled the area; I had become too inhibited to ask questions.

The heat of the day abated. I arrived at the Salvadoran side of the border after the last light from the sun was dying and the offices were closing. The immigration officer charged me a two-colon fee, but I soon discovered that I had to go through a similar routine with the other five offices. As it turned out it was fortunate that a couple of the offices had already closed for the day. The small bureaucrat from customs saw my passport and wanted to try the handful of English words he knew.

"You like my country?" he asked in a somber tone.
The irony of his question hit me. Here stood a man on the other side of the counter wanting a small bribe which he will split with the rest of his corrupt workers asking me if I liked his country.
"Do *you* like it?" I asked like a jaded psychiatrist.
"It is my country. It is not for me to like. You like my country?" he asked again.
"You can see I spent only two days here. I had no chance to see your country."
He pressed me no more.
It was a moonless night. I felt relieved to cross an unguarded bridge to the Honduran side in the dark. The Honduran offices were closed; all guards went home promptly at sundown. I put up in another dingy hotel near the border and slept with energetic three-inch cockroaches as my roommates.

***

In my rear pannier I carried several pounds of maps inside plastic bags. It had taken weeks of tedious research in library map rooms to find good maps for the countries I would travel. Maps for bicycling must be more detailed than those for car travel, showing the smaller roads and, where possible, their condition. Honduras was not part of my plan, and I had no map of the area. The next morning, after I got my passport stamped at immigration, registered my bicycle, and changed money with a seedy character, someone offered me a ride — and I quickly accepted — in the back of a truck for about fifty miles in order to get me back to the margin of my Nicaragua map. Then I rode to the sleepy farm town of Choluteca and stocked up on fruits and vegetables.

I had a choice of roads to the border, so said my map, a short way toward the coast and a long way through the mountains. I asked a group of people at the crossroad if the border was indeed down that short road, which looked about fifty kilometers from where I was. They said yes. I also talked to several more people en route, either when I stopped to drink, or when I stopped for brief conversation, always bringing up the subject of the border because I had learned long ago to ask directions from many. Everyone told me I was going the right way.

I bicycled in an almost uninhabited part of the country on a well-paved road which had hardly any other traffic. The land was dry but green with bushes and small trees. The wind blew against me as I pedaled a steady pace. As soon as I was able to see the border facilities in the distance, four fellows in a car came up and told me that the border was closed.

"Shit," I shouted spontaneously in English.

They knew the word and couldn't help laughing, despite seeing frustration written all over my face.

"No one told me," I said. "Everyone said go this way to the border. No one told me."

"Did you ask them if the border is open?" asked one person.

Their laughing cushioned the sting, but I couldn't understand why anyone wouldn't volunteer that information. Still, I went up to the border to find out the situation firsthand.

The guard directed me to a fat man in his forties who was involved in an intense card game with three others his size. Unlike almost all Salvadorans, many Hondurans are physically large. All the men wore civilian clothes. The boss snorted at me when I appeared, telling me to wait outside, making me think that there might be a possibility of getting through. Why else would he have me wait? I stood in the heat for twenty minutes until he lost his money, then he shouted at me to show him my passport. I felt hopeful. He thumbed through it, as every official does, not looking for anything in particular, then told me that the bridge was blown up and I couldn't get through.

"Why did you tell me to wait?" I asked.

He made a threatening gesture with his arm indicating that he wasn't used to being questioned. I hopped on Angel and briskly pedaled back the way I had come, without stopping, even though my water bottles were empty.

When I returned to the crossroad, I turned south. A mile later, seeing a crowd with plastic buckets surrounding a well, I stopped. Two fellows ran over to take my water bottles as I was dismounting. They returned to the well, pulled up a metal bucket of water, filled my bottles, and told me that I had to go over the tall mountain in front of me, passing San Marcos de Colon in order to get to Nicaragua. Other people around the well told me that trucks would be going up the hill tomorrow, that I couldn't possibly bicycle up the hill. The challenge made it sound appealing. After I thanked the group I took off in the direction of the mountain.

Both sides of the mountain road were crowded with stark brown, baked dirt houses. Some had scant vegetable gardens in front, faded yellow crops on the dry adobe soil. Chickens and pigs ran in and out of front doors. Women had to carry water from the bottom of the hill to their houses. Up above, large electric towers traversed the area, but the wires did not connect with the homes. I had only made it up the hill a short distance when I stopped in front of one of the houses where a soft-spoken man graciously invited me in to spend the night. His two boys were thrilled when I gave them two pieces of fruit from town, and the family treated me cordially in their empty two-room house.

The man and I chatted on the porch. A small moon lit up the darkness. He began talking with pride about being Honduran, but seeing that I was tired, he went inside and listened to his transistor radio. I rolled out my sleeping bag on the porch and put my cycling shoes at the top for a pillow. Sleep was caving in on me when a "political information" program came on. Dubbed over martial music, a deep-voiced announcer praised the Honduran "democratic and military" government. I thought the phrase was an oxymoron. The program aired a diatribe of trite, hollow phrases backed by marching music. If it had been forty years ago one would have thought the fascists were in power. Sleep got to me before the program ended, a welcome escape from the propaganda.

I didn't get a chance to see my host before I left the next morning, for I wanted to climb the mountain while I felt fresh, before the heat of the day. The people at the well were right: it was a tough climb. I don't know why; it seemed only a few thousand feet, and the grade was mild. Some mountain roads are harder than others of equal height and grade. This one required many rest breaks. The local people stood and stared at me with blank expressions, rarely returning my wave. At the top I rode into San Marcos de Colon, then found the Honduran frontier station where a dozen men napped under a huge round tree in front of the army-green building. They didn't hear me bicycle up.

I had enough Honduran money to pay the usual exit tax, but I forgot about the other five offices and their payments. When the man who rubber stamps forms told me that he wanted more money, I stepped outside and yelled, "Cambio." In an instant the shade under the tree came alive as a dozen sleepy figures shot up anticipating business. The money-changer told me that the official Nicaraguan rate was twelve Cordoba to a dollar, and that I should also change with them for eighty to a dollar, which I did. After my papers were stamped, I coasted down the forested mountain.

The border guard, a fourteen-year-old boy, let down a rusty chain across the road, and I entered Nicaragua. However, the border facilities — customs, immigration, and so on — had been destroyed. Burnt wood and broken glass and destroyed pieces of office furniture littered the area around the charred ruins. Two young men carrying guns, one in a faded uniform and the other in civilian clothes, were walking up the hill when they saw me looking at the bombed buildings. One of them said, "You need to go down ten kilometers. Immigration has been moved there."

"How did this happen," I asked pointing to the buildings.

"The war," one of them said with a wry smile. "Where are you from?"

I felt embarrassed to say, feeling somewhat guilty about being from the place that, in reality, blew up the place. I didn't want to be perceived as an enemy. "I'm from the Middle East, but I live in North America."

They wished me well and continued walking up the hill. I felt a spirit of fellowship — happiness — a quality I hadn't yet felt in Central America. I looked at them more closely. Their clothes were worn and ragged. They hadn't shaved. The soldier, who didn't have a uniform, wore army boots while the other had old tennis shoes. Their guns didn't match, unlike El Salvador where every soldier had identical, polished automatics.

From the border facilities I looked over miles of rough mountains covered with dense vegetation. I could see how convenient it would be for an army of revolutionaries to hide. I coasted downhill and quickly arrived at the temporary immigration post: a small trailer surrounded by a half dozen soldiers and an old woman selling homemade snacks on an improvised table. A soldier looked at my passport and gave me a form.

Another soldier took the form when I had filled it out, stamped it and my passport, and returned the passport to me. That was it: no bribes, no fees, no power plays, no harassment, and even though I carried an American passport, these young officials treated me with courtesy.

I bought three tamales from the old woman, then rode another twenty miles through the uninhabited mountains to a warehouse which was used for customs. After filling out another form for my bicycle, a lively, stocky woman in an army uniform searched my belongings thoroughly, the only time I was searched in Central America. Further down the road a teenager in a uniform stood in the middle of the road and whistled me to a stop in order to check that my passport was stamped. A group of soldiers sat nearby in the shade making friendly one-liners about traveling by bicycle, and I asked them where I could refill my water bottles.

"Where are you from?" one man asked.

"The United States," I said. The answer rolled off my tongue unchecked. I wanted to qualify the statement.

"Welcome to free Nicaragua," said another, making me feel silly for thinking it would cause a confrontation.

"Congratulations on your independence," I said. "The eyes of the world are on Nicaragua."

"Thank you. The country is yours," the first man said as he got up to walk me across the street to a wood house. We entered the room and saw a family sitting around a table: a short man of about forty-five, his plump wife, and their two adolescent daughters. I saw an open book and pieces of paper on the table, and I understood that the daughters were teaching their father how to read and write. I felt sheepish about walking in on the lesson. The soldier asked one of the girls if she could fill up the water bottles of this North American bicyclist.

She waved me in and filled my bottles from a large clay urn in the corner. Next to it were a few shelves of provisions for sale and a small refrigerator that had a slip of paper with prices for sodas written in pencil. I bought one as an excuse to listen to the father struggling through the learning process. He glanced up at me when I came in, then returned to the papers in front of him. The mother sat across from her husband periodically nodding her head in encouragement but remaining quiet. I looked out the open door across the street at the soldiers. Two of them were reading small books; one was reading the newspaper *Barricada* which he later told me was the Sandinista party newspaper.

I paid for my drink and thanked the girl who wished me a good trip, and I left the room trying not to disturb the father's concentration.

Further down the road, I again needed more water, but I saw only a military post. I went over and asked if they had water. A private took my bottles to a well and began pouring water from a large tin can.

"It's hard to ride a bicycle, no?" he asked.

I saw almost no other bicycles in Central America until I reached Costa Rica.

"The mountains are hard, but I can get a real feeling for each country," I answered. "How is the war going for Nicaragua?"

"The Yankees keep trying, but they will not pass the frontier because the popular army defends the homeland." He smiled at me. His answer seemed both sincere and automatic.

"I'm from the United States. Does that make me a Yankee?"

He gave me an intense look, searching my face. "No, certainly not," he responded with a tinge of amusement in his mouth. "You come to see. The Yankees come to conquer."

The first night I stayed with a family whose rustic house was on the road near Esteli. We gathered at night to eat beans and rice and a large, thick tortilla. I had heard the mother pounding the tortilla masa with her hands as soon as I entered the house. The family asked me to explain to them why "the Yankees" despise the Nicaraguan government so much. I told them that most Americans don't know what's going on south of the Rio Grande and that it's really the idea of communism that worries them.

"When you go back to North America tell everyone what you have seen here," said the father. I agreed to do that.

I asked why the people here don't see me as an enemy. One young man replied, "We know that there is a difference between your government and the American people. Many Nordamericanos have come here to help us."

At night I slept on the porch near another young man. The next morning, after the family and I had another plate of beans and rice and a tortilla, I began bicycling. Toward mid-morning, I saw a commotion at an intersection ahead. As I got closer, I realized that a fellow in a VW bus had crashed into a tree. People hurried to the site from all directions, and by the time I got off my bicycle, four young men were carrying the bloodied driver out of the car. The crash broke his windshield, and blood was coming from his head and his arm. The men laid him on the grass. A plump woman brought over a cloth to put under his head. Another man, who was half dressed in a military uniform, directed traffic, and another couple brought out a piece of cloth to bandage his head.

"Wait," I said. "I have something better," and I went into my panniers and pulled out a plastic bag that served as my medical kit. I found a new Ace bandage, the only thing I had which would be of use. From another compartment I took out a bottle of iodine which I use to purify water. The woman cleaned the wound with water that a man carried in his truck, and we could see the cut really wasn't deep. She applied the iodine, then wrapped the man's head and let him lie on the grass. Two men in worn army trousers came over and asked the injured man's name and his town. Another two people said that they would take him to a clinic. The crowd dispersed as the man was carried off, and I resumed bicycling.

At a restaurant a short way down the curvy road, I met a local Baptist minister and his family who lived in Esteli. The minister had arrived at the accident scene just after the victim was taken away, and he had seen me there.

"We all know what to do because of the war," he said, "and we have had many years of war."

"People wouldn't have helped others like this in a lot of countries," I commented.

"Because they are afraid," he said. "I know: it was the same here a few years ago. If they can change their government they will change. We made that change, so can others."

"Can a government change the spirit of a people?"

"Yes, clearly. A bad government as we had traps people's divine spirit, robs them of the chance to express concern for each other."

He talked on, making it look black and white: the dictatorship, and my government that supported it, was repressive and evil; fighting against it was the progressive and liberating force of the people, represented by the Sandinista Revolution. "Was it that simple?" I asked.

"Yes. That simple," he replied.

The rest of the ride to Managua was a casual pleasure, with quaint towns and long, empty wooded stretches in between. I bicycled past smoking volcanoes, past outdoor stands where people sold fruit or candy or soft drinks, past a couple of fiestas where ferris wheels swung excited children to the heavens and back to earth, past walls filled with graffiti praising the Revolution, past spirited men and women who came up to me and asked about life in the north, past little girls with torn shirts, smudged faces, and no shoes, past boys playing baseball using a limb of a tree for a bat and a large unripe orange for a ball.

I arrived in Managua when it was dark, and I had a hard time finding a hotel. Managua was one of those sprawling cities; its center was destroyed by the 1972 earthquake and never rebuilt. I have not discovered a comfortable way of asking for hospitality in a city. I got directed to one hotel that wanted to charge thirty-three American dollars a night, U.S. money only. The other hotels were far away, and I didn't want to ride down the unlit streets. I saw what appeared to be a prairie in front of a large building, and decided to stop and camp. In seconds I heard rifles clicking into action, and I looked up to see two people approaching with their guns pointed at me.

"I'm only looking for a place to sleep," I said to their blinding flashlights.

They could see that I was a harmless foreigner, and they put down their guns.

"You can't sleep here; it's in front of an electric station," one man said. He took me inside to the light and drew me a complex but accurate map of how I could get to a reasonably-priced hotel, one that charged a dollar's worth of black market currency.

The next day when I was in a grocery store in a poor area of the city, the shopowner asked me what I thought of free Nicaragua.

"The spirit of the people seems strong," I said.

The store was on the bottom of a run-down wood framed building, the type of building you sometimes see on the TV news floating out to sea after a flood. If I extended my arms inside the store, I could have almost touched both walls. The shelves contained only a few items such as rice and flour and a couple of shelves of rum. The man had four glass jars of gum and sweets on the counter and used a tin box next to it as a cash box.

"It's been four years since the revolution. Has it made the people more prosperous?" I asked.

"Yes, some people. Now everyone has food. We all have to sacrifice to make sure that the campesinos eat. Besides, liberty is more important than prosperity."

"Permit me to ask another question. The number of soldiers here is as many as in El Salvador and Honduras. Don't you think that it might lead to another dictatorship?"

"There is one important difference between the military here and in Salvador. Here the soldiers are ready to defend us, the people. There the soldiers are used against the people. We have to have a strong military, or else everything we fought for will be lost."

A few men and women gathered in the store and agreed with the shop owner's summary.

"Nicaragua has a feeling of freshness, newness," I said. "I hope that when I come back in a few years, and I intend to, that I will find that same feeling even stronger."

"When you come back you can be our guest," said the shop owner, writing his name and address on a piece of paper.

"I will come back," a promise I was to keep two years later.

I spent the rest of my days in Nicaragua riding, talking to people, and being part of the lively New Year celebrations. I saw no other signs of war until I was ready to cross into Costa Rica, where I bicycled past another blown up border facility. The Costa Ricans, or Ticos, provided me with a wonderful cycling experience in their beautiful country. The poverty of the other four Central American countries I had bicycled through disappeared as soon as I crossed the border. Panama, on the other hand, was boring for bicycling; the only interesting aspect of the country, the only thing the country is known for, is the canal. Because the only road between Panama and Columbia is a trail for backpackers and cocaine smugglers, I flew from Panama City to Columbia and continued my journey south.

Down the Spine of the Andes

These were going to be the toughest, highest mountains for Angel and me. I felt disappointed to fly over them at night because I wanted to see them from the air. The plane from Panama was scheduled to arrive at noon, but Avianca, the Columbian national airline, is a national laughingstock. Not only do they make a policy of surprising passengers with their impromptu schedule, they often cancel a city and land somewhere else.

Instead of assembling my bicycle in the terminal — usually a group of people gather around to watch and give advice — then riding out of the airport amid taxis and buses, I stood outside looking for a bus to a hotel in town. A vivacious family whom I had met on the plane saw me standing with Angel and came over to talk to me. They fell in love with my enthusiasm for traveling by bicycle and gave me a ride to a reasonably priced hotel in town.

Bicycling in Columbia stands out as one of my most exhilarating experiences, like riding in Italy during racing season. I hit the streets the morning after I landed, a fiesta Sunday, and rode among dozens of bicycle teams in bright colored jerseys, riding on roads that were closed to cars and trucks.

Males in Columbia don't ride with each other, they try to outdo each other. Being a sucker for competition, I wore myself out on several hard stretches against fellow macho cyclists. I had to hammer hard when riding my fully-packed touring bicycle to keep up with others. At midday, exhausted, I found the main road south and met a lone bicyclist on his Sunday outing. Like most, he was dressed in the most fashionable European cycling gear: shiny, skin-tight black shorts with suspenders over a "wet look" red jersey. I told him where I was going.

"The mountains? It's hard, very hard," he said while holding his wrist in the air and shaking his hand.

Our legs turned faster and faster as we talked, trying to surpass each other while being careful not to show that our energy had already been wasted. A slow moving green bus passed us, and I drafted it (a trick of getting close behind so the bus breaks the wind), waving to my newly-made friend to join. I was using a high gear and made the maneuver briskly, but he, by this time, was struggling. The people on the bus moved to the back and cheered us on, but my friend was having a tough time keeping up, probably because he had worn himself out in similar informal competitions earlier that morning. Finally, with a feeble wave he gave up and turned back. A minute later the bus stopped. A racially mixed group of people got out, gave me spirited congratulations, and told me that they were going to a small party.

"Why don't you put your bicycle on the bus and join us," said the driver, a lively young man who wore his short-sleeve shirt unbuttoned to his stomach and introduced himself as Roberto.

"We can't stand the idea of you being alone on this feast day," said a round-faced woman.

Two fellows carried Angel through the bus's front door before I had time to answer. People put their arms around my shoulder and ushered me in, making me part of the conviviality as soon as I climbed aboard. A song would come on the radio, and they would all sing and clap; someone would tell a simple joke, and the bus shook with laughter.

We went into a black neighborhood via a pothole-ridden dirt road. The people dressed in worn and torn clothing, but their faces carried not a tinge of self-consciousness. Men and women came up to the side of the road when they heard the bus coming and joked with us through the windows. Amid cheers and jeers, two black youths standing at the side of the road turned around and tossed handfuls of talcum powder at us, part of the fiesta tradition.

The bus stopped in front of a painted wood and adobe house that had a vegetable garden surrounded by a picket fence. Five or six people came out and were delighted to discover that their home had been chosen for the party. The neighbors walked over to hear what was going on. We went through the Spanish custom of formal introductions, then readied for the feast. Our hostesses caught, plucked, and cleaned five chickens that had been running in the backyard. Two other women gathered wood and started a fire in the kitchen, a tin-roof shack in the rear with waist-high walls so the smoke could escape from a grated clay pit that served as a stove.

Roberto and three others took me on a walking tour of the neighborhood while the women cooked. We invited ourselves into two homes where we were treated to homegrown coffee and a sweet yellow fruit that has a hard shell and a large seed but tastes like honeydew. I never learned the name of that fruit. The houses had a few tables and chairs on stone floors. Each house had a vegetable garden and fruit trees in front, but no fences divided one property from another. I saw a television in the kitchen of one house. A couple of neighborhood boys took us to the local water hole where boys and girls were swimming in their underwear. Roberto and another man stripped to their shorts and jumped in. I followed them in my bicycling shorts.

When we came back the women sat me down with everyone as if I were part of the family; that is, the men sat down on benches in the covered patio while the women served. We ate boiled chicken with rice and corn. Roberto sat next to me and told me about Columbian life.

"This is a typical meal," he said. "We are in one of the poorer areas of Columbia. You can see that the people don't have much."

I nodded my head in agreement. "But the people are generous," I said.

The young man sitting next to us said with a smile, "Generous and honest."

"I enjoy being with them." I said.

"Why don't you move here?" asked one of the young men.

Nothing would have prevented me from stopping and making Columbia my home. Before I had begun that trip from Mexico City I had again stored my books and clothes in cardboard boxes — six this time — some of the same boxes I had used when I went on the previous long trip.

"Perhaps I'll come back," I said. "Now I have many other places to visit."

Roberto talked proudly about children and family, wanting to make sure that I understood all aspects of Columbian life.

The men and boys sang songs, told witty one-liners, and ate with relish, sucking on the chicken bones and savoring every spoonful of corn.

Roberto stopped abruptly and loudly demanded the foot. His plate already had a drumstick and thigh on it, so I had no idea that he literally wanted the foot of the chicken. He kept shouting for it until the heavyset hostess brought him one of the cooked chicken's feet, and he began sucking on the claws crying, "Ah, the foot, the best part."

The next day, after handshakes and slaps on the back and wishes for a successful trip, Roberto drove me back to a main road. I began bicycling over what looked and felt like tall mountains but were only stepping stones to the Andes. I got into low gear, stood over the handlebar, and pushed. My rear derailleur was out of line, probably because a heavy suitcase had been sitting on top of it in the plane, and I kept forgetting to adjust it every time I stopped. As I was getting into my lowest gear for a steep hill, the derailleur caught in the spokes and snapped. I shortened the chain and put it on a low gear, bypassing the derailleur and allowing me to pedal up hills and coast down. At the top of one long hill I invited myself into a home where I was again treated to royal hospitality by an enjoyable family.

Inviting oneself into a home is an art form that has been lost by the contemporary traveler. I found it to be the best way of discovering the customs and culture of other countries. Following the centuries-old tradition of travelers, I never impose on my host. When I see someone in front of a house I stop and say hello. I say who I am and where I'm from and where I'm going. Then I ask if I can have a space in their front yard to pitch my tent, a request that has never been denied me. In countries where I don't know the local language, I use hand gestures and arm waving as my vocabulary. I don't expect anything more than a place to camp, but most people invite me into their homes. The rules of reciprocity require me to give something in return, make conversation, and take a sincere interest in the lives of my hosts, no matter how tired I feel.

I woke at dawn the next morning and began pumping thirty miles up and down hills in my single gear to a town where I was fortunate to find another derailleur. A Columbian family who lived in a stone house built around a courtyard took me in that evening. Thick tiles covered the floors of their house. The walls were high and stucco, the rooms large and open, containing few pieces of furniture. The dignified young man showed me every corner of the house, introducing me to present and past family members hanging in framed pictures high on the walls. I did a minor repair on his bicycle and answered questions about North America and his greater interest, Spain. In the morning his sister, a stately dark young woman with large deep eyes who walked perfectly erect, milked a cow in the backyard. She made coffee, added the fresh milk, and put chunks of sweet white cheese on top, giving it an exquisite taste.

The real mountains began at the southern end of Columbia near Pasto, where a thin and bumpy road wound its way around treacherous curves carved from the sides of huge barren rocks. The road hung dangerously over thousands of feet of emptiness between crude gullies at the bottom and the cold clouds on top which hid the summits. I began seeing South American Indians in traditional dress: short plump women in layers of brightly-colored petticoats and brown bowler hats, a colored striped cloth tied in front and a child's head looking over the woman's shoulder; small-framed men with narrow cheeks wearing baggy pants, alpaca sweaters, white and brown wool caps with earflaps, who usually smile, almost always bent over carrying bundles, a four-foot high stack of firewood or grasses for animal feed.

I didn't know how to communicate with these people at first, but my shyness was broken after I crossed the border into Ecuador when a farmer who grew half an acre of corn and raised five head of cattle invited me into his tin roof house. He had seen me bicycling toward the village and gestured me to stop. It was still early in the afternoon, but I looked around at the adobe houses painted a pale white, and I felt happy that he had cracked my wall of timidity. I immediately accepted his hospitality. He had a large family with uncles and cousins and grandparents, and all the people wanted to meet me and ask me about life in the North. The young men inspected my bicycle and watch and cycle computer. I gave colored elastic hair bands to the girls. The boys ran their hands over my hairy arms, comparing them to their hairless arms.

Abuelita, the spry matriarchal grandmother, inspected my clothes, laughed at my black shorts, and pulled me aside to tell me how to dress for the mountains. She told me that I had to wear layers of warm alpaca wool. "People who come from the coast lose their heads here and don't know how cold it really is," she said.

One of the men added, "They say in the higher altitudes if you stand still in the sunlight, you can get sunburn on one side of your face and frostbite on the other side."

Abuelita took a particular interest in my journey, though she could not understand why anyone would want to see different countries: "Most of us have seen the world," she said. "I've been to Quito, and my husband has been to Columbia. What more is there to see?"

No one argued with Abuelita, a strong, plump, straightforward woman who had borne twelve children. Without a second thought, she asked me intimate questions that I had to answer, giving me a hard time about being neither married nor a priest, but she didn't suggest a wife for me from among the village women.

She looked at me. "You're too thin," she proclaimed, changing the subject. "Don't they know how to eat in North America?" She stood over me during dinner making sure I ate plenty of bread and corn. When I stood up she looked up at me in astonishment.

"My God," she said, "your height will frighten people. But they're easy to win over. Carry corn with you, and make sure you find a place to sleep before the sun goes down. You will always be able to find drinking water, but you must keep warm."

After that I put on an alpaca sweater over my long-sleeve wool Italian cycling jersey, but I still felt the cold through my clothes when going down hills in the morning or late afternoon when the sun was on the other side of the mountains.

The enchantment I felt while bicycling in Columbia continued throughout Ecuador. People gave me a place to sleep in their homes and treated me well. Their pressed dirt floor houses had few furnishings — perhaps only a few cast-iron kitchen utensils — but the people had a positive spirit. I had to pay my dues to see them, had to climb mountain after mountain, miles of steep, winding grades where my hips and shoulders and arms had to support the pushing-pulling action of my legs. I stood up, pumping, sweating, stopped to breathe, started again, pushed again, struggling up long mountain roads. Trucks whined past me, only slightly faster than I, the drivers waving cheerfully as their old vehicles spewed a trail of black exhaust across the road.

It was election time in Ecuador, and there were daily rallies for the eighteen presidential candidates. In every city people shouted over bullhorns, gathering crowds for their favorite candidate. They took the matter seriously, as if a change in government would make a difference.

On top of a snow-covered mountain I stopped to look across a deep valley at a mountain rounded like an ice cream cone that had delicious white snow melted on it. A group of cars plastered with posters for a candidate named Leon pulled up next to me to share the sheer beauty of the view. Leon got out and introduced himself to me, then began making plans with his team for the campaign in the next city. The cars and I left at the same time, but I let my brakes go and leaned into the sharp downhill curves, outrunning the four-car motorcade, cycling down to the town's main street and running straight into a massive parade for Leon. The townspeople were waiting at the town entrance expecting their leader, but when they saw me coming out of the last curve they sent up a roar of applause.

The denizens were covered in red and green and blue wool capes, carrying posters and shouting slogans for Leon. One person in town who wasn't part of the campaign parade told me that many of the people wouldn't be allowed to vote because Ecuador requires voters to be literate, and the Indian villages were too poor to build schools and teach their people to read. This did not temper the enthusiasm of their campaign.

Finally, after sweating up and down Ecuador's mountains, I stood on top of a long hill, looking over miles of green and brown and white mountains. I descended the mountain through a cloud and ended up on the hot and muggy coast at the southern part of the country. The mist of the cloud felt like bullets hitting the exposed parts of my skin, the windchill making it a brisk, invigorating experience. I descended a thousand feet every five minutes. A few miles later the world changed.

***

The coastal air hung oppressively low, forcing me to lower my head to the handlebar drops to cut through thick waves of hot air and humidity. Bicycling through towns where flimsy wood houses stood on stilts, over dirt-road towns where stray dogs on lean diets rummaged through plastic bags of trash along the street, I finally arrived at Zarmilla, the town at the Ecuador-Peru border. Small bare-chested men and boys with muscular arms, wearing handkerchiefs around their heads, pushed flat hand carts piled high with dime-store merchandise. They sold their goods at a series of stalls along the main street which ran straight across a river and into Peru. Peruvians came across the border, changed money with the sordid briefcase-carrying money-changers who leaned on the rails of the bridge, and shopped for Korean plastic cooking utensils and thin aluminum pans.

After border formalities, I pedaled down a dirt road punctuated with stretches of deep sand, making it necessary for me to get off and walk part of the way. The Pacific coast of South America is a dry desert from Ecuador to the middle of Chile. Two massive corridors of mountains filled with rain and snow run inland from this flat sandy strip.

I reached the town of Tumbis two hours later. Its dusty streets were flanked by painted adobe houses sandblasted and baked dry by nature. A young man selling bottles of soft drinks under a brick of ice told me that the road to Piura, the next main town about 150 miles south, was even worse than I had experienced. He and two other young men who came over to listen to our conversation took me around the corner and pointed to a polished modern bus parked incongruously between the dingy, neglected buildings.

"It's going right away to Piura," they said. Since I had several hundred miles of coast before returning to the mountains, it didn't take me long to decide to avoid bicycling on the destroyed road. I took off the panniers and Angel's wheels and laid it in the underneath luggage compartment, jumping on the front door step as the bus was beginning to move.

The bad roads were blamed on El Niño rains from the year before, storms that brought severe floods west of the mountains. At first I couldn't believe that the damage around me was caused by rain — much of the road surface had vanished — but enough people described the torrent of destruction that I had to accept it as unexaggerated truth. The rains swept away hills, houses, roads, bridges, and changed the geography of the area.

Our hardy Brazilian-made bus had problems negotiating the ruined road, making the relatively short trip in an astounding eight hours, stopping on the way at several beach hamlets where the local people sold the passengers fruits and cola. After several hours on the road we couldn't see out the windows from the dust.

At three in the morning the bus arrived in Piura. People breathed a sigh of relief as they staggered off. Thinking that I wouldn't find anywhere in the city to sleep at that hour, I got on my bicycle, asked an old man how to get to the Pan American Highway, and followed the direction of his arthritic finger pointing down a straight road lined with stately adobe houses which stood white in the reflected moonlight. I found a large open area of sand half a mile outside the city where I set up camp. The full moon overpowered the stars and cast a cool blue hue over the sand, filling the air with a profound quiet, a desert silence. I didn't bother with a tent, preferring to lay down in my sleeping bag and let my soul merge with the tranquillity of the setting.

When I set off the next morning, I was oblivious to anything being wrong. The desert night put me in an inward-directed mood; I neither felt like talking nor noticing the world around me. But I couldn't help seeing that the smooth tarred road that people said I'd be able to ride the rest of the way to Lima didn't exist. Instead, I began riding on a destroyed road that required slow speed and constant weaving from one side to the other, a road which gives a cyclist a sore neck from having to lift the head up unnaturally and concentrate in order to avoid the holes and sharp stones. Peruvians, I thought, must have a different standard for road conditions. A policeman I had asked at the border told me that the horrible road to Tumbis was a decent one. Describing it as worse than bad would have been more accurate.

South Americans seemed so casual about directions. People often pointed to the sky when I asked the way to a town, making it impossible to figure out which direction they were indicating.

People would tell me to go straight — that was the answer three-quarters of the time — but the straight road would end, turn in a circle, or divide into a fork.

Estimating distances was even worse. Most people would say that a place is close or far, either can mean anything. Someone's close ride is another's far. I can tell point to point distances from a map, but in between I often lose track of time and can't estimate how many miles I've traveled from the first point. Once in Ecuador I was standing at a corner eating corn with three Indians, and I asked how far it was to the next town. The first person said twenty-five kilometers, the second said seven, the third said forty-eight.

Nothing but withered desert vegetation surrounded the barren road wide enough for two cars. It was supposed to be the Pan American Highway. Perhaps all traces of the human race had been erased from the earth while I slept, leaving me as the only living being. No insects or birds, no trucks or cars or homes, nothing to alter my self-sustained silence while I bicycled on a road that could have once been laid by the Incas and left to rot.

My compass said I was moving south, and my map showed only one road to the next main town, Chiclayo, so I continued pedaling slowly, trying to avoid the chunks of broken pavement covering the road. Dirt roads cut my speed in half, and that type of road which has sections of disintegrated pavement is the most potentially destructive because of all the sharp rocks that remain scattered on the surface ready to slash my tires and bend my rims. Yet I was in a positive frame of mind, alone, with the optimistic faith that the road would suddenly get better. It got worse.

After forty miles of desolate bad road, I reached a junction which had a road continuing straight and another going toward the mountains. A wooden police control post stood at the right side of the intersection. Two food stands were across the road from it. Random pieces of raw wood were tied together and supported by branches, forming a canopy under which people could eat. A large woman wearing a long drab dress cooked a rice dish on an open fire, spooned the food from the aluminum pot to tin plates, then turned around to place the plates on a rickety table that had two benches near it. Children and women and a couple of men rested in the shade of the guard post and the food stands.

A half dozen children saw me and ran up to look and to sell me clear plastic bags full of mangoes, but I was anxious about the road and went up the stairs of the traffic control post to get information. Three young guards dressed casually in fatigues came out on the porch, shooed the children away, and greeted me energetically.

"We rarely see a stranger here," one young man said as we shook hands.

The situation, they told me, was simple: since all these roads were badly damaged by the tremendous torrent of El Niño, a new direct road had been built between Piura and Chiclayo. I, of course, had taken the wrong road since I hadn't asked anyone in Piura, and if I'd thought what I'd been on was rotten, they said, I should see what was coming up.

"Your best bet is to go back to Piura and take the other road," said another guard.

The third guard said, "Yes, but it so happens that a small colectivo would be going in an hour or two to Olmos." A colectivo is a truck used as a taxi.

I looked at my map. They gathered around me. One guard pointed to Olmos, showing me that it was half way to Chiclayo.

"It wouldn't be bad to bicycle the rest of the way to Chiclayo," said the first man. "The colectivo will take you out of the sandy part of the road."

They announced that their boss, el Jefe, was going to be on the colectivo. At this point the Jefe himself came out on the porch and smiled at me while drying his hair with a green towel. He had just finished a shower. The Jefe was short, in his early forties with a friendly face and soft brown eyes. He wore a khaki T-shirt and a pair of loose-fitting fatigues. Since the guards were welcoming, and since I hate the idea of going back over the same road so much that I'd rather go twice as far forward on a new road, I decided to wait with the Jefe for the colectivo.

The poor people of the world ride colectivos. A truck designed to haul cattle or dirt, a quarter-ton truck or a mini-pickup, becomes the only available public transportation in rural areas. The fare is half the price of a bus. Busses can't travel difficult routes, and they're limited because they can only carry people. The colectivo rider pays for a place to stand, usually in a crowd, while the truck bounces on the rough roads.

In remote areas, people have no other choice; they must passively accept the circumstances. The seats in the front cab are reserved for those who pay extra money, or for a person who by age or social standing is deemed worthy of a seat. No matter how small the vehicle, these colectivos have an attendant who collects the money and takes care of legalities such as submitting a list of the passengers' names to control points such as the one where I was standing.

As we were talking, a different colectivo, a large truck with vertical wooden posts which surrounded the perimeter of the flatbed, drove up to take the western fork going to the mountains. It was the first vehicle I saw that day. The flatbed was jammed so tight with Indians that they looked like crayons in a full carton. As soon as the truck came to the fork and stopped, the half dozen children, each carrying two or three bags of mangoes, climbed over the sideboards of the truck to sell to the parched, hungry travelers. Competition was fierce among the children: they elbowed each other as they climbed over the sides of the truck, stomping on the heads of their captive customers, recklessly hitting bags of mangoes into their faces. The attendant of the colectivo came to the control post and gave the guards a sheet of paper. One of the guards took it without looking at it. The attendant ran back to the truck, and the condensed mass of human cargo was off. I was glad it wasn't the one I had to take.

A few minutes later a fellow on a fat-tire bicycle came up to the control post and handed the guards another slip of paper. Two live lambs were strapped upside down on the sides of the bicycle's rear wheel, each lamb with its legs tied tightly and its head swinging back helplessly under the hot sun. Both creatures were in tremendous pain. I wanted to walk over with my knife and cut them free, but I did nothing. One of the guards who saw them felt the same — I could tell by the way he looked at the lambs. Animals have to be kept alive until they are ready to eat, but I saw no reason for treating them so cruelly. The fellow returned to his bicycle and began riding to what the guard told me was a nearby house.

The guards at the post gave me drinking water from a tank that collected the rain, and I gave them bread and oranges that I picked up at a stop during the eight-hour bus ride.

They made fun of their job, the only sensible response to a senseless occupation. I asked them what they actually controlled because I had passed several similar control stations in various countries and was baffled to know what function they served. One of the guards stood at attention and blew his whistle.

"We control the plants and the birds and the trees and the mountains," he said in mock seriousness. The others laughed.

Even on the busy roads these posts are equally useless. They record meaningless information from locals and foreigners who cross their post, such as name, age, occupation, where coming from and where going, mother's and father's names. The information is often taken orally, so anyone can tell them anything, which I suppose people on the other side of the law do. The guards keep this information in huge log books where, it seems, it would be impossible to find a person's name after hours of intense searching. In fact, the time I rode out of Ayacucho I passed the same control post that I had passed two nights before where they had recorded, among other things, from what city my passport was issued and Angel's frame number. As soon as they saw me return to the post, the guards went to work to find my name and record an exit date, but even though few vehicles passed on the road, and not one foreigner, it took three people a half hour to pull out the correct ledger. There was no telling if it was the correct one or the book that someone had the whim to use two nights before. Unlike the tranquil guard post at which I was resting, Ayacucho was the seat of a massive anti-government revolutionary struggle.

To relieve our boredom I pulled out my Walkman and let one of the guards listen to a cassette. He immediately recognized Beethoven. I don't know why I should have been surprised — Beethoven is as Peruvian as he is American — but I was surprised. He got carried away listening to the sound of the symphony.

My camera equipment I showed to another guard and then pulled out my pocket battery shaver, my cycle computer, and other bits of modern technology which I thought would interest them. They were fascinated, examining everything carefully, then launched into a discussion about American rock music, a subject on which they were more up to date than I.

The person who had sympathized with the lambs said, "Michael Jackson. He moves very well. And the Bee Hees. We like them a lot."

"The Bee Hees?" I said. "Oh, yes the Bee Gees."

The Jefe joined the conversation and talked about American movies. He had just seen an American film called *The Day After* which depicted what life would be like after a nuclear war. He asked me if such a war is possible. I replied, "Yes, certainly it's possible."

The people who operated the colectivo that the Jefe and I were going to take arrived and went to eat at one of the stands. The driver was short and dark and had no distinctive facial features. He parted his full head of hair on the right and wore clean clothes that were too big for him. The attendant, a thin man with a crooked nose and dry, empty brown eyes, wore pants that were so wide that the gathers under his belt left his waist looking like a drape. His hands and face were soiled with permanent dirt. He had a sedated look and imitated the driver's every move, acting like his shadow.

I went over while they were waiting for their meal, stood ten yards from them, and negotiated a price for transporting Angel and me over the next sixty or seventy miles, past the bad part of the road to Olmos, the same destination as the Jefe. At first they wanted an exorbitant price, 30,000 soles. We settled on 5000 soles, a bit over two dollars. I figured that was about double what the locals would pay. I knew that if I hadn't negotiated hard people would have thought of me as a sucker.

The colectivo operators had the air of the authorities I had met in El Salvador, and I felt an immediate repugnance for them. The driver looked like a man who beat his wife; his attendant looked like a cross between a fly and a rat. My gut feeling was to snub their colectivo, but I rationalized my need for a ride in their truck, a small, light-blue Japanese pickup.

I strapped Angel on the side of the pickup and sat on the hot sand in the middle of the intersection with fifteen others. The air was as dry as the Sahara; the sun shone ruthlessly over our heads. When the attendant gave the go ahead, the passengers stepped on the back and found places for themselves and their baggage. I was the last one to climb over assorted packages and boxes and squeeze my legs inside the rear gate while the rest of my body was well outside. When we were ready to leave, the driver drove us to the front of the guard post, and the Jefe came out. I almost didn't recognize him, for now he was dressed in a polished uniform with stripes on his shoulder and gold braids on his hat. With dignity he got in the front and carefully put the glimmering green officer's hat on his lap.

Apart from a large-framed Spaniard who made great sweeping gestures with his elegant ten gallon hat, the colectivo carried an assortment of dejected individuals. A man with gray hair announced that he was sixty, thus making himself the group's unofficial spokesman, philosophizing freely about life and the nature of existence. He sat on one of the two narrow benches and told the story of a man who lived nearby who was over a hundred years old.

"How wonderful," replied the Spaniard, "a century of life."

His words left his mouth and fell heavily on the air. The Spaniard's enthusiasm for living conflicted with the mood of the group. He was clearly not from that area.

Next to me in the truck stood an innocent-looking walleyed girl about fourteen and her mother, and next to them a fat woman who looked drugged. Her drooping eyes were watery, and her face never felt a smile. If inertia took a body, it would look like hers. There were also two barefoot Asian-looking Indian girls about ten or twelve in red and blue dresses who each carried three chickens. The chickens' legs were tightly tied together by a string; the children carried them upside down like plastic grocery sacks and squeezed them among the rest of us, but one chicken kept making noise and tried to flap its wings and get free. It didn't want to hang on a string and struggled for better treatment. I noticed that the Spaniard kept looking at it, but no one else paid it any attention.

Wanting to break the conversational ice, I gave a mango that the control guards had given me to the walleyed girl and another to the sixty-year-old man. She took it graciously, thanking me, but the old man pointed to a sack of mangoes at his feet that he was taking home, making my gift superfluous. The girl kept the mango in her hand and remained quiet.

The dust caused by the pickup remained suspended in the dry air. The talk between people took on a slow, lethargic tone, centering on the prices of goods. Peru was suffering, is still suffering, will suffer for at least another generation, from economic disaster and run-away inflation. The price of goods from mangoes to wristwatches was out of control. Clothes were twice the price they had been two months previously; food prices were skyrocketing, making life hard for all citizens; imports were impossibly priced. The gallant Spaniard astonished everyone by relating that his cream-colored linen hat cost 15,000 soles, about seven dollars. He stood in the corner of the truck ready to wave his hat at the few people we passed. At first I thought that he knew them — he waved so affectionately — but that was his way.

The rest of the people in the back conveyed a bleak and depressing picture of life. Their bodies looked inert, without energy, and they had long morbid faces which had never had reason to smile. Through the side mirror I could see the Jefe sitting calmly in the front seat. The sixty-year-old man continued to philosophize; his life experience had given him profound ideas on the meaning of existence, and he shared various pointed comments freely with the unappreciative crowd.

"Life is hard without money and water, and when it's hard there's no joy," he pronounced, like Tiresias proclaiming a prophecy.

The noisy chicken kept fluttering its wings, incessantly complaining about its fate on a string. It became increasingly difficult to ignore.

The guards at the control station had been right: the road was a nightmare, a mixture of sand deep enough to bury a case of mangoes and rocks that stuck out higher than a car's bumper. All bridges had been washed away, leaving not a trace, not the slightest clue, that bridges had ever spanned the banks, making it even more difficult to believe that the road had once been the Pan American Highway. I found it hard to imagine that the rains the year before could have washed away houses and roads, and I hadn't believed it until I was told dozens of times.

"There's oil in the mountains," said the old man after several people had complained about their thirst, "but not a drop of water anywhere."

"Couldn't the water have been collected from the rains last year?" I asked the seated sage, but he turned away from me.

The harshness of the sun made the area stark and ugly as the colectivo slowly drove the tortuous road. The drug-eyed woman began nodding her head with sleep, a remarkable feat, like falling asleep on a tilt-a-whirl. From time to time the attendant would listlessly hit the side of the truck. The driver would stop and turn off his engine. One or two people would struggle out with mangoes and their belongings, give the attendant a few coins, and plod off in the deep sand to their houses. People didn't seem happy to arrive at their destination, and no one came out of the house to greet them when they heard the sound of the pickup.

Their dilapidated homes were surrounded by fences of deadwood. Raw pieces of wood, the trunks of small trees, were tied together to form the wall and fences, many of which sagged into the thick dark-colored sand; a few random desert plants managed to cling to life. Cattle and goats roamed freely, the only other sign of life. I never saw anyone taking care of the animals. We passed a couple of empty villages where children sold melons on an improvised table near the road, but I couldn't see how they had any business. Our colectivo didn't stop except to pick up or let down passengers.

The small pickup emptied until there was room for everyone to sit on the benches. The polite walleyed girl and her mother got off and walked to their shack. The drug-eyed woman got off and walked away without taking her eyes off the ground. The children with the abused chickens got off; the one chicken continued making noise, but the others hung silently. Neither the Spaniard nor I could take our eyes off them until they got out of sight. With each person went mango crates, boxes, and bags. It boggled my mind how much baggage — human and otherwise —fit on such a small vehicle.

Later, we were about to cross another sandy bottom of a dry river, descending to the riverbed and crossing under where the bridge had been. But another car was coming toward us, one of the two or three cars we saw, and it began crossing the long span of the riverless sand. The driver, no doubt inexperienced on bad roads, forgot the first rule about going over sand, never to stop, and got stuck in the middle, his spinning tire trapping him further. Our driver stopped before going down the bank, turned off his engine, and he and the Jefe got out.

I too jumped over the side because I thought we were going to walk down to help the others push the car. This wasn't necessarily altruism; we couldn't pass until the other car had gotten out of the way. The driver took a piss; the attendant followed suit. I was too afraid to go over and give the people in the car a hand, for I thought the colectivo might pass me and leave me behind, so the Spaniard and I looked on until two women and one man, passengers of the forlorn car, pushed it out of the sand trap, the car fishtailing until it got on firmer ground. When they finally managed to come up out of the riverbed and had gotten to where we were, the driver of the car asked if the rest of the road was as bad. Our driver and the attendant laughed at him, making sure he understood how foolish and inexperienced he must be. The Jefe told him that although the rest of the road was awful, only a couple more spots were long and deep.

A few more passengers got off until only three remained. The sixty-year-old man talked to the Spaniard about hard times, the lack of water and money, talking in a sorrowful monotone. He was probing his life and pouring out his observations to the affable Spaniard, who held his hat in his hand ready to wave to children and adults. Finally, with the wind blowing his words toward me, the old man stood up solemnly and spoke with feeling a profound truth sixty years of living taught him, saying: "La vida es pobre."

It wasn't that life is hard, or that life involves struggle, or that life is unfair, but that life is poor, and he wasn't talking about money: he had arrived at a spiritual truth. Despite his age and his philosophical understanding of the environment he faced daily, he was wrong: such a life is not poor, it's bankrupt. It's cruel and it's empty and it shouldn't exist. The blacks in Columbia, the Indians in Ecuador, were no less deprived.

As we came closer to Olmos, our destination, we picked up new passengers, people who had been sitting on the sand by the road waiting for this unreliably scheduled ride to take them five or ten miles to town. The hot sun lowered as the small truck, again filled with passengers, pulled into the sleepy town of Olmos where the Jefe and the Spaniard could take a bus to Chiclayo. I lifted my bicycle down and put on my panniers. The driver and his attendant tried to get more money out of me, but

I didn't even listen to them. They stood next to the pickup ridiculing me.

I bicycled down the unpaved main street to the edge of town and into a Shell station. I began washing my arms and face from an oil drum of stagnant water. A bunch of children came up waving plastic bags of mangoes. They stood in a circle, staring. I bought a bag from one boy who asked my nationality. "Nordamericano," I said. No one else said a word. They stood around me staring while I washed, just stood there, as if they too hung on a string.

**

A harsh headwind faced me on the desert road, all the way to Lima. It came straight up from the south, hurling sand in my face, tearing my resistance as it had in Wyoming. I fought to keep a fifteen mile an hour pace. A bicycle with packed panniers is a poor aerodynamic design. It's like pulling a parade banner without vents through a strong wind. Even though bicycles are the most efficient use of human power for movement thus far designed — and they are quiet, non-polluting, of low-cost, and maneuverable — they can't handle strong wind.

Mountains are also hard to bicycle. The rider struggles the incline in low gear, standing and pushing pedals, sitting for a minute then standing again. But then comes the crest, an end to the physical strain, often followed by the thrill of coasting down. But winds are ruthless. They never end, and after exerting enormous energy little is achieved: no thrill, no accomplishment, only the deafening roar of the wind that ruins the peace of bicycling while sapping all the rider's strength.

My only technique to fight the wind is to focus my mind on bicycling by counting strokes. With single-minded concentration I push one pedal after the other, concentrating on the main pedaling force, the quadricipital muscles in the thighs. I thrust the ankles and pull the toes up against the straps, keeping head and shoulders down, arms tucked in, not allowing my mind to register fatigue until the end of the day: no sightseeing or picture taking, just hard bicycling. This determination gives me the aggressive energy to stomp on the pedals and confront the adversity that is knocking me in the face. From my biased perspective there wasn't much to see on the Peruvian coast except sand and a couple of unexciting cities.

I rode at night. No bicyclist likes doing that. It's dangerous and aggravating. You hit potholes because you can't see the road surface, and you have to take unusual precautions every time a car passes and blinds you with its lights. But the wind was calmer at night, the air cooler, and a large moon hung overhead. I felt that I had to ride at night when it was easier to make up for time lost to the wind.

Late one afternoon when I was seventy-five miles from Lima, I came to a stop and fell over. I had tightened my toe straps so hard that I couldn't release them in time when I stopped. Two guys hauling mangoes in a slow-moving truck saw me dabbing iodine on my knee and offered me a ride into town. I accepted. I didn't know how tired I was until I tried to stay awake and make conversation along the way. They asked me about life in the U.S., about movies and rock music, about my trip.

Finally, I couldn't hold onto consciousness any more, and woke before dawn in the front seat of a truck parked in the middle of an immense outdoor market. I saw people and trucks setting up for the day's business. The driver of the truck saw me wake up and came over.

"I'm sorry we made so much noise and took so long," he said.

"When?" I asked, rubbing my eyes.

"When we had to fix the tire," he said. I pretended to know what he was talking about. "We thought it would be bad for us too, but we managed to get a good place here."

After I brought them coffee and helped them take out more crates of mangoes, I thanked them, walked Angel around trucks backing into stalls, and began cycling to the center of the large city.

There I met a friend of a friend whom I surprised by telling that I wasn't interested in visiting the famous museums and tourist places: I'm a terrible tourist for such things when I'm on a bicycling trip. It takes only a few minutes of passing through the lifeless halls of such places before I burn out and want to leave. I was anxious to get away from the coast and back to the mountains. The museums have enough tourists visiting them, but only a few go to the villages.

It happened to be Lima's 449th anniversary, so the town held a crowded fiesta in the main square. The first part of the fiesta was dull: people sat on the long cathedral steps waiting impatiently for something to happen. Hundreds of men, women, and children walked around the square aggressively selling small packages of chewing gum and individual cigarettes and pieces of candy. Stalls selling sweet junk food stood all around the square.

Two or three people would march around the square beating an Indian drum, and dozens of others would flock around them, jumping over others' shoulders to see what was happening. From a small street a dozen yellow-robed Hare Krishna devotees marched through the square chanting. A crowd gathered around and followed them, probably thinking they were part of the celebration. The mayor gave a speech, then the serious festivities began. People formed groups with people from their own village, playing traditional tribal music on reed flutes and drums. Every group had its own melody. The crowd came to life. People danced and clapped as if they needed the memory of their roots to snap them out of their inactivity, as if their present culture in that brutish city was false, unreal, and unfulfilling.

Next morning I re-greased my bearings, changed to dirt tires, and psyched myself for the 16,000-foot climb over the first corridor of mountains, alongside train tracks that boast of being the highest railway in the world. I discovered it wasn't as hard to bicycle as I expected: a one hundred mile road followed rivers through the scenic mountains. Road crews were working on re-surfacing the parts destroyed by El Niño. People from the towns and villages along the way saw me climbing and ran over to the road shouting "bravo," a great morale boost. I found a hotel near the top of the snowy peak where I shivered myself to sleep under three thick alpaca blankets and completed the climb the next morning.

***

The llamas and alpacas stopped when the boys did. All eyes turned to me in disbelief. Breaking into an infectious and disarming laugh, the boys looked up at the black clouds and waved at me to quickly follow.

The rain started when we were a few feet from their straw-roof adobe house. It wasn't just rain; suddenly there was a wall of water between us and the front door, so that by the time we ran in we were baptized, fully immersed by nature. Thunder cracked all around, and every time it did the teenage boys broke out laughing a laugh of innocence, and I joined in as if we had known each other for years.

Within a couple of minutes a small man in his forties, with a wrinkled face and a big smile under his straw hat, came in and greeted the boys in Quechua, the old language of the Incas that is still widely spoken in southern Peru. The boys called him Tio, and Tio warmly welcomed me to their home as if it were a mansion; his voice and attitude was one of obvious pride.

"You're on a trip," he said. "It's good to have you here."

He began making dinner amid spontaneous laughter from the nephews.

"I'll fix your puncture," said the oldest, looking at my deflated rear tire.

"OK," I replied, and was instantly shocked that I would allow anyone else to do even the slightest repair on my bicycle. I pulled a patch kit out of my panniers, and the three fellows set to work finding the hole and patching it by the dim light of the open door.

"The road is bad and gives me many punctures," I said, and they all nodded in agreement.

It was one of Peru's main roads between Cuzco and Puno. Peru has only a handful of paved roads. Almost all the mountain roads are dirt.

After climbing over the first corridor of mountains, the road descended into the long plateau, the altoplano, which runs through Bolivia, hovering between 10,000 and 14,000 feet. The people there, mostly segregated Indian communities, dressed similar to the mountain people in Ecuador. They told me that each village has a slightly different dress — a different style hat or different petticoat colors — so that a trained eye would know each person's village by one's dress.

The cycling days were beautiful. The sun shined over the mountains and warmed the valleys, lighting up the streams and waterfalls, highlighting the herds of cattle, llamas, and alpacas. I bicycled through dozens of Indian villages and stayed in the homes of people who grew fruits and vegetables, raised animals, and remained isolated from the grave problems of their changing country. Their life involves a daily struggle for survival; the soil is as hard as the weather is harsh. I saw no tractors: they worked by hand, stoop labor, and they had to fight to make things grow. It takes a dozen people two weeks to pick as much corn as a combine can harvest in an afternoon. Men and women carried the harvest on their backs and briskly climbed up and down almost vertical hills. It wasn't unusual to see a woman walking down the road, carrying a large load on her back, spinning thread, and breast-feeding her child all at the same time. The child hung in a woolen sack around the woman's neck and shoulder.

Many of the mountain roads were terrible to bicycle, some filled with deep mud, where I had to walk. My feet and ankles were heavy from the weight of it, my back, face, and arms were sprayed with it, the steep grades I walked were slippery with it. Mud filled my derailleurs and jammed around my brakes. Rivers rushed over the road surface — deep rivers. I wouldn't be able to see the rocks on the bottom. Sometimes I successfully crossed, riding right across. Other times I didn't make it and fell into the icy water, cursing, grabbing my bicycle with heroic strength and running over to the other side, worrying about my equipment, cursing, shivering. The rivers raged. If someone else was around, we tried to help each other, rolled up our pants and dried ourselves on the other side.

In Tio's house the boys closed the door and lit a candle. Within a few minutes the smoke from the small fire that Tio made filled the windowless, chimneyless house.

"Windows make it cold," one of the young men told me.

But Tio used the few gathered twigs for the fire sparingly, making sure all the heat went to warm the two pots balanced between stones.

"This dinner will warm you and dry the cold mountain rain from your body," Tio told me.

The nephews sat on logs placed on the dirt floor around the fire. They spoke a mixture of Spanish and Quechua and laughed at every word that came from my mouth. Outside, the thunder moved away, but the heavy rain continued. I thought about having to bicycle through deep mud the next morning, and I mentioned it to the boys. Their eyes opened wide, and they uttered sounds of excitement, making me feel childishly thrilled by the idea of splashing mud.

Tio's house was about a hundred miles from Cuzco, the center of the Inca empire, now a popular tourist center since it is the starting point for visits to the Machu Picchu ruins. The nephews said that they went to school a few hours a day and spent the rest of the time farming, taking care of the animals, and laughing.

"The animals become our friends," said the oldest. "We need alpaca for wool and cows for milk, but they are part of our family."

I had a little bread and fruit and gave it to Tio, and he was able to put together a decent meal for all of us. First Tio gave us each a boiled corn on the cob, then a handful of the corn kernels which he had dry roasted. The smoke from the dark one-room house gradually rose through the thatched roof and left us with the clear, brisk mountain air and the sound of the rain. We ate, shared, and laughed together.

"Can you see better with your glasses." asked Tio.

I took them off and gave them to him to try on, and the nephews roared with laughter. I went to my bicycle and dug in my panniers while the oldest nephew brought over one of the paraffin lamps so I could see. I pulled out a pair of sunglasses and gave them to Tio. He was so touched he hardly knew what to say.

"Thank you, thank you very much. I will wear them often."

Tio and his nephews sat me near the fire so I could warm my hands. After we finished talking and laughing, we all wanted to sleep. The boys gathered up a bunch of straw lying on the floor and laid it down in the corner. One of the youngsters put a candle next to the straw, and from my rear rack I took off my sleeping bag. The boys took special interest in it, feeling the nylon while zipping and unzipping it.

"Is it better than alpaca?" asked one of the youths.

"Try it yourself," I answered, and they all took turns in and out of it.

"Does everyone in North America sleep like this?"

I tried to explain that I needed the bag because I often slept outside, then said good night and got into the bag fully dressed.

They spread three or four covers at the other corner of the house, laid down with Tio in a row, and joked themselves into silence and sleep.

For me the Andes was a place to think. In the day the clouds came close to the ground and crowded me into the handlebar. The stars accented the blackness of the night. Only the larger cities have electricity or running water. Hordes of running children filled their days with play while men and women worked the land. When I came to a city during a festival I would see a glimpse of their rich Inca heritage stretching back millennia. The people put on their most colorful dresses, danced, played hand-made musical instruments, and sang. They have many festivals, but that represents only a small part of their life. The daily living of most involved farming, buying and selling at open-air markets, taking care of children, weaving, building, and socializing.

The sound of Tio and the nephews' gaiety woke me in the morning. How they loved life! After I said good-bye, and all of us regretted the moment, I was ready to again hit that foul road. Mud no longer bothered me. I rode straight down the center of the road toward Bolivia, singing all the way. Busses and trucks passed me, drivers honking, passengers waving, oblivious to their tires spraying me with more mud.

A natural line around the Andes divides the Indians from the Europeans on the rest of the continent. When I crossed the border into Argentina and rode down the majestic mountains to sea level and faced the Chaco marsh, I gradually saw fewer Indian villages as the area became more developed and Westernized. Quite abruptly, there were only Europeans, and when I saw a fair-haired woman in a skirt, nylons, and make-up, I had to bring back to my mind a world I had forgotten. From there I rode across miles of rolling earth to Rio and took a plane to South Africa.

East African Swamps

It was a stupid accident. I had taken the road for granted when my front wheel skipped over the edge, and down I went. I had fallen on a new asphalt road on the edge of Mtengo Wa Nthenga, a Malawian village of about a thousand people. Half a dozen shops lined the road, and clusters of huts were scattered nearby; a typical market town sitting in the midst of trees and bushes and plots of plowed brown soil.

I was in tremendous pain as soon as I hit the pavement, but I quickly pulled myself over to the shoulder of the road to get out of the way of a car I heard coming up fast behind me, one of the three or four vehicles I saw that entire morning. The car, I discovered later, was driven by the local parish priest.

I had ridden through the village just before my fall. The villagers near the main road had stood silently, their eyes following my progress. Suddenly I fell. Their heads stopped. No one said a word, and I couldn't ask for help, but soon I looked across the road pavement and saw a few dozen bare black feet crowded in a semi-circle in front of me. My head tilted up. I saw a jumble of worn and faded clothing. The men wore polyester pants and short-sleeve shirts fraught with holes. The women wore colorful cloths wrapped from their knees to their chests, like sarongs around their round bodies. The villagers stood in front of their sharp shadows. Their ebony faces, weathered by many afternoon suns, registered no emotion.

Every eye was staring at me. I'd grown accustomed to being stared at by crowds, and even at that ego-humbling moment as I lay on the pavement, their stares didn't bother me. Sitting in pain, my head hanging in my arms, the center of attention of this semi-circular silent and unmovable crowd, I felt strangely pacified.

I asked quietly in English if there was a doctor near, but no one understood me. They remained silent, all eyes intent on me. English is the official language of Malawi, but not many people speak it outside the big cities, and few speak it well. The

137

tiny country of Malawi has over twenty distinct local languages, Tejawa being the language of the central region where I took my fall.

After some time, a young woman in a bright yellow and blue dress with flowers printed on it came through the crowd and sat on the ground next to me. She carried a child tightly on one hip. No one spoke. I turned to look at her. God, she was beautiful: smooth and defined facial features, rich soft eyes, a graceful lean body, and ebony complexion without blemish — skin that I wanted to reach out and touch as one would want to touch a velvet cloak or a silk gown. Her face looked gentle and kind and warm.

She untied the knot on the center of her dress, took out her breast, and gave it to her child. The crowd remained still, looking alternately at the two of us. She turned her head to me and broke the silence: "You are in pain," she said, half question, half clairvoyance.

"Yes," I said after a pause. "I think I broke my hip."

I began to feel the heat of the pavement and looked at the crowd. There was another meditating pause.

"There's a little hospital in town," she said calmly. She spoke English fluently.

I looked at her, then turned to the crowd. It took me a while to appreciate what she had said, a hospital in Mtengo Wa Nthenga. I raised my head and said that perhaps I should go there right away, but she stretched out her arm in front of me, gesturing me to stay while she directed a couple of young men to bring the doctors and their ambulance.

Two fellows suddenly emerged from the group of onlookers and ran down the road. A few minutes later a tiny Renault station wagon with a small red cross on the side window came up the road and found the crowd.

"Here are the doctors," the woman told me.

The semi-circle parted, and two nuns in white flowing robes walked quickly toward me. They were the first non-Africans I had seen in many weeks. I heard them speaking Spanish. Their voices were like a balm on my aching hip. One of the sisters looked me in the eye and saw my bicycle. I knew she understood the situation. Speaking Tejawa, she motioned for someone to remove my bicycle. Two other men came forward at her direction to carry me into the backseat of the Renault, what the woman called an ambulance. I gave myself up to their care as they tried to put me gently on the seat. I thanked the lovely woman in the flowery dress who remained sitting on the ground nursing her child while she watched the crowd disperse. I never saw her again.

The sisters took me to their hospital, a small dispensary. They and a third Carmelite nun ran the facility. One of the sisters looked at my hip and knew that I needed an X ray. Another nun graciously drove me to the hospital in Lilongwe, the newly declared capital of the country, about twenty-five miles south of the village. Earlier that day I had bicycled through Lilongwe with the intention of buying food, but it was Sunday, and all the shops were closed, so I continued north until my hip met the pavement.

When we arrived, the small nun who drove me and a buxom nurse whose muscular black arms were bursting out of her white uniform pulled me out of the car and placed me on a cart. I moaned all the way to the X-ray room. A young African doctor who had just finished his training in Holland told me that I had nothing broken, but I couldn't believe him. I couldn't move my leg. He had to show me the X ray: a big bruise but no cracks.

I spent a week on my back in the paying ward of the hospital. The broad-beamed nurse put me in a room with eight other patients. The families of two patients also lived there, sleeping and cooking meals as if it were their home. I say paying ward with reservation since a bed with three unexciting meals costs five kwacha a day, about four dollars. There were about seventy-five paying patients and 400 non-paying.

The hospital was a sorry affair by Western standards. The staff would run out of clean towels and sheets, and no one would be assigned to wash more. One bathtub served the entire floor. At times there was no hot water, so dishes and patients were washed in cold water. No one complained. In the three non-paying wards they served either a porridge or nsima, a kind of tasteless cornbread that is the standard nourishment in south and east Africa, while the paying ward had rice and chunks of meat. Twice during my stay there was no food. "It's finished," a nurse announced as a statement of fact, and that was it. Compared with the poor villages, the hospital was luxury. For me it was salvation.

When the wheelchair wasn't in use, I'd sit in it and wander around; otherwise, I hopped around on one foot using a wooden chair for support. Gradually I became friends with several patients and visitors. At night a group of twenty patients, some missing a limb or with a nasty rash, would sit on the floor in the hallway and sing the most melodious gospel music I had ever heard. The sound echoed through the cement-block corridors, down the open air courtyard, and into the warm night.

At the end of my stay a short, thirty-year-old Franciscan brother who had the face of a black St. Francis presented me with a cane he'd carved for me. By that time I was able to limp with it, although any awkward or sudden movement brought an explosion of pain. The good sisters came for me with their car, took me to their mission, and put me up at the priest's house next door. There the Malawian priest, a large man in his forties, confessed to me his feeling of conflict when he'd seen me lying on the pavement.

"I could see you were in great pain when I passed you," he said in a BBC English embellished with a native accent, "but I did not think I could be of any help."

"It doesn't matter," I replied. "The people helped me."

"If you had waved me to stop, I would have."

"The sisters took care of me."

"I was almost out of petrol. I did not even think I had enough to get to Lilongwe to fill up."

"It turned out fine."

"If you were not near the town I would have stopped. I was sure you would be all right."

On Sunday he gave a sermon about the need to take positive action. He lectured people about washing themselves and keeping the village clean in case they had more visitors like me. He asked people to come with machetes the next day and trim the large lawn in front of the church, a dominating but simple hall built of concrete. The service was filled with people sitting on small square mats placed on the concrete floor. Women and men were on different sides. The elders sat on chairs near the altar. One of the elders saw me sitting on the floor in the back and brought me a chair: everyone knew about the way I hurt myself. Anytime the priest mentioned me, the congregation turned their heads to look.

The Carmelites and their mission were an oasis of comfort. They ran an active clinic and worked with the surrounding communities. It was their busy time, right before the corn harvest. Those who had not considered the future, or had sold their corn from the last harvest to buy beer, were left destitute. Many families owned nothing but an empty mud house and the clothes they wore. The mission ushered them through their hard times, not only by helping them when they needed medical care, but the nuns visited people in their homes, ate with them, and showed them how to wash their babies and recognize health hazards. I could see that there was a bond of affection between the nuns and the villagers.

Sister Angelica, the nun in charge of the clinic, gave me two injections of a vitamin B complex, and I felt ready to bicycle three or four days after leaving the hospital. I could ride better than I could walk; I still needed my cane for walking, but the easy circular pedal movement put little pressure on my sore hip. The Carmelites and several villagers advised me to wait until I was better before starting out again, but I was anxious to get on the road and see other parts of Africa before the rainy season changed dirt roads to mud. I thanked everyone, and began riding again.

The road, as I said, had little traffic. Apart from trucks hauling beer in waxed cartons like quarts of milk, I hardly saw a car an hour. Gasoline was expensive; a gallon probably cost ten or fifteen times as much as a nsima meal. Keeping an invalid's pace, I bicycled fifty miles to a fairly large town called Kasunga and spent the night in a fleabag hotel. Two fellows who had seen me bicycle through town insisted on showing me the sights. I limped around with them, cane in hand, through the few paved and dirt streets. They showed me the bus station, stalls for the open-air market, and the handful of shops in town.

Hills caused problems while bicycling; I couldn't push down with my right leg, and it was difficult to ride my packed bicycle up the hills with only one power leg. Getting on and off the bicycle was also a chore. I had to lay it on the ground, grab my injured leg, lift it over the struts, and gingerly lift the bicycle up between my legs.

After riding the entire next morning, I came to the edge of a game reserve. I love these peaceful places where wild animals roam free, but whenever I stopped for rest or water, people warned me about the danger of cycling through the game park, and considering that it had hills, that my hip was still weak, and that I couldn't get away if an elephant charged, I decided to take a bus through the area. I used to consider taking a bus or accepting a ride a form of cheating, like buying and wearing a racing T-shirt but not racing. Gradually, I began accepting my own limitations and didn't need to prove myself so much.

The bus ride took as long as if I had bicycled. It dropped me off at the top of the mountains looking down on picture-postcard Lake Malawi, near the same spot where Dr. Livingston, the area's first modern white explorer, pointed down and asked the local natives what they called it. "Nyassa," they said, which means water in their language. The adventurous doctor thought they were telling him the name of the lake, so it stayed "Nyassa" until a few years ago when the government changed it to "Lake Malawi." Whatever the name, it's smooth and blue and beautiful, and it's free from bilharzia, the serious disease that makes many African lakes and rivers unswimmable.

I began making my way along the lake's shore, pedaling conservatively, and finally finding myself in the town of Karonga, a city of dirt streets and shops that had nothing to sell. I gave away the food I had bought from the men and women who sell on the side of the road by the lake to the beggars in the city. At Karonga I had the choice of taking a 150-mile paved road back through Zambia and then to Tanzania, a two-day trip in my condition, or going straight up a dirt road to Tanzania. The second route, it seemed from my map, was about twenty-five miles. Various people standing around the town told me that I would be able to take a boat across the border, but I couldn't get accurate information about this boat. I wanted to get off the main road, and since the dirt road was much shorter, I took it. It turned out to be a tire-destroying road full of sharp rocks, but after twenty miles I reached the Malawian border station in good spirits, my hip without pain.

At most border crossings, the distance between one country's checkpoint and the other's is usually not more than a hundred yards. A couple of times I remember going a bit further, but usually once you reach the first checkpoint, the second is close, over a bridge or something. I thought I was almost at the border, ready to cross the Songwe River and ride on a tarred road that would take me through Tanzania. By the time I got to the wooden shack that housed the government border facilities the immigration officer had left for the day. On my gentle insistence, a policeman who kept telling me to return tomorrow finally, but reluctantly, stamped my passport.

"This is no longer an international crossing," he said to me in an authoritarian voice. "The few foreigners like you that try to make the crossing get turned back."

I learned from two men who came into the station, each carrying a seventy-five-pound metal can of cashews from Tanzania, that there used to be a ferry on the lake, but it stopped running years ago when Tanzania and Malawi had an argument, and now the crossing is used only by locals.

Maintaining the cocky notion that I have a good way with border officials and can pleasantly distract them with my bicycle, and since I thought I was already near the border, I said I'd rather take my chances than go back on that terrible dirt road.

I limped across the street to drink a cup of tea, merrily waved to the border people, slowly went through the ritual of getting on Angel, and started off down the road, ignorant of what was ahead.

The road was covered with sand and became narrow right away, too narrow for even a small car. I bicycled around banana trees and clusters of highly-populated mud huts, but the sand became deep and almost threw me. I had to quickly remove my feet from the toe straps and sling out my legs to keep balance, a jerking motion that shot pains through my hip. After several miles on this trail I could ride no further because the sand became too deep, and by this time my hip was throbbing from the sudden agitations needed to keep my balance. Once I fell over and took a long time getting up again. I lay there wondering why no one improved the road since it was the only way to Tanzania and relatively well-traveled.

The locals thought the sight of a white foreigner quite strange. They were exceptionally friendly; they waved, said a word or two of greeting, usually with an expression of astonishment, and never took their eyes off me until I was out of sight. Just off the road I could see many poor villages. The thick vegetation would be cleared away, and I would see a cluster of thatched-roof mud huts.

I don't know what kept me going. I had no business continuing and should have stopped and asked someone if I could stay for the night. The people would have been hospitable. At one place where I stopped to rest my hip, two men offered to help me back to a doctor. But I always get excited near frontiers and become anxious to cross to the new country. It's a childish feeling, and it clouded my thinking. This feeling was accented after spending so many days off the road. I had the notion in my head that I had to cross the Songwe that day, so I stubbornly carried on, only to find that the road turned into a swamp. I took off my shoes and began wading. What else was there to do?

It turned out to be a thoroughly unpleasant swamp with a muddy, slippery bottom, and the last thing my hip needed was unstable feet. I held the cane in one hand and Angel in the other. In no time the dark water went up to my bottom bracket, hubs and saddlebag panniers. One small-framed man with mahogany-colored skin who lived in a hut on the edge of the swamp saw my plight, came over quickly, took my loaded bicycle without saying a word, and carried it on his shoulder to an oversize rowboat about 200 yards away, a feat I can't perform even in my best condition. I waded behind. The water came almost up to my waist, and I slipped many times, sending jitters up my hip. Somehow I climbed into the boat where a half dozen passengers and a ferryman sat waiting. The ferryman began to move the boat, gondola style, across the Songwe River (I assumed it was the Songwe). It was getting dark by this time, and the mosquitoes were out en masse. I swallowed four B-1 tablets which are supposed to keep those vicious insects away by emitting a subtle odor from the skin. It never works for me, but I keep trying it.

The boat stopped midstream, and the passengers got out and began wading again. One of the passengers who wore cut-off pants grabbed Angel, unconcerned with whether I wanted him to or not, and carried it across a worse swamp to semi-dry land. Again, I waded behind with my cane, arriving when it became completely dark, and being greeted by the sound of several women crying. I had befriended a man in the boat who spoke some English. He told me that someone had died, and the women would stay up all night grieving. I was lucky to meet this fellow; the dozen words of Tejawa I learned in Mtengo Wa Nthenga were useless in this area. He and two other relatives who were also in the boat were going to take me to their four-hut village for the night, about a two-mile walk. I dreaded the idea of walking further, for, as I said, cycling was no strain, but walking still came hard.

I shook the water out of one of my panniers that had fallen in the murky river, and then we were ready to walk down the dark footpath. I walked, pushing Angel down a one-man trail that wound through an area of rectangular African huts. Many people lived nearby. Every few yards I saw a paraffin lamp burning behind the bushes and heard the sounds of people talking and singing. Unable to see my way, I stoically limped behind, slipping several more times and gnashing my teeth in pain, afraid that I'd finally surrender to the urge to stop and sleep without putting up my tent. This crossing would have been difficult enough for someone with a good pair of legs, but for me with a seventy-pound bicycle, it was masochistic.

When the pain became too much I told my friend that I couldn't walk further. He said that he would take me to the local chief's house just around the bend, and he would ask him to give me a place to sleep. "Of course," I said, knowing that in Africa I always need the permission of the chief to sleep in his village.

This chief was terribly jolly, one of those blessed people who enjoy life and disarm misfortune. His round flabby face enshrined a perpetual smile and when one of the women who lived there brought out a stool for me to sit on and converse with this happy man, the harsh swamp-crossing experience drifted out of my hip into oblivion. He wore baggy trousers rolled up to his calves, an old safari jacket over a white T-shirt, and a large floppy hat. He spoke English fairly well, and he nearly collapsed with laughter when my other friend told him in Swahili that I was traveling through the country by bicycle. He slapped my knee and told me that I was most welcome to spend the night there, a gesture which slightly surprised me since touching a stranger is not an African custom. I asked him about mosquitoes, and his white front teeth flashed out of his dark face.

"Yes," he said gaily, "we all get malaria."

He made malaria sound so inviting that I regretted taking pills to prevent the disease.

"This is banana area," he explained. "In south they like eat maize. Here they eat banana. Too many banana." Maize, or corn, is the staple of much of Africa.

"I saw plenty of banana trees, but I also saw a lot of rice growing near the lake," I said.

"Yes," his smile never leaving his face, "but people love banana."

This was true enough, for the next night when I stayed with a family on top of a hill overlooking miles of green valleys, we ate fresh bananas, fried bananas, boiled bananas, dried bananas, and mashed bananas. For three meals there was nothing but bananas, except once when the host passed around what he called "cow meat," which looked so slimy that I couldn't bring myself to eat it.

The chief and I sat on stools surrounded by a few people who sat on the ground, and by a half dozen huts in an area that was cleared of the heavy tropical vegetation. After our cordial visit, he directed two women to prepare a hut for me. I really wanted to sleep in my mosquito-proof tent, but I had to keep my obligation as guest. Buzzing mosquitoes keep me from sleeping. I can often rig my tent indoors and hold it up with ropes. But this hut had mosquito netting around the bed, a luxury I had not seen in other African villages.

In this part of East Africa rectangular huts are common, while in the south round huts are found. Both types have a thatched roof, hardened dirt floor, and no window. The sides are made by applying clay onto a structure of branches. Cooking is done in a separate hut or outside. The huts usually have no furniture, not even the crudest chair, but here I had a bed, table, and one of the two chairs the woman brought out for the chief and me to sit on. I took off my muddy clothes, slipped into my sleeping bag, and felt the tension flow out my body and mind. The quiet sounds of the tropical night soon put me to sleep. Then, and for many days after I had hurt my hip, I could only sleep on my back.

The next morning a profusion of light came through the open doorway. I felt strong. The chief had someone heat up a small bucket of water so I could wash and shave. A woman carried the bucket on her head and led me behind a cluster of banana trees to a private area carpeted with banana leaves where people wash. I washed off mud and dirt, dressed in clean clothes (though slightly wet from being accidentally thrown in the swamp), then met the chief in the cleared area at the center of the cluster of huts. He introduced me to his son, saying that he would accompany me to the river. It was then that I discovered that I had not crossed the Songwe River the night before, but was still in Malawi. The swamp I'd waded through was just that, a swamp. I still could not believe this was the only route between Malawi and Tanzania.

I said a fond farewell to the chief and walked with the heir apparent up the slippery footpath to the river, where we saw a fourteen- or fifteen-year-old boy skillfully paddle a hollowed out tree trunk canoe across an intense brown current. The river was not wide at this point, perhaps seventy-five feet, but it flowed fiercely. I looked at the canoe and didn't think I'd be able to get my packed bicycle across safely, but the chief's son tried to allay my fears.

There was no dock on either side, so everyone that wanted to cross the river had to wade in mud to get to the canoe. I saw a woman sink down ankle deep in the mud on the riverbank. I asked the five or six people there why someone didn't cut a few branches and tie them together to form a dock, something I could have done in an afternoon, rather than traipse through the mud. Although they understood what I was saying, no one understood my mentality.

After we watched the canoe transport people back and forth, it became our turn. I had a piercing mental image of Angel falling in the raging river, and I was apprehensive. The chief's son and I put the bicycle in the boat, and I hobbled in and steadied the bicycle, holding it ever so tightly. Two other passengers followed me into the boat.

The oarsman paddled upstream straight into the raging current. The canoe shook and swayed. We sat low in the boat, but the bicycle stood up high; it would be the first thing to go if the boat leaned too far.

When we had gone out a few feet from shore, the boy oarsman turned the canoe broadside so it could be taken by the current. We immediately began moving fast downstream. The boat leaned. The two other passengers held on to the side of the tree-trunk hull. I held on to Angel. The oarsman began paddling furiously to make it across the raging current to the other shore. Everything around me began spinning, but the shore came closer, and finally we were out of the current. I never thought that climbing into ankle-deep mud would feel so welcome.

There were more small swamps to cross before I could put on my shoes and begin riding. The vegetation became less tropical. The footpath gradually became wider until it was an almost acceptable dirt road that went in front of more hut-filled communities. Everyone was surprised to see me; the men would generally make a gesture of greeting; the women would just look. After a few miles I came to a teahouse, crossed a bridge, and felt ecstatic when I saw a paved road where there was an inconsequential building marked, "Customs and Immigration." Anyone could have easily missed it, and I debated whether or not to go in since the words of the Malawian exit guard came back and began to haunt me. I decided to stop, thinking that at most they would give me a lecture but surely not turn me away after such an arduous trek. How could they?

A sleepy air hovered over the border post. A young man sitting in the shade of the building fetched the immigration officer from his house next door, a man about forty, slightly potbellied, wearing a green uniform. Like most government workers in former English colonies, he spoke excellent English. Acting the role of an official, he took my passport and began thumbing through all my stamps.

"This is not an international crossing," he said definitively, but I didn't think much of his words since I was already there, feeling as if I had won a battle.

"But I already have a Tanzanian visa," I replied.

"I'm afraid you're going to have to go back and come through Zambia."

There was no way I was going back, but after a little conversation I discovered that he was not going to allow me entry. He took a mild negative interest in my South African stamps, but since I had gotten my other African visas beforehand, this was not the stumbling block. Ready to betray every moral conviction, I delicately hinted about bribes, about doing anything in order to gain entry. I described my leg problem in detail, the depth of the swamps, and the agony of crossing, but he would not give in. We came to a dead end. He would not yield, and I would not go back through the swamps, not even if he put a gun to my head. Finally, he said that his boss, the chief officer, would be back at one or two o'clock, and I could talk to him. I looked at my watch. Ten in the morning. I had to buy that plastic digital watch for about $2.50 in South Africa after my other one stopped.

So I waited, contemplating whether to sneak off down the road or take my chances with the new officer. It could be a serious offense to be in a country without the proper papers, but there was no way I'd go back. If they denied me access, I would sneak around and go through anyway, but I didn't want my passport stamped "refused." When the officer had gone home, I checked the three rubber stamps in the office and thought about stamping my passport myself, but I had the sense that reasonableness and humanity would triumph over the uncompassionate routine of the obeying of laws.

When the first officer dropped his official stance, we got to be good friends. He invited me over to his house for a nsima lunch, that ever-popular African meal. He, his wife, and three children ate with their hands, but they offered me a fork and knife. By that time I was quite comfortable eating with my hands. Someone had gone to town and told the chief officer that a foreigner was waiting at immigration, and about three o'clock he arrived. A flamboyant man in his late twenties dressed in civilian clothes, he wore his hair in an afro which overflowed onto his forehead, unlike most people who wore their hair close cut. He sat me down in the inner office and went through the same routine as the other officer. I couldn't get a feeling for the man; I couldn't tell if he was a dedicated follower of rules or a man looking for a large bribe, so I didn't know how to act toward him.

"This is not an international crossing," he said mechanically. "You have to go back."

"I can't go back."

"We have to enforce the law."

"I can't go back. My leg is too painful. Can't we call someone in the capital and see if an exception can be made? I'll pay for the call. There must be something that can be done."

"No. You have to go back."

We talked this way for a few minutes until it felt useless to continue. I discreetly took my passport so he wouldn't stamp it, looked incredibly pained, and quietly rose to leave. I had been accenting my limp to try to gain as much sympathy as possible.

"Sit down," he said after a pause. "Give me your passport and currency declaration."

I had no choice but to respond.

"It says here you have one hundred U.S. dollars, fifty pounds sterling, and seven Zambia kwacha, besides travelers checks."

I sensed an opening but didn't trust my feelings. Many countries are fanatically concerned about the amount of currency travelers bring in and take out. Tanzania changed money at the official rate of about twelve shillings to an American dollar, while the black market rate was over eighty shillings to a dollar. Currency controls are made upon entry and exit in the foolhardy attempt to combat the black market.

"What does it matter if you won't let me in," I said.

"Is that all you have?"

"Yes," I said truthfully, "That's all I have."

I couldn't see which rubber stamp he picked up, but he began to stamp my passport and my forms.

"Can you make it through the country in fourteen days?"

Those words sang in my ears. "Absolutely," I replied unemotionally.

"Our country has many mountains."

"I've been over much higher mountains. Look at all the stamps I have in my passport."

"You must be out of the country in fourteen days," he said handing back my passport. I still couldn't get a feeling for him. I didn't know if I was supposed to pay him or if I would go to jail for suggesting it.

"You have done something for me," I said tactfully. "Is there something I can do for you?"

"No, nothing." But as we were stepping out of the room onto the front porch he added, "That watch you have on looks very nice. Perhaps you can make it a present to me?"

I hesitated a bit. Where would I be able to get another at a reasonable price? He saw my hesitation and asked, "Do you give it willingly?"

"Oh, yes," I said, holding my breath. "Very willingly."

The first officer came over and congratulated me, for indeed I was a happy man. Then he asked me if he could have a tube of tire patch glue. Willingly, I gave him my spare glue, and was off, singing, laughing, and waving at the natives who were astonished at such a sight.

Near the Lion's Roar

Nothing worked in Tanzania. The few trucks in running condition had no diesel. Stores had empty shelves — completely empty. Restaurants had no food to serve. Bakeries had no bread to sell. Sewing machines had no cloth to mend. Land not scorched by drought lay fallow or was not put to good use. Roads paved before the 1963 independence were neglected and disintegrated. The few road signs planted by the British stood so rusted and faded that they were unreadable. People stood idle, often looked downtrodden, unable to change the situation. But beer, warm beer, beer brought in by special trucks, beer that men bought with whatever wages they earned, was almost always available in the villages.

The country abounded in beauty. Mountains covered much of the country: some green and purple in the setting sun stood majestic and fertile; others harsh and rocky with sparse growth. Thousands of wild animals roamed freely in the game parks. I bicycled close enough to elephants and giraffes to see their eyes. Monkeys and baboons crossed the road in front of me. Herds of zebra and impala grazed all around. Red and blue and orange birds flew overhead. I knew that big cats and hyenas roamed the parks near me.

The sky extended from horizon to horizon, and in the evening the sun glowed a rich yellow-red, then made way for a sky full of stars and a profound feeling of peace, a dark black peace.

Drinking water was brown. Straight out of a well it was given to babies and old men. I put a drop of iodine and a chlorine pill in it and drank it through a charcoal purification filter. It tasted so awful that only when I felt desperately close to dehydration could I bring it to my lips.

I rode past dusty villages of wood or mud houses where people sat in the shade of a leafy tree eating a little corn. In the northern part of the country there were villages of Masai. They tended their cattle with spears; boys twelve years old, with dangling ear lobes and cow dung in their hair, carried spears as long as they were tall, stood on one leg like flamingos, wore torn and dirty robes, and walked straight over vast dry, desolate areas with their animals.

One day in the middle of the country, when I was tired from bicycling on a ruined road, I saw a town on top of one of the many hills. On my map I read the name Mtmada. I discovered that it was a stop-off for busses. A half dozen food stands with oil lanterns lit the center of the town on both sides of the rocky brown road. A young man with rich dark-chocolate-colored skin who had been on a bus that had passed me a mile back, came up and shook my hand, introducing himself as Nathan and telling me that he was a Christian. Speaking reasonable English, he invited me to eat with him.

I leaned Angel on a building, and we went to one of the stands run by his sister. He didn't introduce me. She gave us full plates of rice and vegetables. We ate after the sun had set, the light of the dozen lanterns illuminating the town's center. While we were sitting on stools and eating, I saw women with cloths wrapped around their straight bodies walking down the hill to the well at the bottom. They returned with urns of water which they carried elegantly on their heads.

"Couldn't a plastic pipe be extended to the top to make it easier for the women?" I said.

"There are no pipes here," Nathan replied.

"A hundred meters of pipe can be brought from Dar es Salaam," I said. "Someone can bring it on a bus."

"The village is poor," he replied. "We have no money for pipe."

I paused, and thought. The money these stands charge for a meal amounts to pennies of black market currency. The country has very few industries; plastic pipe probably has to be imported, making it expensive. A local alternative has to be found. I turned to him with the excitement of a bright idea:

"Then you can use bamboo. There's plenty of that around. In a few hours two men can hollow it out and join it together by trimming one end and enlarging the other end."

"The women have always brought the water this way," came the reply.

Perhaps I was wrong, trying to impose my idea. I can't know that my way would be better than their way. But I continued because it seemed so practical: "It isn't the matter of a pipe. If two people can build a pipe, another two can build a farm," I reasoned.

I knew nothing would come of my idea, not that Nathan and the others were lazy, but for some cultural reason that remained a mystery to me things would probably not change. Should I have started the bamboo project or remained a silent observer? I decided to leave things as they were.

I put up for the night in a room of a building that served as the town hotel. I had a square room with a wood bed and two oil lamps. Nathan came the next morning to take me to tea at a different stand on the main street. He told me that many people in town were weak and sick, and asked if I could give him medicine and dollars. He didn't want Tanzanian currency.

"I made a currency declaration when I entered the country," I said. "If I leave with money unaccounted for, I could get into trouble."

Many townspeople were observing our conversation. Nathan's voice became more despairing. I thought that the night before he and the others must have talked about how to approach me. I took out a salve that the Carmelite sisters had given me for my hip. I had been using it on my hip every day, for it hurt, and I still walked with a limp. Nathan took the salve and gave it to someone standing nearby, not interested in knowing what it was for. I pulled out iodine and antiseptic pads used to wipe wounds. Nathan took them from my hand without seeing what they were, giving them to another person who came over.

"I don't have anything else," I said.

"Can you give me five dollars?" he pleaded.

I sat down, then stood again. Five or ten dollars wasn't going to make much difference to my currency declaration. I took out a ten and gave it to Nathan, feeling uncomfortable. Saying good-bye, I mounted and began bicycling, looking at the women carrying urns and plastic buckets on their heads.

The road leaving Mtmada was even rougher than the road approaching it. The few people who lived there had no good water. Toward the middle of the day I saw two houses near the road and stopped to rest. An old woman gave me a glass of tea and a bowl of rice while six children played around me. Two men came over to talk to me. One, a man about twenty-four, had been to school in Dar es Salaam, but had returned home to support his family.

Another young woman inside the house had a small baby, not yet six months old. I could see the baby unnaturally struggling to breathe.

"Does the baby need a doctor?" I asked.

He talked to the mother, a small timid girl no more than eighteen, and said to me, "The woman in the next village told her not to worry."

"Is that woman a nurse?" I asked.

"She has had many babies," he said. "She knows children."

I looked at the child. The mother walked to the other side of the room, wet a towel from a jug, then put it on the child's body. I felt the child's hot forehead. The man and I walked out of the room and sat on chairs. The playing children had moved away.

"I know very little about medicine." I said, "but I can see the child needs medicine. She wants to cry but can't. Don't you think she needs to be taken to a clinic in Dodoma?" I thought that Dodoma was the closest city.

"We will take her," he said, but I wasn't sure he would.

Two other barefoot men dressed in shorts came over and sat down near me in silence. We heard the sounds of birds and a slight wind in the trees. The four of us sat around the table. I had nothing to give anyone. We heard the faint footsteps of the mother walking around the room. No one talked. A half hour later, feeling extraneous, perhaps fatalistic, I got on Angel and continued down the road.

When I came to the end of the time allotted by the border official, I made my way to Tanga, a large town near the coast south of Kenya. On my way to the town I had been thinking about replenishing my supply of food, about eating a healthy meal and drinking fruit juice or bottled drinks. For many days I ate and drank almost nothing. But when I arrived in the city I felt intimidated. I had been too long in rural areas, and I felt uncomfortable among the rush. I rode through the town without stopping to buy one thing.

On the other side of the town I found a restaurant and stopped to ask for a bowl of nsima.

"I am sorry," said the owner. "It is finished."

I started mentally kicking myself for being so irrational and not stopping in Tanga for at least some fruit. There was nothing else outside the city, but I wasn't going back. Another day, I thought, and I'll be in Kenya.

Since the sky was pink with the setting sun, I asked two men where I could spend the night. They said "manager," and pointed me in the direction away from the sunset. Thinking that "manager" must be the new way of saying chief, I followed one of them as he led me through a row of houses to a clearing behind tall mango trees. I saw a large two-story European house at the end. The man went ahead of me and talked to someone in Swahili. A white man in his early sixties came out, looked at me, and told me in German accented English that I was most welcome to stay. The change of scene put me in shock.

A servant took my bicycle to one of the guest rooms, a room as splendid as in any elegant hotel. He sensed my disbelief, saw my fatigued face, and tried to put me at ease by being exceptionally kind. He took me to a refrigerator full of wine and soft drinks and bottled water, then told me to give him any clothes that needed washing, which I did gladly.

The European turned out to be a genteel Swiss who had managed a Tanzanian farming company for thirty years. He and his cordial wife showed me their home and treated me to a dinner of chicken, roast potatoes, and peas. A black dressed in a white uniform served us as formally as if we were in a five-star restaurant in Paris. I chewed every mouthful and savored every taste, including the cake and ice cream that followed.

"We go to Switzerland every six months," said the wife, "and bring back different foods to eat."

"Nothing goes to waste here," said the man. "Everything gets eaten by someone."

"Tell us about your travels in Africa," requested the wife.

"Much of Africa has been hard going," I said. "I tried to require only what I thought an African would, but I come from a different world. It's difficult to adjust."

My two gracious hosts understood what I was trying to say. We moved to the sofas in the sitting room. "We've been here so long we consider ourselves Tanzanian," said the wife. "Tell us about South Africa. We hear many different stories. What's it like between whites and blacks there?"

"I'll tell you a story," I said. "I rode into a town to rest, a black town. The hills and the heat were as taxing as they are here. I bought a bit of food at a supermarket and sat under a tree to eat. A group of people down the road were looking at me. A minibus driver came over and told me that the people there had taken up a collection for me, and he wanted to give me the money. Everyone contributed a few cents. I must have looked done in and worn out."

The Swiss man said, "So here comes a white man into a black township, and the people, who I guess were poor, wanted to help him by giving him money, even though they themselves are oppressed by white men."

I nodded.

The wife added, "You'll often find blacks doing such things."

"I tried to make a joke out of it," I continued, "saying that what I needed was cooler weather and fewer mountains, not money. A couple of the people came over and talked to me. They couldn't understand why I wanted to travel by bicycle."

"I suppose a lot of your friends don't understand that either," interjected the wife.

"True. But these people thought that there might be something physically wrong with me. They had to make sure I was all right before I left their town. The next town was sixty or seventy kilometers away."

"Here we work with the people, and they appreciate us," the man said. "Do whites and blacks work together in South Africa?"

"Another story," requested the wife.

"One day on the road I met a white man who drove into the African villages selling plastic buckets and pans out of his pickup. That evening when I was staying with a black family, I asked one of the men why blacks don't sell to each other. He told me that the priorities of whites and blacks are different. 'We want to be free, but we don't want to be white,' he told me."

"Yes," the wife said, "And why should they be like whites?"

"You have many stories," said the husband.

My hosts and I spoke about the local political situation. I felt they were too careful to not criticize the socialist Tanzanian government. The next morning they gave me bread and cheese and chocolate, and I bicycled up a sandy road to the Kenyan border. Several times I stopped, needing something to drink, but found only distasteful water. By the time I rode twenty miles I had either eaten or given away all the fine food I had. Two days later I reached Mombassa, a city full of supermarkets and modern shops.

While standing in line at the central post office I met a talkative old Britisher with khaki shorts and a hard shell jungle hat. Without my asking, he told me that he'd been in East Africa for thirty years.

"You must have seen a lot of changes," I said.

"A lot of places have gone to the dogs," he said. "Before we pulled out," he added, speaking about the days when Britain ruled, "we left them with everything: roads, railroads, factories, farm equipment. The whole lot."

We both bought stamps for our overseas letters.

"What do they have now?" he asked as we walked out together. "Don't tell me. I know. If we didn't build it, it doesn't exist."

"Perhaps building roads wasn't the thing that was needed," I said cautiously, but he wouldn't hear of it.

"Those were grand days," he said. We saluted each other, and he walked down the street with brisk determination.

On the main road between Mombasa and Nairobi I came to the edge of a game park and contemplated whether to stop for the night at one of the few houses or ride through. A game park is no place to be after dark, and the sun was on its way down. A sign said that a hotel and restaurant and gas station was thirty miles away, in the middle of the park. Man Eaters, it was called. I assumed it meant a place where men eat. I continued riding, reasoning that there would be at least a village there.

Although tourists visit Kenya, its game parks and scenery pale next to Tanzania. I saw giraffes and a herd of twenty elephants on the way. I stopped and watched them as they roamed wild and free, walking miles, playing with each other. All around me was open savanna with vistas for miles.

Toward the end of the day I caught my first view of Man Eaters. It looked small. I approached and saw only one building, an Esso gas station, a clean and modern oasis of civilization in the middle of a rough and empty land. White painted metal chairs and tables stood in front of a shaded food counter on the side, and next to it, behind the station, were two old railway cars. A large unused restaurant took up the second floor.

Looking around, I saw a slim chance for getting a decent night's sleep. I went up to an attendant and asked for the manager. A sympathetic-looking young man named Benjamin with a short afro came forward. I explained my dilemma and asked if I could stay the night.

"The rules say no one can stay after dark, but you have no where else to go, so we must bend the rules." Logical fellow.

He showed me around. "We are going to change these railroad cars into a hotel, but we're running behind schedule. These were the original cars of the Nairobi-Mombasa line." Then he took me upstairs to the empty restaurant and showed me a wall with incredible large photographs — a montage of lions attacking people. One picture — I have no idea how such a fantastic shot could have been taken — showed a lion jumping up to a railway-car window and pulling a man through the window, the lion's paws grabbing the man's head, and his mouth taking the man's neck. I could see the raw power in the lion's body and legs.

Benjamin explained the story to me: when the railroad was being built, the workers encountered a pack of man-eating lions near the spot where we were standing. These lions killed many people and terrorized the work crew. Finally, the railroad imported a game specialist, and he successfully killed the pack, which turned out to be about six man-eaters.

"Are there still lions here?" I asked.

"Yes," said Benjamin, "but it's been a long time since they've hurt anyone."

"Nevertheless," I said, "I'm certainly glad I made it here where I'll be able to sleep safely indoors."

"Indoors?" he said. "I'm sorry, but you can't sleep in the building. You can put your tent right next to it."

The only other time I had slept in a game park was in Zambia where people put me up in a group of huts in the middle of nowhere. The people there worked in a tsetse fly control center. Tsetse flies, they told me, were also called sleeping flies because their bite puts people to sleep. The government erected various control posts around the park to keep the tsetse from spreading.

These control posts seemed to me relatively useless. I had been bicycling behind a slow-moving truck on the road from Lusaka when I saw signs directing traffic to stop. The truck drove into an enclosed area and stopped. I came up behind. Two old guys woke up from a deep stupor and went along the sides of the truck and around me with long-handled white butterfly nets looking for the tsetse. Their eyes were hardly open.

They could have been church deacons recovering from a long sermon taking around the collection plate.

A jovial young man in charge of the control post talked to the truck driver and then to me, asking me about my trip. The old men finished their half-hearted inspection, sat down on the benches, and soon continued their sleep. The young man told me to go two miles down the road and turn into a reddish-brown dirt road. The people in charge of controlling the spread of the tsetse have huts there and would give me a safe place to stay. The men spray insecticide and put up physical barriers so the fly doesn't spread out of control.

When I arrived they not only put me up safely in an empty hut, but served me a big meal. I didn't need to worry about animals; besides, that game park in Zambia contained few lions, certainly no man-eaters.

Benjamin and I looked at the other pictures on the wall of the empty restaurant: a picture of a lion finishing off a human, a picture of two lions roaming around a railway car, the railway cars that now stood outside.

"Surely you joke about sleeping outside," I said to Benjamin. "I thought you told me there are still lions around, and with the drought they'll be hungry."

"You have nothing to worry about. We haven't had problems with lions for many years."

"Yes, but have you had anyone sleeping outside?" I asked.

"Well... I tell you they won't come close to the building. You'll hear them tonight, but you won't see them."

He took me down and introduced me to the people who worked at the cafe and the service station. A white man with a group of four black men came in, bought gasoline, drank tea, and drove off.

"It's getting dark," Benjamin said. "We have to go."

He pointed in the direction of a group of five huts about a mile away, which I had seen from the second floor. "It's dangerous to walk home after dark," he said. "Lions, you know."

"I see," I said, "but you say I'll be safe sleeping near the building."

"Yes. You'll hear them but not see."

I went outside to the back of the building. As the sun set, the gates around the building closed, all the lights in the building went off, and everyone who worked there, the people who pumped gas and worked in the snack shop, quickly got into a car and drove away — too quickly — leaving me alone next to Man Eaters. I staked my tent as close to the building as I could, then used a couple of sticks to support my bicycle on the other side of the tent as a visual barrier to the lions, a silly symbolic effort. I didn't have one thing to put my hand on or keep under my head to give me even an illusion of security, not even a camping knife; the most dangerous thing I carry is a paring knife. I crawled into the tent and tried to believe that I was safe, tightly closed my eyes and thought about the conversation of the night before when I slept in the house of a school teacher.

Her husband had met me on the road and invited me to stay at their house. She and I had talked about our experiences teaching English. Her whole family had spoken it fluently, as do many Kenyans. We also had talked about dowry, or as anthropologists call it, bride price. In some countries the bride's family must pay the groom or his family for taking their daughter, but here in Africa as in the Middle East the groom's family pays. The price varies on how well educated, sturdy, pretty, and industrious the woman is, and on economic conditions of the region. I had heard of a bride being given away in Malawi for two chickens. I could have bought a chicken for two dollars of local currency. But in Kenya the situation was different.

"We've had bride price of as much as a dozen cows, jewelry, and a house full of furniture," said the school teacher. "But the important thing is for the family to know that she's going to someone who will be nice to her."

While I was thinking of the conversation I sank into a shallow sleep. It ended when I heard a deep-throated groan, and then a forceful, fearful roar. It sounded a hundred yards away. I turned over and tried not to cower, repeating in my head the few words of comfort from Benjamin. The roar continued and lasted well through the night, but I felt lucky that the tremendous awe-inspiring sound came no closer.

When I looked out of my tent I saw the sun coming up, and I knew that it was going to be a bright day. I put on my clothes and cycled into my shadow amid nature's awakening.

The Hashish Trail

Veiled women gathered in clusters, talking while slowly creeping toward the barricade. Inch by inch they moved forward. The chief officer became outraged at the advancing women's audacity and ordered his men to drive them back. The guards yelled, threatened, swung their clubs, and pushed the crowd back twenty yards behind a yellow line on the ground. As the guards turned their backs, the women, undaunted, inched forward once more, replaying the scene again and again.

The women wore traditional full-length Moroccan dress. Some had red candy-striped blouses and long white skirts; others wore all white — that is, what was once white — the rest wore solid black. Their gowns completely covered their bodies; only their eyes and hands showed. From a distance they looked like a group of nuns. Incompatibly, they wore old tennis shoes with knotted laces, deromanticizing their time-honored dress. A group of working class men joined the women and became part of the inch forward/rush back game with the guards. The men were dressed in cheap European clothes. Men and women remained in separate groups, but a few men went over to talk to a few women. I sat in the morning shade watching the movement while waiting for the man who stamps passports to begin work.

Eventually, I realized that the men and women were preparing to smuggle boxes of cookies and bottles of alcohol. The men brought the items and gave most of them to the women who put them under their ample dresses. Some of the bottles and boxes they gave to the guards who took them without any attempt at discretion. However, the gifts did not affect the way the guards treated the crowd, which had gradually grown to over a hundred. The guards continued shouting, swinging clubs, and shoving every time the chief officer gave the order. After they had enacted this drama a few times, they caught a young man, threw him to the ground and pretended to strike him. We watched him cower, then anxiously run back to the crowd of men when he was free.

There seemed no apparent reason for the guards and the crowd to play such a game. The men and women were obviously domestic workers who crossed the border daily without presenting papers. The guards didn't need to keep them waiting; forcing them to stand at a line twenty yards behind the barricade was an exercise without meaning. The crowd gained nothing by the process of creeping forward. Each side played a power game which ended when, at the chief officer's whim, the guards raised the barrier and shouted for the men and women to move quickly, threatening them if they didn't hurry. The crowd, which had seemed so eager to run across, sauntered slowly through, talking to one another as they went. The play was sheer perversity.

A half dozen Germans arrived at the border and became indignant that the man who stamps passports hadn't arrived. They focused their attention on the rubber stamps sitting idly on the desk inside the immigration window. Two of them came over to me, the only foreigner, to ask about the situation.

"I'm sitting in the shade because I don't want to pay a bribe," I said to them. "The fat man inside behind the desk asked me to give him some money for stamping my passport. If you choose to cross right away, then go in and give him a few deutsche marks."

They talked it over among themselves and decided to wait. Two Moroccans came over and told me in French and Spanish that they were from the tourist office and were going to help me get my passport stamped. I had done my homework on Moroccan border formalities, and I said that I didn't think I needed help.

The border had no business being where it was, one of those historic quirks that make unnatural national boundaries. On top of the North African coast across the water from Spain sits Ceuta, a leftover city claimed by Spain after the Spanish moved out of most of North Africa, a Spanish Dunkerque.

I arrived there by a slightly circuitous route: from West Africa to Spain then back to the African continent. I had flown over the Sahara from Nigeria to Madrid, unsure if Angel was below me in cargo. Several unsavory characters who roamed the Nigerian airport said that if I didn't give them dollars, Angel wouldn't be on the plane. The next morning I waited around the Madrid baggage turnstile and watched all the other passengers pick up their bags and clear customs, leaving me standing with my panniers at my feet in an empty, echo-filled terminal. A half hour passed. Wondering if I would be able to continue my trip, I went to the baggage office, but no one was there. I headed toward a glass cage with an "Iberia" sign over it. A porter appeared in front of me. "Por Usted?" he asked, carrying Angel, apart and tied. I calmly said yes. Caressing a bicycle would, I'm sure, have made me slightly suspicious and have led to extended questioning by immigration officials.

I bicycled south through Spain to the port of Algeciras near the Rock of Gibraltar, then boarded a ferry to Ceuta. I got the last ferry, arriving in time to see a full moon hovering over the city like a giant orange street light, a sight that brought exuberant cries of "magnificent," "beautiful," and "incredible" repeated in a dozen languages, for news of the spectacle spread quickly on the ship, and tourists flocked starboard to gaze at the romantic sight.

That evening I slept in a Ceuta campground and came to the border early the next morning, in time to watch the cat and mouse game between the crowd and the authorities, eager to begin my ride across Morocco, Algeria, and Tunisia.

At nine in the morning a tourist mini-bus full of other European travelers arrived at the border. Everyone asked the same question: "Why couldn't one of the other officials standing around stamp passports?" A mustached guard stepped out of the office, waved his arm as if he were pushing air in their direction, and rudely told everyone to wait. A minute later the person who had asked me for a bribe came to the immigration window and began grabbing passports and madly stamping, opening a passport anywhere and stamping without looking. When I got mine back I saw that he had stamped over my Brazilian visa, making his stamp hard to read. The other travelers must have had similar results.

The fellows from the tourist office came over to me and wanted five American dollars for helping to get my passport stamped. I laughed. They insisted. I tried to ignore them. One stepped in front of me, implying that I had to pay to pass. I said I'd tell the guards. He put a grin of defiance on his face. I threw him a dollar, and he ran off; the other boy followed.

At the end of the border complex I stopped at a cafe to get a sandwich made of French bread stuffed with ground chick peas and tomato sauce. My bicycle remained in my sight, but part of the left rear pannier leaned on a post, and during the half minute that I turned to pay the man, a seedy fellow about twenty was unzipping one of the pockets on the pannier and diligently searching among the array of malaria pills, spoons, and tire irons for anything valuable. He looked up, saw me standing over him and stopped short.

"Tranquilo. It's nothing. Tranquilo," he said fearfully backing away with his arms crossed in front of his face like I was going to hit him.

Others around observed what had transpired but did nothing. My appraisal of the situation was justified: I couldn't let Angel out of my sight, not even for a few seconds. I mounted my bicycle, sandwich in hand, and headed down the road to Tetuan, eating as I pedaled, feeling that it was going to be uncomfortable to be in a country where I had to worry about my possessions.

In my travels, I noticed that former French colonies, such as those of North Africa, have never given up their French ways. The English usually left the indigenous colonies' culture alone. They exploited the land and resources, created a servant class and a national dependence. But they didn't alter daily life significantly. The French, on the other hand, wanted to possess their colonies, to make the native population French. They undermined the local language and replaced it with their own. While many people in former English colonies don't speak English, in former French colonies the upper and middle class and most of the lower class speak perfect French. They cut their hair in a French style, dress in French clothes, eat French bread, drive French cars, and drink French wines. Some native North Africans don't even speak Arabic.

I rode in front of Mediterranean resorts that had buildings surrounded by white-washed stone walls topped with broken glass. As I entered the white city of Tetuan, I grew increasingly uncomfortable, and although I needed to change more money, I decided not to stay in the town. A young Moroccan on a motorcycle came up and rode next to me, asking me in a friendly way where I was from. I told him.

"Man, that's great," he said in English while we rode side by side down the street. "I work two years in the States, in a circus.

You've come here on the best day. Once a month the Berbers come down from the mountains to sell their goods in the market at half price."

"I'd like to see, but I want to ride more miles today."

"Come on. I'll show you around the bazaar and get you the best deals."

"I can't buy anything. Look. I have no room. I can't carry another thing."

"Of course, but come and look. I'll give you a tour."

I didn't want to seem rude, though I had a feeling which told me not to go. He led the way, and I bicycled behind, passing white houses surrounded by high white walls and black iron gates. An old man who looked after belongings sat at the market entrance. I judged him as honest and left Angel with him. The circus worker and I walked under the market archway, quickly passing fruit vendors, brass sellers, herb shops, and trinket shops. Men and women sold from tables, push carts, or from a cloth spread over the ground. Bargaining was tough; women showed the merchant how damaged his fruit was and pretended to walk away. The merchant waved them back and made them a counteroffer. Almost all the women in the market dressed in clothes similar to those I had seen at the border.

After walking through various narrow streets we arrived at a carpet shop where the owner greeted me as a long-lost friend, sat me down, and told a boy to fetch tea. We talked cordially in English on a variety of subjects, from politics to Arab customs to life in America.

"Do you like these carpets?" the owner asked.

"Very nice," I said looking around.

"Kelim is our specialty. They are hand made, and they can be yours for less than you think."

"Thank you, but I'm on a bicycle. I can't carry anything."

"Of course. But allow me to show you some."

They took my herbal tea away, cleared the room, and began presenting the colorful carpets on the floor in front of me.

"Do you like this one?"

"Very nice."

"How about this one?"

"Very nice."

"Which one do you like better?"

"They're both very nice," I said, thinking about Angel sitting vulnerably outside the market entrance.

"We're brothers. We can make you an excellent deal on this one."

"I can't take it on my bicycle."

"We can send it to you. Look in this book at all the people from around the world that we have sent carpets to."

"I don't have the money for such a nice carpet."

"You can use Visa, Master Charge, American Express, and travelers checks. Which card would you like to use?"

"Please, I really can't buy any. I don't have a house to put it in."

"You can make a lot of money selling these carpets in the States," said the circus man. They stood on both sides of me, making me feel as if I were a captive being interrogated.

"Each carpet is hand knotted," added the merchant. "This one has 40,000 knots. We'll ship it to you."

"I'm sorry. They're beautiful, but I really can't."

"Yes you can. Make me an offer for the one you like."

"I'm on a long trip through many countries. I can't buy your nice carpets."

"This is your golden opportunity. It's an investment. You can sell it for twice or three times as much. Which one would you like?"

"You brought me in as a friend, not as a customer. Why did you pretend to be my friend?"

"It is our tradition, to sell and to bargain. These carpets are becoming scarce. We want you to have one."

We continued for one hour, a thousand one-liners, finely tuned and thoroughly practiced. Finally, they realized that they were going to get nothing from me, and the circus man accompanied me out of the market.

"You need to give me $10 for guiding you around," he said half way down one of the shop-lined streets.

"All you did was waste two hours of my time."

"We're brothers. We need to stick together and take care of each other." His voice had a tone of threat.

We walked past a table of men smoking a water pipe. I thought about Angel. A group of three large women were haggling over the price of vegetables with a small merchant who wore a white cap and stood on the other side of the boxes. I mentally kicked myself for not following my better judgment. A boy no older than ten stood behind a cart carrying a mountain of dates. I was afraid to stop and buy some. I walked faster; the circus man followed. I came to the market gate and looked to my right; there stood Angel exactly as I had left it, the old man watching over it. I paid the old man, thanking him, and threw the circus man the equivalent of two dollars to be rid of him.

Relieved at my regained freedom, I bicycled southeast, toward the Rif mountains. A spiral road wound up the side of a cream-colored craggy mountain, scratched into the side of the huge bare stone, noble and majestic. Each turn yielded an even more magnificent panorama, a regal view of miles of natural beauty. Across a ten-mile crevice another line of bald mountains rose above the green earth. I bicycled up into thick clouds which gave me visibility of only ten yards, climbed even higher above them and looked down at cloud-covered valleys. There, men dressed like monks, in solid-colored robes: dark blue, white, black. The women wore nun-like headdress without veils and kept their bodies fully covered by thick gowns. At dusk I was four or five thousand feet above the sea, not yet at the top. I found an abandoned house and set up my tent near it, making sure that no one saw me; the experiences at the border and with the circus man made me uneasy about asking for accommodation.

The Rif mountains are infamous as the hashish capital of the world. That I knew. I didn't know what was to follow. Along the road every male aggressively signaled me to stop and tried to sell me a black ball of hashish. They didn't just try to sell it, they wanted to force it on me and, I felt, take everything I owned if they could. They would see me cycling up the hill and would run to the road, urging me to stop in half a dozen languages. Their entrepreneurial forcefulness terrified me. Cars stopped in front of me, and the drivers got out, pieces of hashish the size of a golf ball in hand, urging, being friendly, promising, shouting, threatening, wanting me to go home with them. Scooters and motorcyclists rode next to me and pulled hashish out of their pockets. The size and price of the hashish would have made many Americans I know ecstatic. A boy about fifteen tried to gallop his horse next to me. One group formed a human chain across the road to get me to stop. I felt attacked on every side. Boys nearby threw stones when I didn't stop. They were terrible shots.

I rode into Katama, the center of the Rif mountains, tired from running away from people, hungry because I hadn't been able to buy anything to eat, since I was attacked by the hashish network every time I stopped. A minute after I entered the town cafe, eight unsavory-looking men in their late teens and early twenties surrounded me. Their eyes were deserted, containing no evidence of having at one time contained pupils. Their faces were unshaven, their clothes dirty and mismatched, and their bodies thin, a malnutritioned thin.

"You want to buy hashish?" I was asked non-stop in French, Arabic, Spanish, English, and German.

"I need something to drink," I said, irritated, not wanting to be forced out of the cafe.

"Bring him tea," ordered a tall man with a blotchy beard. "Let's make business."

Angel sat half inside the door, an arm's reach from my chair, and they saw that I wouldn't take my eyes off it.

"You know that hashish is illegal for foreigners," I said.

"Come to my home," said another young man with brown-blond hair. "We smoke and listen to music, and we make business."

A man in his forties brought me a large glass of hot tea with various herbs in it.

"I have to move on."

"You go with this man," said another.

I kept quiet, sipping my tea and trying not to let these mischievous boys who shoved balls of hashish under my nose irritate me.

"Do you do anything beside sell hashish?" I asked after a silence.

"Hashish is our only business," said the tall man. "We have the best."

I looked at their disheveled appearance and rotting teeth. "In other countries people who make a similar business become rich," I said.

"Here, many people make the same business. It's hard."

"I know," I said. "Dozens have been trying to sell to me."

"You come home with me," repeated the light-haired teenager. "You will have a good time."

I stood up abruptly. "It's damn uncomfortable to have dozens of people try to sell me something I can't buy."

The group surrounded me, everyone except the tall man who remained calmly seated. A couple of people said simultaneously, "You go to this man's home," pointing to the fellow with light hair. I didn't say no. Looking instead for a way to escape the situation, I moved to the door. Two people let me pass. The light-haired young man walked out the door and took a few steps. I looked at Angel's freewheel to see in what gear the chain went over, then hopped on it with a great sweeping motion. The young man thought I was following him. I turned suddenly and jammed the pedals to get a jump on them and made a dash out of town. I almost succeeded. Two of the gang followed me on a small motorcycle. The passenger in the back had a knife in his hand. I unhooked my pump and started swinging at them, as I do when I'm attacked by dogs. I saw them turn back, leaving me alone on the sparsely traveled road.

My senses told me not to ask anyone for accommodation, and my sensibility told me it would be unwise to camp. A gray-bearded man who sold bread on the side of the road told me that the town of Bui Nadfa had a hotel. I bicycled there, found the slum hotel by asking a couple of young people, carried Angel up the narrow dark stairway, and put it in the room to which the landlady directed me, a sizable chamber with a tile floor and a shuttered window that overlooked a dirt square. A bed with a metal headrest stood near a fractured table and two old chairs.

No sooner had I closed the door than four smartly uniformed national police burst into my room and requested my name and passport number. Word about my arrival in the town must have spread like a California grass fire. The policemen were decent and polite officials who recorded the information in a book and wished me a good night.

When they left, a Moroccan soldier who was also staying at the hotel came into my room and offered to share his dinner with me, showing me a fish which he had just roasted in the landlady's kitchen. I wanted to sleep, but Ibrahim was jovial, a good soul who wanted company. He was a new enlistee from the western part of the country. I took out the bread I had and a jar of Spanish jam, and we sat down at the table to begin the fine meal. After a few minutes we were interrupted by two local gendarmes carrying guns. They came in briskly, as if they were surprising us. Sadness covered Ibrahim's face like a sheet, giving me an immediate feeling of dread.

"Get your things together and come with us," said the first gendarme in French. He was heavy, dark, and wore an immaculate uniform. My dinner companion stood up, knocking his chair to the floor. The gendarme turned to Ibrahim and ordered, "Search the room. Look under the bed."

The two gendarmes struck me as a mismatched pair: a large stern man with a thick black mustache who stood like a statue of a military hero and his pale skinny cohort who waltzed nervously around the room. A dozen thoughts flashed in my mind: they were going to rob me, shoot me, beat me, plant drugs on me, extort me, and probably imprison me.

Ibrahim moved slowly, making a half-hearted show of looking under the mattress. I could tell that he sympathized with me, but his dejected expression only made me more worried. The thin gendarme shuffled his feet; the fat one barked orders. They followed me as I carried Angel down the steps, then walked on both sides of me through the dirt streets to the police station.

We walked inside. A large hardwood desk that was cluttered with papers stood in the front part of the room. In the rear a plain table stood under a bare lightbulb that hung halfway down the fifteen-foot ceiling. A small dark cell was off to the side in the rear. The walls were a pale green, without pictures or flags.

"Take everything out of your bags," said the commanding gendarme as soon as we moved to the rear part of the room. "Take everything out of your pockets." He turned to the beam-thin gendarme: "Search him."

The fragile light-skinned one danced aimlessly around me and clumsily tapped my pockets and under my arms. Then they went to work on my equipment.

When I had taken every single thing out of my panniers and handlebar bag and placed them on a table, when I had unpacked and spread out my sleeping bag, tent, and camping mattress, then I understood what they were looking for: ironically, the very substance I had spent all day avoiding. They examined minutely, looking for hashish or anything valuable. Clothes were shaken out, pill bottles opened, maps unfolded, film canisters unscrewed, spare tires and tubes squeezed. They took their time — and my time — doing it. The thin gendarme grabbed my Walkman and listened to it until he wore down the batteries, disregarding the vociferous objections of his stern colleague.

"I was trying to get away from them," I said in poor French.

"Untie that," demanded the commandant, pointing to the sleeping bag.

He went through all the tools, handling each one. The last item was the cane which I had been given by the Malawian friar. Although I no longer needed it, I still carried it. I anguished: Where would they plant the hashish? How much will I have to pay for my freedom?

"Put everything back in." His face was a picture of disappointment at not finding hashish.

"Is there a problem?" I asked. He didn't respond.

I quickly threw everything into my panniers.

"Sit down," he ordered, pointing to a straight-backed wooden chair in front of the large desk. The other two sat across from me.

I tried again: "Is there a problem?"

"Amount of money you are carrying?" asked the gruff one.

"It's all in travelers checks. I only have a little bit for bread." I showed them my travelers checks. I didn't tell them I had cash stuffed in Angel's handlebar.

They stood up and talked among themselves. The big gendarme told the little one to fill out a form. The dancer opened drawers and cabinets, running back and forth looking for a form until he made the stern one dizzy. The stern one growled and yelled, telling him to use blank paper. The thin one took out four long blank sheets, put carbons in between them, and straightened them in the typewriter.

"Which one of these names is your father's and which is your mother's?" he asked pointing to my passport. "Where is your Spanish exit stamp?"

"They didn't stamp."

"Ah, a problem," said the commandant. "And I can't see your Moroccan stamp."

I pointed it out. He spent at least a quarter of an hour studying it, and blaming me for not being able to read it.

"How can we fill out the form," the austere one said. "This is really a problem."

He launched into more questions: "How long were you in Spain? Where were you before Spain? Where are you going? How long do you plan to spend in Morocco? In Algeria? How old were you when you left Lebanon? In which town in the United States do you live? When did you leave? How many brothers do you have?"

The skinny one typed with two fingers, searching the keys for each letter. First he typed the question, then my answer. By the time he was through it was past midnight.

"Is there any problem?" I asked again.

The large one finally responded: "No." Then he stood up, indicating that they were not interested in me.

"Go back to your hotel. You can get your passport in the morning."

"Why is it you treat me this way and not the people who sell hashish?" I asked the thin man without accusation.

"There's no law for them," he said to me in Arabic, as if it would make sense to me.

I returned to my room, leaned Angel on the wall, dropped on the thin mattress, and slept uneasily. The next morning at the first sign of light I showed up in front of the police station, but it was closed. I repacked my panniers in front of the building, oiled the moving parts, and waited for someone to arrive. A man across the street brought me a glass of tea. Without my relating my experience of the night before, he told me that the authorities think every foreigner comes for hashish.

"That's too bad," I said. "It's a beautiful country."

"It's more than too bad," he replied, "but the hashish peddlers control everything here."

After collecting my passport from a gendarme I hadn't seen before, I tried to put on swift miles to get past the Rif Mountains. Gradually, the offers of hashish were replaced by demands for cigarettes or money from boys standing on the side of the road. My paranoia remained acute, enhanced by two other delays where unfriendly gendarmes conducted other detailed searches of my bicycle. The first time two gendarmes sat in their car for forty-five minutes looking through my passport, complaining that my entry stamp was an illegible blur on a Brazilian visa. The second time a gendarme asked for foreign money, saying with a sinister smile that he wanted to add it to his collection. I gave him a note of worthless foreign money and watched him run off.

Finding somewhere to sleep that night caused renewed apprehension. I certainly didn't want another hotel experience. I found a clump of trees and hid there like a fugitive, afraid to put up my blue tent which might attract attention. Over the dusty earth I spread my camping mattress and my sleeping bag.

The next day I cycled hard to the flat, dry inland, arriving at Oujda, a town near the Algerian border where I had to get an Algerian visa. I hadn't been able to get it before because I had a South African stamp in my passport. Several countries won't allow visitors who have been to South Africa. I had gotten all my other African visas before I had the South African consulate stamp mine, but I forgot about Algeria. The South African visa was slightly obscure, but if someone spotted it he or she would have to refuse me a visa. Then I would have to go back from where I came, back through the hashish hell.

"Please fill out four forms and give us four pictures," said the clerk at the consulate. My passport was taken to the back office. I waited a formidable amount of time for the processing of the forms, sitting in a small office amid a dozen women, some veiled, some not, wondering anxiously whether the officials would see my South African visa. After an hour, the clerk yelled my name. I rose to walk to the window and was met by a wide smile on the clerk's face. We looked at each other intently.

"Here is your passport," he said.

I took it. The women huddled closely around me while we all looked through the passport trying to find my visa. I turned the pages. One of the veiled women stopped me by putting her large finger between the pages. "There's your visa," she said, pointing to a red rubber stamp written in Arabic and French. Her fingernail was painted bright red. The other women and I read the visa together. Realizing that I had been given permission to enter, I grabbed the clerk's hand in both mine, thanking him until he blushed. The woman who had spotted my visa said, "God be with you on your trip." The rest of the women echoed the blessing as I left the room. The ride to the Algerian border took a half hour.

A worker on the side of the main road saw me riding my bicycle in front of the hazy red sunset, and he took up his shovel and walked quickly to the main road.

"Greetings," he said at a distance, in Arabic. "You look like you're coming from far."

I stopped and put one foot on the pavement. "I've been riding from months," I said.

"Welcome, welcome," he said looking me in the eye and taking my hand. "My name is Rashid. Our home is over the bridge. Come."

He took my bicycle and began rolling it down the dirt road. We walked and talked as the last minutes of daylight escaped the sky, crossed the concrete bridge and walked into the town, greeting people as we passed. We watched shopkeepers lower their shutters and arrived at a house in the center of the main street.

Rashid opened the door to a courtyard and asked me to wait while he told his family that a guest was coming. I heard the voices of women moving to another part of the house. Rashid came out and ushered me inside the room to meet his father, two brothers, and a handful of other relatives who lived there. They stood up when I entered. Rashid introduced his family with pride, giving each person's name and relationship clearly — "This is Ali, my mother's brother's son" — the person came forward and gave me a sturdy handshake, then returned his hand to his heart, as if meeting me was his spiritual honor.

They lived in a four- or five- room house with bare stone walls and a tile floor. We talked in the living room, sitting on a few wicker chairs and a divan that I was later to use as a bed. Three ornate paintings of Arabic calligraphy hung on the wall; the room had no other furniture or decorations. A white tile bathroom consisting of a toilet, bidet, sink, and shower stood adjacent to the courtyard. I wasn't shown any of the other sleeping rooms. The men and boys dressed in ordinary Western clothes, but although the days were hot, none wore short-sleeve shirts. In deference to their culture, I bicycle in long pants through Muslim countries.

"How did you come to Algeria?" one of Rashid's brothers asked. He and most other men wore a mustache.

"I bicycled through Morocco," I said to their shouts of enthusiasm. "Three days ago I crossed the border and rode here."

"How do you do it?" asked a cousin. "Isn't it hard? And in Morocco?"

"Morocco was hard because many people sell hashish there. I had to run from them."

"What a pity," said the gray-haired father, "but you are now among friends. You are the first person from a foreign land that we have had the privilege of having in our home."

A woman's voice called for two of the men to come. The rest of us moved the chairs back and made a space on the floor to spread a blue cloth. The boys brought in plates of rice, French bread, chick peas and meat cooked in tomato sauce, and boiled green vegetables. They put the plates in the center of the cloth. We sat on the edges of the cloth while another boy put a plate and spoon in front of each of us. The father started serving, passing the first heaping, steaming dish to me, then putting a dish in front of everyone else, the oldest to the youngest. The sight of the food made me suddenly feel hungry, but everyone waited until we were all ready to eat before starting.

"We farm the land in front of the village, on the right side of the road," said the father. "Most people are going to the cities for work, but the cities are crowded. This is our father's home, our grandfather's land. We can't forget that."

"Why did your family leave Palestine?" asked a cousin of Rashid.

"They were forced to leave," I said. "We now live in America."

"Have you taken an American wife?"

"I'm not married." Everyone stopped eating and looked at me, filled spoons suspended mid-way between their plates and their mouths. I realized that I better add something. "In America people marry later."

"I'm sure your father will find you a good wife," said one of the boys.

The subject needed changing. "I felt the difference between Morocco and your country as I rode across the border. The Algerian border guards felt sorry for me because I didn't have much money, so they didn't force me to change money at the bank rate."

"We will give you some money," said Rashid.

"I don't need it, believe me. You have already given me so much by opening your home to me. God has blessed me by allowing me to enter your house. In your country each time I stopped, people would give me something, a loaf of bread or an ice cream. If I ate in a cafe, they didn't want to charge me."

"You are our guest. You worked hard to come and see us; it's our turn to share with you what we have."

"What have you learned in all your travels?" asked Rashid's cousin.

"I've learned that people learn how to behave from the society. For example, each of us is capable of generosity and cruelty. If generosity is important to a society, each person tends to be generous. If the society encourages cruelty, it brings out cruelty in people who would otherwise be generous. I'm fortunate I found generous people in this house; I saw goodness in Rashid's eyes when we met on the road, and I felt it when I met each of you."

"Your presence is a blessing to our house," repeated the father.

We talked long into the night, about life in their land, about America, France, international politics. The men were more knowledgeable about history, including American history, and current events, than most of the American college students I had in Chicago. When it came time to sleep, they insisted that I take the divan. The two cousins, who I guessed usually used it, rolled out a mattress on the tile floor near the door and slept side by side. We awoke to the sunlight coming through the open door, then had bread and tea for breakfast while exchanging more compliments. The men gathered outside to watch me bicycle over the bridge and out of town. I saw them standing there until I could no longer see their outline.

A few days later, when I was on the eastern side of the Algeria, I was traveling down a small hill when I saw another touring bicyclist near a river. I turned from the paved road to the dirt road, and we introduced ourselves.

"I was born in Algeria," he said, "but I'm French and live in France. It's easier for you to speak English, no?"

"Much easier," I said. "I haven't spoken English for a long time."

"I learned English in school; I need the practice."

"Where have you been bicycling?" I asked.

"In Sahara," he answered. "It's beautiful there. People always help each other. Giving comes naturally to them."

He took out a white cloth bag of sweet dates and shared them with me. When he saw I enjoyed them, he wanted to give me the whole bag.

"I've learned that from Sahara," he said. "You give to others when you have. That's how it works: everyone gives."

"I was afraid to go into the Sahara alone. It looked like too much of a challenge. I also felt I couldn't spend the time; I need to go to India before the rains, and I'm already very late."

"Ah, India. My favorite country," he said, "although I've never been. I have a special place in my heart for Gandhi. The people in Sahara live like Gandhi, full of peace. They know how to live without worrying about money or possessions."

I accepted his opinion.

"Do you speak Arabic?" I asked.

"None. Many men in the desert still speak French. They've had many years of our rule," he said.

I ate more dates. They were sweeter than those available in the north. "Do the desert women wear veils?" I asked.

"Some men of the Tuareg tribe wear veils," he replied. "You rarely see women. I stayed in a village three months and never saw a woman. They have their own side of the town, and the men have theirs."

"Sounds very traditional," I said. "I'm sorry that I didn't include the desert in my trip. Next trip."

"It can be difficult traveling," he said in an excited voice. "Sand fills the road. Sometimes a storm comes. The sand hits with fury. It can cut like a sharp knife and burn your skin."

"What do you do in a sand storm?" I asked.

"There's nothing to do. What can anyone do? You wait until the storm passes, then you go on. When you go into Sahara, go by camel so you won't need to stay on the road."

I gave him a souvenir that I had bought in Sevilla. When he discovered that I had very little local currency and couldn't change money until after the weekend, he took out the equivalent of $20 and wanted to give it to me.

"Take this. If I need something, someone will give it to me."

"Tomorrow I'll cross into Tunisia." I said. "I can eat these dates today. Someone else can use the money."

We embraced in friendship then returned to the road, bicycling in opposite directions. I found a lightly traveled road through plowed lands, and crossed into Tunisia full of warm recollections of generous people.

Lines Written on a Ferry From Tunis to Palermo

I leave you Africa,
    Vast land where the sun brightens the heated day,
    Where a profound darkness fills the night.
    So many trees, so many animals, so many shrubs,
    So many rivers, so many mountains, swamps, deltas, savannas,
    Insects, flowers, birds, babies, so many minerals and metals,
    Fruits and grains — the wealthiest poorest land where hunger
    Erases plenty, and the countryside teems
    In nothing.
    Nothing, stark naked nothing, rising out of opulence like
    Kilimanjaro towering its white peak over the plains
    Darkened by bodies of living beings.

I Leave you Africa,
    Land of tribal chiefs and animal dowries, of scarred
    Bodies and sacred rites and packs of vulnerable
    Children, of women carrying burdens on their heads
    And hard-working idle men. Of boys hunting with spears
    And girls doubled over wells of brown water.
    Land of clay and manure; open, expansive, beginningless.
    Land of big cats looking for prey, villages seeking
    Survival, of old men lingering in spent lives;
    Young men, shackled by tradition.

I leave you Africa,
    Black and White land that generates humanity.
    You have brought me to my knees,
    Knocked all sense out of me,
    Destroyed what I held to be real.

I leave you Africa,
    Uneasily.
    Sahara dividing White from Black;
    Tree lines dividing dead White from living Black;
    Apartheid dividing White lavatories from Black latrines.
    White over Black, surrounded by Black, rich Black.

Climbing the High Road

A couple of minutes after I arrived at the mechanic's shop, the changing of my bearing cup had become a community project involving plenty of joking. To act as translator, some boys fetched a man who must have claimed to know English. The poor fellow came forward slowly, his shyness making it obvious that he knew no more English than I knew Nepali, but everyone was having too good a time to care.

The crowd surrounded Angel and me, looking, pointing, and laughing. The general excitement made that moment as fresh and alive for me as it had been when I first began distance bicycling five years before. I was a solitary enigma in a cohesive community. Earlier that morning I had caught my first sunrise view of Everest from a Buddhist hill shrine near Dhulikel, a town on the other side of the Kathmandu Valley. I was heading in that direction until I realized that the rear axle that I had been nursing since Delhi wasn't going to hold the load on the rough roads ahead. It was the second axle of the trip; the first died somewhere in Turkey, expiring after too many bad roads.

The little translator flushed when his knowledge of English was required — I understood as much from the hand gestures of the mechanic — but I pretended to carry on an intelligent conversation with the poor fellow so he wouldn't blow his cover. Initially, I only went there to buy a bearing cup and put it in myself, but I soon realized that working by myself wouldn't have created such joviality.

The cycle mechanic sat cross-legged in the dirt outside his shop. Since it had no windows and hardly any space, he used the shop to store materials and worked with his two sons outside in the light. Although the people around Dhulikel were predominantly Indian, there was a strong Tibetan influence evident in their round high-cheekbone faces.

Cycles, as they're called in Asia, are prolific, but they aren't anything like the one I was riding. As with other Asian mechanics, this man worked on those single-speed clunkers that weigh a ton, so he knew nothing about the new bicycle in front of him, but he took up the role of an expert in order to prove his ability to the people gathered around.

"Crooked," I think the man said, and everyone echoed his words, sending a ripple of laughter down the crowd.

"New one," I kept saying. "I do it." But it was no use.

First the man had to figure out how to take off the freewheel, the cluster of gears on the rear wheel, and after letting him look it over for a minute, I gave him my freewheel-remover and showed him what to do, helping him only when he needed me. Everyone gathered, closely watching every move and responding as one voice. I then gave the man my cone wrenches so he could take off the axle and get to the root of the problem.

I pointed to the thing I wanted changed, and he went about replacing it, not allowing me to touch it. By this time, every little move, every surprised expression was met with vigorous audience participation.

The translator, sensing that he wasn't going to lose any prestige, became part of the conviviality.

"He do very good job," he assured me.

"OK," I replied, bringing a murmur among the group. "OK" is a universal expression they associate with Americans, and they got a kick out of hearing someone actually saying it.

I helped the mechanic put the new bearing cup in, angling it to offset the bend in the hub, and then we put the entire thing back together. Naturally, a round of tea followed, and the gentleman next door at the teahouse had already added a couple of pieces of wood to the fire under the water pot in anticipation of the extra business.

"Where your friends?" A man asked through the translator, but I threw off the question and made jolly talk about the mountains I saw a few hours earlier.

"Good road?" I asked pointing toward Everest. I asked out of habit. The roads I knew intimately: every night for months I pulled out and studied maps and atlases and then traveled the roads in my sleep.

The group turned their heads as one person, first in the direction my finger pointed, then back to me. A half second of silence was replaced with a tumult of laughter. A couple of people slapped me on the back, and I took out a plastic bag of sweets to share while the man who ran the teahouse filled the glasses. We laughed some more, laughing until there was no laugh left in us.

I aim for mountains, and I've spent years bicycling up and down them. Covering all continents and going above tree lines, snow lines, population lines, puffing from lack of air and looking down at the clouds over deep drops from roads that barely hug steep grades. I've climbed numerous ranges — forwards, backwards, and longways — bicycling on roads that make me dizzy, grades that made me weary, and heights that made me stupid. I've been up and down hundreds of different mountains, but I never knew what a mountain could be until I hit the Himalayas.

They towered above the villages. Defiant, jagged hunks of rock covered with snow, capable of leveling egos, and taming and astonishing mortals. White on white, white on black. The sight was spectacular, but the feeling, the tingle in the spine I got from being surrounded by all this, I'll never be able to forget. The pictures I saw of them before arriving did them no justice: the bodily sensation I felt was tremendous. The mountains, worshipped by the local people, seemed to call out almost audibly, enticing courageous foreigners to risk their lives.

It took thousands of miles in the saddle before I saw those mountains and the natives living on them. My mind tried to understand the paradox of majestic mountains and simple people, severe mountains and gentle people. I came to be impressed by mountains, and mountains I saw, but it was human beings that penetrated my emotions.

Nepal was going to be the climax of my trip. I had it all figured out: I was going to ride the trails of these fantastic mountains, to meet a challenge that few dare to aspire, a crown to another solo trip around the world. I rushed all the way, cutting short my time in other countries to make it before the rainy season, arriving two months behind schedule: afternoon showers had already begun.

I had nurtured a several year old dream of experiencing the Himalayas. When I bicycled in India before, the monsoons had lingered late and I couldn't make it north to Nepal because of intense flooding.

This time, after landing in Delhi, I followed several hundred miles of flat, hot, Indian roads until I crossed into Nepal and saw through the wall of dense, humid air a line of mountains that suddenly rose from a dull umber earth. A square sign written in both Nepali and English modestly proclaimed: "Hill road begins." Here continents had collided in a forgotten age, and the force of that collision had shoved up these mighty Himalayas.

Lucknow in northern India was unforgivably hot. The 120 plus degree temperature doesn't begin to describe the stickiness, the heaviness, the strangulation, the fatigue, the oppression of the heat. Walking a few steps through the dense air was excuse enough to collapse and have a cold drink, which often meant a carbonated bottled drink kept in the shade.

Midday was stultifying; I'd ride for ten minutes and have to take a break at a water pump to soak my head. The locals got a big kick out of this. A group of men and boys would first gather around me and look me over carefully. Someone might reach out and touch me, then they would inspect Angel.

The heat ravaged my body and began to scramble my brain. Human beings are so affected by climate: physically, culturally, and emotionally. It's one of those banal truths too obvious for analysis. In hot climates people usually socialize more, while in cool climates people become more industrious. To keep going I had to reach down into myself and unleash energy from every sinew, every muscle, every fiber of tissue, forcing myself over inch after inch of blistering road until I saw the promise of relief from the mountains. Because cycling creates a breeze, albeit a hot breeze, the journey through this gruesomely scorching land was possible, barely possible.

I took a two-bit hotel room north of Lucknow and spent the night in an increasingly bad mood, running in and out of the cold shower trying to keep my temperature down. I swear I drank no less than five gallons of liquid that day, but I couldn't eat. A bad sign: not eating would quickly bring me to a dead stop. Knowing that food for a bicyclist is like gas for a car, I had to force myself to eat.

Indian food only fueled my negative attitude. My body can't tolerate hot spices, but in India there is little choice. Even the cucumbers sold by squatting men on the roadside stands were garnished with chili powder. I always asked the vendors not to put the hot stuff in my food, but too often they thought they knew better than I what I should eat. Before going to a country which uses heavy spices I spend months training my mouth by eating progressively hotter foods until I can tolerate the condiments like a native, but having to face only a succession of spicy food, especially when the heat destroyed my desire to eat, made me distraught and unhappy.

To compound the negative, Uttar Pradesh province, one of the most densely populated areas in the world, has hardly an unoccupied space, making it difficult to stop and rest without collecting a crowd. I'm accustomed to spending at least part of my time alone. If I don't have times of solitude, talking to people becomes hard work, harder than bicycling, and I found myself getting annoyed at the people who were, for the most part, only being friendly and curious.

I woke before the sun and made my way north, bicycling through village after village, looking in vain for relief from the mind-destroying heat wave. By 9:00 a.m. it was painfully hot. A young man in a dhoti whose skin was the color of ripe prunes would pedal his clunking black single-speed bicycle furiously, keep up with me for a bit, then trail off, only to be followed by another fellow on a fifty-pound bicycle. No time for rest. I was becoming desperate for relief from the food, the heat, the crowds, the flat earth, the idea of bicycling. Not a rational dislike, if there is such a thing, just a general blanket of loathing and disgust, and even after years of experience, after sensing that such feelings only turn in on themselves and lead to humbling situations, I could not neutralize my aversion.

The sun beat down mercilessly on the pavement and reflected raw belligerent heat in my face. Amazingly, people carried on their business. Too many people, I was beginning to think: someone should do something about the population explosion. People became obstacles I had to get away from. Why don't they believe in birth control? My fuddled mind began seeing humanity gone to chaos. My brain was boiling in my skull.

I became increasingly rude and short tempered, motioned people to leave me alone, and only forced a smile on my face when I wanted to use their water pumps. I told boys to keep their hands off Angel, refused invitations for tea, and barked like a marine at anyone trying to be friendly, something I had never done even when facing harsh winds or intolerable bureaucracies. My irascibility got out of control.

"What is your native country?" began the man on behalf of a group that surrounded Angel, me, and a water pump.

I tried to answer that and the other questions politely.

"My dear, you cannot ride this road in the day. Come in for a cold drink." He pointed to a thatched-roof hut that served as the village community center and restaurant.

"If I don't make it to Nepal soon, the rains will come, and I'll again miss out on it," I said.

"My dear," he said after the smile left his wrinkled face, "you need to rest. You cannot go on under such a sun."

"Don't tell me what I can't do," I barked, hearing my control snap like dry twigs underfoot. I washed my mouth again with pump water, grabbed Angel away from the others, and rode away from the surprised faces without a good-bye.

Riding down the road with this hair-trigger hot-headed attitude, and stopping at every river or pump to cool myself down, each time being surrounded by males and their questions, my mind was turning over muddled thoughts. I could answer their questions without listening: my native country is the United States; I'm making an Indian tour by bicycle; these are gears; I'm not married, but will be when I get back; the bicycle cost 2000 rupees; I arrived here two weeks ago, and yes, I like your country. Some answers true; others only meant to appease. The same answers to the same questions.

I avoided stopping in the towns because I didn't want to be surrounded by people pounding me with questions. It was too hot to talk, and they annoyed me, both the people and their questions. Too many people; too many obstacles. Trucks and busses passed with hands waving, but I made no response; something dramatic would have to happen to change my attitude.

I traveled in this frame of mind for two days, until I was stopped short by something I saw in the distance: a flash of color, a group of women on the opposite side of the road. I thought it must be some kind of festival. The color of a group of women in saris is a striking sight. My curiosity perked me up, and I pedaled briskly to see what was going on.

I approached. The women stood behind a truck, and a few young girls were kneeling on the pavement in front of them. The men gathered in groups, talking. The women and children were making a noise, but I was too far away to tell what it was.

Strange. I couldn't make it out. I pedaled a bit faster to get a look at what I perceived as festivities, for God knows I needed a distraction. Then, upon approaching the group, as I slowed down, I was able to identify the sounds coming from the cluster of people.

Crying. A chill went through my hot body. Moaning and heart-wrenching wailing. Reaching the group, I saw a bloodied girl near the back tires of a truck that had just passed me. Flies had already gathered on her still form.

My eyes turned away quickly. I pedaled relentlessly until I cleared the town, then I gagged. I wiped my eyes with pieces of napkin I had in the pockets of my jersey, just to see the stretch of road before me.

The women cried in profound grief, an anguish which brought my senses in line with reality.

That evening I rode into the Indian equivalent of a truck stop. The owner and his sons tried to welcome me and make me feel comfortable. Their food wasn't loaded with spice, so I was able to force down a meal. The father cooked, and his sons brought tin water cups and generous helpings of yellow rice and diced vegetables. I wanted to continue riding in the relative cool of the night, but my body rebelled, so I stayed and tried to get some sleep on one of the dozen burlap cots that lined the road.

The truckers came in with their assistants, usually relatives who tell the driver if it's clear behind him, jump out and pay the road taxes along the way, and provide companionship. They came in, put river water in their radiators, ate dinner, and slept near me on the open cots that lined the shoulder of the road. Hearing them through the night kept me in that space between sleeping and waking, but I was too exhausted to move down the road and set up my tent for deeper sleep. Too hot to sleep, eat, or move; I just lay on the end cot yearning to go up the steep roads to the cooler mountains, and I couldn't get either the tiny form of that dead girl or my hateful disposition out of my mind.

After the tragedy, when people approached me, I looked them in the eye, humbled, and answered their questions, one after another, about my native country, my bicycle, and my trip. I took men to tea and gave money to those who asked, and it leveled me to realize that I needed such an incident to snap me out of my ill temper.

Going the most direct way to Nepal, I got back on the National Highway, a small paved road where two meeting trucks would have their outside wheels on the dirt. Of course they would be madly screeching their horns, but they do that with or without seeing anything ahead of them. The road had its share of traffic: water buffalo, cattle, goats, ox carts, walkers, bicyclists, busses, trucks, and an occasional car. The road passed through towns lined with stands.

India remains a specialty market, for although the big cities have large stores, most people specialize. On top of a cart a man squats on the balls of his feet and sells bananas, while another deals only in mangoes; one boy pushes a metal ice wagon selling cold tap water for less than a cent a glass, another sells herbs, another sells juice, or cold drinks, or padlocks, or fabric, or tea, or bicycle parts. The bigger towns have stores, and they too specialize, but all cities have an ample supply of outdoor vendors who make their living off pennies earned.

Then there are the restaurants, often called hotels. Fancy ones only exist in the big cities, while even the smallest village has at least one straw-roof shack that has two old wooden tables and four benches on a dirt floor. Someone cooks the food over an open flame in the back room, and they serve a daily menu of three or four dishes. People come in, wash their right hand, mix their food up on their plates, and dig in. A complete meal of rice, dahl, and vegetables costs as little as twenty-five cents.

About a week after leaving Delhi, I made it to Nepal. It had been a struggle which had taken a lot out of me.

The town at the Nepali/Indian border hasn't made it on the map, but it was a wildly lively place, like the hustling foreign street scenes popular in old movies. The locals on both sides of the border were trying to sell soft drinks and ice creams to travelers, offering taxi rides, bus rides, rickshaw rides, trying to get people to stay in their dollar-a-night hotels, and offering to carry bags for a dime, trunks for a quarter, and tourists for a negotiable fee — anything to anywhere. In the midst of this frenzied activity were travelers from all countries — prominently, a Czechoslovakian mountaineering team with a large truck of equipment and an Australian continental trucking expedition — but I also saw plenty of trekkers, rafters, hang gliders, backpackers, teachers, and an anthropologist. I was the only bicyclist, and out of force of habit I drilled the people leaving Nepal about road conditions.

Immediately after receiving another stamp in my crowded passport, I rode a few miles to Lumbini to see the Asoka pillar marking the Buddha's historical birthplace. Asoka, the third century B.C. ruler who conquered northern India, Pakistan, and Afghanistan, had a spiritual awakening after he personally led an invasion of a small country. He saw the suffering caused by war, permanently renounced armed conquest, and took up the moral tenets of Buddhism. He granted religious freedom, preached a positive doctrine of personal growth, and inscribed many of his teachings on pillars such as the one at Lumbini. Asoka even established a branch of government to do good works among the common people, and through him and his respect for all life, animal and human, the teachings of Buddhism ceased being a doctrine of a little-known sect and flowered across and beyond his kingdom, becoming a major religion. Like all heroes, he has been semi-mythologized, but he has been an example to me of what is possible. Seeing the actual pillar he built, as well as being with the monks who lived on the site, raised my spirits.

At the base of the mountains, just before the "Hill Road Begins" sign, a woman selling cold drinks called me over for a glass.

"You need to regain some energy," she said in fluent English with the standard Asian sing-song.

It was obvious that my weariness and fatigue showed; I'd been months on the road, probably too long, but the last few days in the violent heat wave had drained me more than all the months put together.

"What is the road like up ahead?"

Without asking what I wanted to drink, she smiled and opened a bottle of soda that had been sitting under a block of ice in an old metal Coca Cola case that looked as if it belonged in an American gas station during the 1930s.

"It is not possible to take the road by cycle," she said. "It is very difficult."

Of course it's possible. If it's possible to go a mile on a bicycle, it's possible to go a thousand miles. If it's possible to go up one short hill, it's possible to go up a hundred steep hills. You pedal one foot, then the other foot. You ride one mile, then the next mile. It's only not possible when you can't begin, and you can't begin if you only do what you've done before, whether it's waking up an hour early or bicycling around the world.

"I'll try," I said.

She smiled back, and we made casual conversation about the heat. I drank the cool drink, thanked her, and left, only to look back and suddenly realize that this was the first native woman I had talked to since leaving Delhi. In India strange men are not allowed to talk to village women. If a man invited me to his home I could talk to women in the house, but usually women moved away from me.

The first peaks after the "Hill Road" sign were small, not more than 6000 feet, but I felt immediate relief from the choking heat. It's a tremendous sight: miles and miles of completely flat land — nothing higher than an ant hill — and suddenly these mountains loom ahead. On the Indian side they are pale and barren, but the north side is rich in forests, rivers, exotic plants, and colorful birds.

After a hundred miles of up-and-down road, I looked below at the Pokhara Valley and got my first sight of the giant peaks off in the distance: Annapurna, Dhaluagiri, and Machhapuchare. Standing quietly so far away, no one could take those jagged white cones seriously. Trekkers on their way to the bases of those giants in the western part of Nepal leave from Pokhara, while those going to Everest leave from Kathmandu.

Pokhara saved me. After spending a couple of days in a small hotel luxuriating in intense sleep, I casually strolled around the town talking to tourists and recovering from India's heat and my irascibility. I rarely get to see tourists when I travel, but Pokhara had no shortage of other travelers, mostly young people from Europe and Australia with backpacks, who flock there in search of either a spiritual awakening, a social understanding, an experience in natural beauty, or the adventure of climbing the trails.

After taking a curvy river road from quiet Pokhara to hectic Kathmandu, I replaced my touring tires with trail tires and changed the positions of my panniers. When going up mountains I like to have most of the weight on the front wheel, while on flats I keep my bags behind. The back tire takes most of my body weight. When back loaded, I go through three back tires for every front one.

The day after leaving Kathmandu the rear hub had to be replaced by the cycle mechanic, translator, and half the town of Dhulikel, and in the afternoon I bicycled at a leisurely pace towards Tibet, passing a variety of wooden temples and kids who clasp their hands in a prayer position and say "namaste" (greetings) and then extend their hands for "baksheesh" (alms). Nepal is a unique mixture of Hindu and Buddhist. As I traveled closer to Tibet, the people changed physically from dark Indo-Europeans to Mongolians and religiously from Hindu to Buddhist. The Nepalis have blended the two religions, and foreigners find it difficult to distinguish Buddhist temples from Hindu.

The main road, a surprisingly easy one to ride since it followed two of Nepal's many rivers, went through a village every ten miles, but I occasionally detoured up the hilly trails to more remote villages, or found a scenic spot and spent hours watching the powerful jagged white peaks looming ahead, still miles away. From the brown hills around me grew a wealth of green vegetation and an array of variegated blossoms. Birds streaked with striking colors flew from tree to tree — crimson, copper, indigo — their colors contrasting with the faded villages that were limited to shades of brown.

I came to Baradisi near the Tibetan border and then took a trail east, toward the bases of the mighty mountains. I had planned to go to Thami and Namche near the sacred mountain of Khumbila, not far from the starting point of Everest expeditions, but the road was getting too rough. Afternoon rain turned it to mud, forcing me to walk Angel just about all the time. I almost wished I hadn't brought it, but on the other hand the local people wouldn't have treated me so well. There's something seemingly magical about a lone bicyclist arriving at a 12,000 foot village: it unquestionably elicits hospitality.

So close was I that I felt that if I had a rope I could have lassoed the mountains I spent so long trying to reach. The sound of avalanches bounced off them. It was a bad year for climbers: several had died from avalanches that year. People said the climate changes were caused by deforestation.

The afternoon rain came down briskly when I arrived in a town on the crest of the road. The only man outside stopped what he was doing and looked up at me for a moment, as if to make sense of the sight before him, then motioned me into the town cafe. I entered and sat down. A few men sat around talking and joking, and although I understood nothing, I knew that they talked about what all men talk about in cafes. The woman who ran the place put a hard-boiled egg and a cup of tea in front of me. A child crawled around the floor finding things to put in his mouth, occasionally using a table leg to pull himself up. The mother, the one who served me, bent down and calmly took things out of his mouth.

The men made conversation with me through a person who spoke English. "What is America like?" one asked.

A fair question for which I have never had a good answer, especially in places where the life-style seems so different from that in the U.S. Try describing elevators, garbage disposals, and credit cards in Pidgin English.

"America is a big country," I said looking around, trying to regain a picture of a forgotten land. "Life there is like life here: people work, eat, have families, and live in towns."

The men nodded, but I felt dissatisfied with the answer and added, "America is a rich country. People work hard, drive automobiles, fly in airplanes, and live in big houses, but our people are the same as your people. They want good things for their children."

What would you say?

"What food do Americans eat?" another person asked through the translator.

I looked around at the eager faces. "People eat eggs and rice and potatoes and vegetables. Most people eat animals."

The differences that at one time seemed huge shrank under the similarities of a common life. I wandered around the countryside alone, thinking about the similarities. I camped in various spots away from civilization, and did what I had come to Nepal to do: look at and listen to the mountains and the sky and the birds and the trees and the rivers and the teeming earth. To feel a manless, idealess, emotionless, and beautiful place.

After riding and walking further into the mountains, I stopped near a river in a valley to scrape mud from my bicycle. Half a dozen Tibetan kids came out of the brush and stood around watching. All had running noses and coughs. I don't know what sickness they had; it seemed more than a round of colds, but I didn't have anything that would help them. I had begun the trip with plenty of first aid material, replacing items along the way. But all I had left were two bandaids and iodine. Maybe the sickness the kids had was nothing — they certainly didn't act sick, jumping and playing with each other — but my intuition told me otherwise.

They led me to the man who ran the village restaurant on the main road, and he offered the hospitality of his house, insisting I stay for the night. I planned on pitching my tent near the white water river and sleeping alone next to its roar, but several people had gathered in the restaurant and joined in welcoming me to their village, making it impossible for me to turn down such hospitality. There friendliness and close community spirit made me feel like one of them, and I treated their offer as a privilege, even though I knew that outside the safety of my tent I would be eaten by mosquitoes.

The children crowded outside the restaurant to stare at the lone foreigner who was surrounded by their elders.

"No have friend?" one man asked.

I looked up at eyes all turned on me, dark almond eyes inside delicate-featured faces which expressed both rural simplicity and parental concern.

Using plenty of hand motions I acted my way through: "I could not find anyone else crazy enough to come with me."

I laughed, and they all laughed with me, bringing the issue to a comfortable end. Laughing came easily to them. I must have presented a humorous figure, bedraggled and slightly crazed. Many also felt sorry for me since I traveled by bicycle instead of on the back of a truck, but the tone of their voices expressed no sorrow.

When the last orange rays of dusk left the valley and gave way to a dark sky, the dim light of candles, paraffin lamps, and a few flashlights allowed the men and women to finish cleaning the dishes with the water sitting in the heavy earthen jugs. Then the horde of running children became quiet and left us alone with the sound of the river. I had exhausted my few words of Nepali and the village's educated man had spent his meager English, leaving us running on sign language. My host then took me up a ladder, worn smooth from decades of climbing, to the sleeping quarters. Using gestures and recycled foreign words, he showed me a place to sleep on a rickety balcony that overlooked the village compound and the suspended footbridge that swayed across the river. Three old wooden houses lined the opposite bank while the main part of the village consisted of a half dozen two-story wooden structures that had neither windows nor doors.

A baby cried intermittently from the next house, and when its cry stopped, it gave way to the eternal thunder of the river. A small moon lit up the village; all I saw from the balcony was the dirt street and the old houses. I couldn't see the river, but I heard it constantly, nurturing my thoughts, mingling with my thoughts, drowning out my thoughts.

I laid out my bed roll, just as they were doing inside the house. One person slept on the other end of the balcony, and six or seven people were inside the open doorway near my feet. I slept in some of my clothes, just as they were doing. We became united in a common experience.

They had no money, no education, no health care, no home conveniences. It was the type of place where I left Angel with its fancy gear out of my sight for as long as I wanted and knew that no one would touch it. I use nothing but the best equipment. One of the lenses of my camera would cost more than the entire village.

Whose values are askew, ours or theirs? I touched the weather-beaten wood rail and looked through the window of the crying baby's house. The mother tried to quiet her child.

It was not much of a place, just the typical anonymous frame-built village having nothing more than necessary for eating and sleeping. There were no toilets or stoves; people cooked over a clay oven using bits of gathered wood. They washed in the gray rocky river whose roar echoed in the mountains, and drank the water from one of the many streams that feed into the river. Women brought the water to the village in buckets on their heads.

They grew grains on terraced mountains near the village, carried the harvest on their backs, and either spread it on the road so that trucks, busses, and ox carts would separate the grain from the chaff every time they drove over the yellow heaps, or they beat the grain on rocks. The mixture would then be sifted on flat wicker baskets over their heads. The operation involved the entire community.

There was plenty of food, plenty of water, and no need to modify tradition.

The baby's cries disturbed my peace and kept me thinking. My trip was scheduled to end in a couple of months, and with it this world I was now so much a part of. The rush of the river remained a dominant force in my mind. For the people I've met here, the trip had no end. From birth to death they lived on a constant camping trip, a motionless, changeless group experience, a communal arrangement that began at least eight thousand years ago and was not scheduled to end until outside forces interfered.

A truck roared up the hill. Unusual. Most trucks only travel the mountain roads during the day. I heard its whining die into the rush of the river. The baby wailed again while everyone around me seemed peacefully asleep. Privacy is a concept unknown here. No walls, fences, or room dividers. No having one's own nook or cranny. Intimacy is public. Someone's values are askew.

I had been ready to get back and talk about the experience of riding mountains, but this village gave me something more important than a subject for conversation: real people who seemed to accept nature and lived humanely in the middle of giant mountains.

A jet intruded high overhead, its sound faint over the sound of the river. Many villagers have no more than the clothes they wear. I rubbed my tired eyes, but my mind wouldn't let me sleep, probably because of the mosquitoes buzzing around my head. I felt overwhelmed by recollections of their kindness to me. It seemed nothing out of the ordinary for them to accept me unquestioningly.

Reaching into one of my pockets on the back of my orange jersey that I was using for a pillow, I felt my cycle computer and pushed the button to tell me the time, then pushed the button for the light. I felt some crumbled napkins near the computer. I pushed the button for miles traveled and again pressed the light button. Damn good computer, tells me everything I need to know. I put the computer back and felt for the crumbled napkins. My bottled up emotions let go. I laid on my back reliving my experience in Africa and South America and the Middle East while listening to the sound of the river wobbling up and down against the shore.

When I get back, I'll have to tell people about this great adventure. I probably won't be able to describe these people and their spirit of unity. I'll speak in clichés, talking about majestic mountains instead of hospitality, about solitary adventure rather than the identity of villagers as human beings.

The baby cried, and I found myself worrying about him; the river's white water rush, echoing in the mountains, never abated. I tossed this way and that, and finally slept, waking to the sound of sweeping. I looked down at graceful women in colored saris bending double, cleaning the dirt street with hand brooms made from twigs.

I stayed in other villages and got to know people. The mountains were there, but their presence no longer dominated my thoughts. I listened instead to the sounds of children and men and women. They talked and I listened and we enjoyed each other.

Finally, the day came when it rained hard, and the men talked about its being the real beginning of the rains, meaning snow at high altitudes. It was much later this year than it usually is. Everyone knew that it was time for me to go, so without ceremony I took the road down to Baradisi and then back to Kathmandu, where I changed to touring tires, adjusted the brakes and derailleurs, and headed on the paved roads across to Darjeeling and then down to Calcutta, always looking back until I could see nothing but flat hot earth.

Chinese in a Bad Tone

In the afternoon I turned off the paved road into an open area. A six foot by six foot wooden shack that was used as a snack shop stood twenty yards from the road. When the three young men inside saw me, they stood up and moved close to the counter of the shack. They all wore loose, knee-length shorts and short-sleeve shirts with wide arms, making their bodies look even more slender than they were. I smiled and said hello by slightly bowing my back, then took out my water bottle and put it to my lips while tilting my head back to indicate that I wanted water. Understanding immediately, one of the fellows came out of the shack, took my plastic bottle, and filled it from a pump on the side of the shack. I bowed again in thanks and sat down on a rock under a nearby tree to drink and relax.

I had completely given up on my phrase sheet a short time after I crossed the border into China from Hong Kong.

A few other men in the area came over and joined the people from the shack. They stood four or five yards from the bicycle and looked at it, discussing among themselves the curve of the handlebar and the workings of the drive train. One of the men came over to me, pointed to the handlebar, then put his hand on his lower back and hunched over to indicate a back ache, meaning that using a dropped handlebar must hurt. I shook my head and tried to show what the position was like by getting up and sitting down while remaining bent. Another man pointed to the rear derailleur. I stood up and walked over to the bicycle. The group, which had grown to about ten, came slightly closer. I shifted both derailleurs while picking up the rear wheel and turning the cranks, pointing to the chain changing gears. They stood with their heads forward and their hands behind their backs, making sounds of understanding.

A couple of people tried to ask me questions in their language. I guessed it was about where I was from and where I was going. I pulled out the map I had in the front map case and showed them where I was going, but the names of towns were all in the Latin alphabet. They had no idea that the map had anything to do with their country; I could just as well have shown them a picture of the Irish countryside. But one man took my map, and they began a brief discussion. I pointed to one of the roads on the map and indicated that it was the road running in front of us. They tried to follow what I was saying.

Another man wearing a loose unbuttoned shirt was desperately trying to ask me a question. He asked in his language several times, using a different vocabulary each time. He asked with his hands and his face, making a wide number of gestures. I smiled and shrugged my shoulders to indicate incomprehension. He became more animated. I still couldn't understand. Finally, he grabbed a stick, squatted over the earth, and began drawing Chinese characters in the dirt. This time he was sure I would understand, for although there are several Chinese languages and dialects, the written language is standard.

Triumphantly, he looked up at my face expecting an answer to his question. A moment of silence followed. The smile slowly slid off his mouth and hit the dirt when his eyes met my expression of non-comprehension. The men around began to laugh at the scene. I took the man's elbow and brought him to his feet. We walked over to the store where a large jar of red drink sat on the counter. One of the shopkeepers came over. I pointed to the jar and put up two fingers, one glass for him and one for me. From my handlebar bag I brought out a pamphlet written in English and showed it to him, indicating that this was the way we write in my language. He looked puzzled, but when we sat down together and began drinking what tasted like a berry juice, his need to have his question answered disappeared.

Since the government of Burma does not allow foreigners on their roads, I had to fly from Calcutta to Thailand. I landed in the Bangkok airport dreadfully worn out, physically as well as mentally. I had spent eight continuous months on the road, mostly in impoverished countries, day after day of riding into a new village, of meeting new people, of exciting times as well as frustrating times. From the ride through India and Nepal I had contracted various diseases. All but one went away; I was left with miliaria, a debilitating fever and rash caused by exerting myself in the infernal heat. I felt awful. At night my back became full of sores that no amount of scratching relieved.

I bicycled fifty miles out of Bangkok, past the noisy mass of traffic until I reached quieter roads, then realized that I didn't have the energy to tour both Thailand and China. The heat and humidity was almost as acute as it was in northern India. I returned to the airport and took the next plane to Hong Kong.

After putting my bicycle together at Hong Kong airport, I bicycled the busy streets to the central district. The material opulence of the city stood as a naked contrast to the material emptiness of parts of Africa and Asia and Latin America where electricity and running water are unknown, where shoes are scarce, where if it was too long after harvest people hungered.

Along Hong Kong's streets are shops side by side selling Nikon cameras, Apple computers, Seiko watches, 1000-year-old eggs, Asian jade, Arabian silk, Russian mink, African ivory, Sony radios, Hammond organs, Korean VCRs. Between them, with not an inch of free space, are white tablecloth restaurants, hamburger parlors, massage parlors, hotels, supermarkets, fruit stands, money-changers, herbalists. I rode down the street scratching my head in bewilderment at this crowded overabundance which had naturally combined with a crude form of consumerism.

Inside a skyscraper the China tourist office gave me a visa, but they were sure that the authorities wouldn't allow me to bicycle between cities. In 1980 I had applied to the governments of China and the Soviet Union to bicycle alone through their countries. The Soviet Union gave me a flat no. China said I could join one of the organized bicycle tours that had begun shortly after the United States and China opened diplomatic relations. I could neither bring myself to ride with a group nor afford the exorbitant cost of such a trip. In the three years that followed, China became more open, and I thought I would try my luck at the border.

The morning after getting the visa I began my climb to the Chinese border, through what are called the New Territories, winding my way through a series of towns along the coast of the Pearl River delta. Evidence of Westernization faded as I left the greater Hong Kong area. Instead of surgically clean shops selling the latest electronic fad, people haggled over fruits and vegetables in litter-filled outdoor markets. Instead of metal and glass high rises, I found a series of eight-story poured concrete apartment buildings. Outside each window a pole sticking straight out was suspended for drying clothes, row after row of underwear hanging where a flag might have been. As I rode further out of the population areas, single or double story homes replaced the apartment buildings. The congested city traffic ended, giving way to miles of open farmland and hills.

Two miles from the border I stopped at a checkpoint and proudly showed the guards my visa. They told me that I needed another permit to cross the border by road, advising me instead to take a train over the border.

I spent the evening in a seedy hotel near the train station, turning the dial on the TV to *Love Boat*, *Gilligan's Island*, and wrestling from Oakland, California. That night I felt seriously ill, but the next morning I joined the rush hour throng at the local train station. The train authorities had a rule against taking aboard a bicycle, but the young station manager, who was summoned over for his advice, sympathized with me and wrote out a luggage tag.

"You're carrying luggage on it," he said justifying his action. "If you carry it aboard like suitcase, it doesn't violate the rule."

The other employees felt relieved at the way the manager was able to turn corners around the rules. I could see that no one wanted to stop me from taking the train. Two stops later, I walked Angel up and down stairs and through the various official departments inside the large windowless station which housed the two countries' border facilities. I was the only non-Chinese in the chaotic atmosphere. At one end of the station, where everyone else was boarding another train to Kwangchow, I spotted sunlight around a door and walked out onto the street to begin bicycling, expecting that the authorities might stop me at any time.

I was immediately struck with the feeling of a city being built. Cinder-block high-rise apartments dominated the center of the city around the railroad station. Cranes stood over the skyline, constructing more such buildings. All the streets were newly paved and wide; the main streets were built for eight lanes while the smallest city streets could accommodate four. In the center of major intersections, policemen sat inside round concrete cubicles ready to direct traffic, but only a few trucks and almost no cars could be seen. Concrete was poured for parks where people were expected to sit on concrete benches around a few planted trees.

What impressed me most was the number of people riding heavy black bicycles; hundreds of men and women bicycled in neat rows on the right side of the streets. Other people walked on the concrete sidewalks. There were few shops.

Merging with the flow of bicycles, I followed my compass west, arriving at a major intersection. Unlike Hong Kong, the few road signs were only in Chinese. I looked at my phrase sheet which I had kept with the map. "Where is the road to Kwangchow?" I repeated it to myself until I was ready to try it on a group of young people standing at the intersection. They wore casual inexpensive Western clothes. I coughed to get their attention, then proceeded with the question. They laughed among themselves embarrassedly, afraid to look directly at me, making signs of incomprehension with their hands. I repeated the phrase twice, slowly, pronouncing each syllable as it was written in the phonetic translation. They looked at each other and smiled. "Kwangchow, Kwangchow," I repeated, pointing down each road. More embarrassed smiles. I showed them the phrase sheet which also had Chinese characters.

"Ah, Kwangchow," they said in unison.

"Yes," I said, "Kwangchow."

"Kwangchow," they said again, "Kwangchow." One young man pointed me to another road and made hand signs for me to turn left. I said the phrase word for thank you, but it only brought blank expressions, so I bowed from the neck and waved my hand.

After bicycling a few minutes on that road I came to another junction and was again unsure about the way to go. I approached the policeman who stood inside his concrete cubicle. Curiosity brought over six other bicyclists. "Which is the road to Kwangchow?" I asked. Same response. I showed him the Chinese characters.

"Ah, Kwangchow," he said, and the other bicyclists repeated the policeman's words.

"Yes, that's what I said, Kwangchow."

"Kwangchow," he said again as if he was correcting me. He pointed down the street, rolling his finger in a spiral to indicate that it was a long way off.

Apart from the few police who directed traffic, no guards or military were visible along the route, so I continued. The road passed villages and farms well irrigated by the vast river delta. The houses were modest, two or three rooms. People were busy with the land, planting and harvesting by hand. Rows of women wearing loose trousers, light-colored blouses, and large straw hats, were bent over in the fields, slowly working their way from end to end, digging, cutting, tying. They used oxen and buffalo to help carry loads. I bicycled slowly over the hot green earth, stopping often to rest. Unlike India, most people left me alone, although they studied me at a distance.

Toward late afternoon, the number of walkers and bicyclists increased, a sign of a large town. I guessed by my map that it must be Dongguan. When I arrived at the town proper, I decided to again try my phrases on another group of young men standing at the corner. I had practiced to myself until I knew the words without looking at the sheet. "Where is a hotel?" I asked. Everyone looked shyly at each other. I tried again, still no response. I showed them the Chinese. They repeated the same words I spoke. I said something in English. They laughed, timidly.

Two boys made signs for me to follow them. They got on their black bicycles and accompanied me around the busy streets of the city for a mile. After we bicycled on a street where people sold fruits and vegetables on outside tables, we came to an elegant new hotel that sat like a massive monument above the earth. I never stay at hotels like that, I said to myself. Not only are they ugly, sterile, and expensive, but they are exactly what I wanted to get away from.

This feeling had been reaffirmed toward the end of the previous trip when I had been intending to fly from Madras to Malaysia. In the push-shove chaos at the check-in counter a dozen people, including me, were bumped from the flight. The airline put us up for three days in what people call an elegant hotel that had a swimming pool, air conditioning, and five restaurants that charged ten times (no exaggeration) what the neighborhood restaurants charged for a meal. Around the corner men, women, families sat begging on the street, living in mud hovels which they erected on the sidewalk, surviving only a step away from death.

Although Dongguan didn't have people living in such poverty, I didn't want the same situation, to stay in a hotel that sat like a fortress, pretending that it stood in Florida or Bavaria rather than China. To make it picturesque, its architecture had an undercurrent of classical Chinese, as if it were a novelty, just as Londoners might put on their mantle a Chinese vase for decoration. Yet, with my communication problems, and because I was feeling physically worse, I didn't have the resolve to look for something else. Asking for accommodation was out of the question. I thanked the two boys who brought me and found a room in the hotel. A Chinese couple and I seemed to be the only people in the 200-room complex.

One of the clerks spoke some English, though at first I couldn't understand what he was saying. I think he was able to read the fatigue on my face.

"I've been too many months on the road," I told him.

He and another clerk helped me carry Angel to my room, then at dusk he returned to take me to the large, two-story garden restaurant. Like the hotel, there wasn't a soul there, although at least a hundred tables had full place settings on them. Two young ladies took me, the only customer in the enormous building, up stairs and sat me at a table for eight, the only table without place settings. Six other young ladies in uniforms stood around a service counter whispering and shyly laughing among themselves.

"Dongguan Hotel new," said the clerk as he sat down with me. "Visitor come later."

Two of the women came over, laid an elegant European place setting — three plates and six pieces of ornate silverware — then quietly ran back to their other four companions. The clerk said it was forbidden for him to eat, but he was happy to sit with me and ask questions about America. Our conversation echoed throughout the restaurant.

"I had problems talking to people in your language," I said, producing my sheet of phrases.

He examined the sheet, then handed it back to me. The ladies at the front table were looking over curiously, but when I turned my head toward them, they looked down quickly, bashfully, and talked among themselves.

"Words are true for Mandarin," he said. "Not language here, but people understand. But in China words have tone.

China words have four tone. You say words in different tone, words have different understanding."

"Yes, of course," I said. "You have to use the correct pitch." I remembered reading the diary of a missionary in Southeast Asia who had constant problems with pitch. A word he spoke in one pitch had no resemblance to the same word spoken in a higher or lower pitch.

"China language like singing song," said my friend. I asked him how to say the names of towns in the area while I marked the pitch over each syllable. I thought that if I could say those names in the proper tone, I would be able to point down the road and ask if I was going the right direction. After a good deal of coaching, and plenty of hand over mouth laughing from the ladies around the serving counter, I got to the point where the clerk approved of the way I said each name.

At night my body felt worse. In addition to the rash which erupted with bubbles of water under my skin, I was tired of not having a home, a base, a place of my own, of having to exert physical and emotional energy day after day, of riding all day and having to be sociable as soon as I got off the bicycle. The next morning I woke exhausted, sweating. My usually voracious appetite had disappeared. I forced myself to the outdoor market. At the first stand I selected a few pieces of fruit from an honest-looking woman's table, then held out a handful of paper money. She chose the ones she needed, and I began bicycling slowly west, making sure not to overtax myself.

At the first fork in the road I approached a man standing at the corner and said, "Kwangchow?" then pointed at the two roads. It gave me a proud feeling when he raised his hand to the left road. A short time later someone else directed me to a ferry that I needed to take over the wide river which was alive with activity. Our metal barge slipped through the brown water among junks and wooden house boats and fishing boats. Men stood and poled some of the boats; others flowed with the current; several had loud motors which conflicted with the serenity of the river scene.

On the opposite shore I continued bicycling on the flat land. Gradually the number of bicycles around me increased. The countryside ended, and the big city began with its cheaply constructed high rises and well-paved roads. We bicycles had special lanes, while the small amount of traffic, mostly public transportation, used the rest of the road. Traffic lights and policemen stood at major intersections. The new streets were three times as wide as they needed to be, but the old streets in the central part of the city were tight. Everyone looked at me; many smiled or nodded their heads, but no one tried to engage me in conversation.

I stopped at a corner where a man and woman cooked in a large wok heated by propane. They worked in a permanent tent-like structure and served people who sat on stools placed on the sidewalk. The owner greeted me eagerly, indicating that he was going to make something special for me. I leaned Angel on a nearby telephone pole and sat down for a hot meal, although I had no appetite. In a minute people gathered around my bicycle and began inspecting it. They stood or squatted a few feet from it, looking at the differences between Angel and their heavy single-gear bicycles. Although I was in a big city, I felt no need to keep an eye on Angel.

Shortly after I sat down, one man with a sincere face made signs for me to stand up so he could compare his height with mine. People around us joked at the foot and a half difference. Another man brought over a studious-looking woman with glasses who spoke English, so I could tell them where I'm from and explain about my bicycle.

"You only need wide tires on dirt roads," I said in answer to one man's question. "These thin wheels are as strong as yours but much lighter. The roads here are good and don't require fat tires."

"It has only happened recently that the roads have been made smooth," said the translator in good formal English. "We are building our country."

"Yes, I can see that China is concerned about its future," I said. "In the West the accent is on the present. Somewhere in the back of our minds is the idea that we're living in a temporary world that could end, will end, any time."

She didn't understand what I said. "America serves as a model for development," said a young man through the translator. "We want more production, more farms, more factories."

"I don't think you know what you're getting into," I said. "America has paid a high price for its economic development."

When she translated, two older men nodded their heads in agreement, but most didn't agree.

"Our goal is not capitalism," said the translator, her words well pronounced. "It is industrial development."

One of the old men said to her, and she translated to me, "If you have industrial development you will have moral decay."

There was more argument among them on this issue. Each person let the other finish before speaking. These people took these philosophical questions seriously, as if they had regular discussions on such crucial topics.

"From what I've seen China looks prosperous and well developed," I said. In my mind I compared it to India.

"This area is one of the most developed in China," responded the translator. "If you go to the east you will find the country much more poor."

When we had finished our conversation, the translator drew me a map to a budget hotel where the backpacker-type of travelers stay. I felt weak and exhausted, and rode there to rest in an almost empty dormitory of a large but unadorned old stone building.

I tried to recuperate for two days between outings to see the sights of the large city. My head felt feverish; my body sluggish. At night I couldn't sleep for the tormenting rash. Two days later I began riding west over flat earth covered with farms and villages. Every parcel of land was used. People tilled the soil, raised pigs, herded flocks of geese, sold vegetables by the side of the road, tended children. Everyone seemed engaged in some activity: walking, trotting, balancing a pole over the shoulder with wooden buckets of goods hanging from both ends, bicycling with loads on their rear racks and top struts.

I bicycled to Fatshan, Samshui, and toward Wuchow, impressed with the feeling of freedom and lack of authority. I bicycled slowly, stopping at almost every store or shack, hoping that the illness would pass. Illnesses on the road usually last a day or two, caused by eating or drinking something foul. I had drunk the water everywhere I went. But each day I felt my energy more drained until I was unable to carry on any longer. In all my bicycling I've had times when I had to rest for a day, but never before a time when I had to turn back.

I decided to return to Hong Kong while sitting for two hours in the shade of a large tree at the edge of a village. A couple of people came over to look at the bicycle. We tried to communicate by making hand gestures at each other. One of the villagers rode off on his bicycle and returned a few minutes later with a boy of about thirteen who greeted me in understandable English.

"I'm very tired," I told him.

"You need doctor?" he asked.

I realized that I must look sick. "I think I need rest," I said. "I've been riding many hours a day, drinking a variety of water and eating so many different foods."

In some places people have not the slightest idea of germs. Boys who serve food at restaurants in India bring around water by carrying the glasses from the top, putting their fingers in each glass.

He didn't understand most of what I said. "Perhaps you need medicine," he added.

Before I started I had taken all the recommended injections against diseases. "I want so much to go deeper into your country," I said. "I feel I haven't even started. But I think I'll have to do that on another trip."

He translated what I said. Another person with gray hair who had been sitting with me for an hour said something which was translated by the boy: "China always be here. You come back when you more better."

One of the men brought me a bowl of fried rice, and the others forced me to eat part of a yellow melon. I got up to leave, looked at my map and found different roads to return to Kwangchow, where I took the train back to capitalist Hong Kong, still feeling weak.

From Hong Kong I flew to Japan where it was slightly cooler. I stopped at the factory where Angel was made, fifty miles out of Tokyo, and they presented me with a new seat to replace my torn one and a small ceramic bicycle. Determined to see two temples of two different Zen sects, I pushed my body around the country for a week until my energy came to an absolute end. I flew to San Francisco. A few days in the cooler climate cured me of the fever and rash. When I was well I took Angel over the Golden Gate Bridge and stopped in the middle, high above the water. Cars and busses and trucks hurried back and forth, making the pavement tremble. I felt the wind tearing my hair and the sun warming my face. I looked over at the hills on both shores. It was a wonderful day for a cross-country ride.

Afterword:
Seventy Words for Water

The biggest obstacle facing travelers is not dishonest people or wild animals or bad roads; it is not disease or food or bad water or diverse languages. Problems make travel an adventure which can, depending on a mixture of the traveler's ability and attitude and luck, enrich the traveler's life. The biggest obstacle to travelers is governments.

Governments partially or completely close their countries to outsiders: either the officials make it difficult or impossible for travelers to enter, or they restrict the movement of travelers, forcing them to stay only in the major cities, allowing foreigners access to one or two roads.

In war-torn areas, officials may be genuinely concerned for the safety of travelers. Often the reasons for barring travelers are less obvious. Some countries consider foreign influences, such as dress and behavior, offensive. In their insensitivity to local customs and values, travelers have ruined or overrun many societies and their cultures. Closing or restricting border movements seems to be a prudent form of self-protection. Other countries want to select, choosing the travelers that please them, travelers that spend money or come from friendly nations.

However, the world does not belong to governments; it belongs to us, all of us.

I have two pleas, for travelers and for nations.

I see travelers, men and women, going into European churches wearing shorts and skimpy tops, even when posted signs ask people not to. This is culturally insensitive. If we as travelers think that the church-goers have hang-ups or need to be liberated, then we are imposing our cultural values, being what anthropologists call ethnocentric.

Prudent travelers try to discover the manners and sensibilities of others, whether they are traveling to Louisiana or Zaire, and try to behave within the other's social framework.

No one can dump all ideas and prejudices before beginning a trip. We usually don't realize what prejudices we carry with us. Rather, travel makes us generally more open to new cultural values, especially if we travel with an attitude of discovery.

I look forward to a world without frontiers, a world where we all can travel freely. I feel optimistic that such will be our world in the next century. This does not mean that I hope every country will be the same. I hate seeing fast food joints in foreign cities. But I feel it is important that we move away from the limiting idea of nationalism and think of ourselves as members — guests or patrons — of this entire planet.

My plea for open access to travelers is not particularly aimed at Burma or Albania because they won't allow foreigners. Western countries, where the concept of the nation-state evolved, have tremendous barriers to stop non-Westerners. I believe it is up to Europe, North America, Australia, and other industrialized countries to break down the barriers erected by a desire to protect their nations against foreigners. Our nationalism must give way and allow a greater internationalism to evolve. I believe it is up to Western countries to rise above the myths of advanced and backward people and nations, of superior and inferior, developed and undeveloped. At a time when the attitude of many is to close borders for self-protection, we have to realize that real protection comes with more openness and understanding.

Through travel with an open mind, we can, perhaps, evolve to a greater understanding of our planet as one place that belongs to all of us.

Other Books Available From Mills and Sanderson

The World Up Close: A Cyclist's Adventures on Five Continents, by Kameel B. Nasr. Discover the essence of humanity through various cultures by vicariously wandering the world by bicycle. $9.95

The Alaska Traveler: Year 'Round Vacation Adventures for Everyone, by Steven C. Levi. With maps and cartoons, this is a unique insider's guide to gold panning, stalking big game, windsurfing, dogsledding, etc. $9.95

The Portugal Traveler: Great Sights and Hidden Treasures, by Barbara Radcliffe Rogers and Stillman Rogers. A companion to fascinating places to eat and sleep, festivals and other events as well as insider tips to enrich your visit. Includes city maps. $9.95

The Cruise Answer Book - 1989: A Comprehensive Guide to the Ships and Ports of the Americas, by Charlanne Fields Herring. The premier guide to the cruise ships, itineraries, ports-of-call, and shore adventures awaiting vacationers. $9.95

Sicilian Walks: Exploring the History and Culture of the Two Sicilies, by William J. Bonville. Self-guided tours (with maps) of Sicily and the adjacent Italian mainland. $9.95

Bedtime Teaching Tales for Kids: A Parent's Storybook, by Gary Ludvigson, Ph. D. Eighteen engrossing stories to help children 5-11 work through problems such as fear of failure, sibling rivalry, bullies, divorce, death, child abuse, handicaps,etc. $9.95

Your Food-Allergic Child: A Parent's Guide, by Janet E. Meizel. How to shop and cook for children with allergies, plus nutrient and chemical reference charts of common foods, medications, and grocery brands. $9.95

There ARE Babies to Adopt: A Resource Guide for Prospective Parents, by Christine A. Adamec. "Dispels the baby shortage myth and teems about the choices available."- *Parents Adoption Pipeline*. $16.95 (hardcover)

Winning Tactics for Women Over Forty: How to Take Charge of Your Life and Have Fun Doing It, by Anne De Sola Cardoza and Mavis B. Sutton. For women left alone through separation, divorce or death, "this title presents many positive, concrete options for change." - *The Midwest Book Review* $9.95

Fifty and Fired: How to Prepare for it - What to do When it Happens, by Ed Brandt with Leonard Corwen. How to deal with getting forcefully "restructured" out of your job at the wrong time in your career. $9.95 / $16.95 (hardcover)

Aquacises: Restoring and Maintaining Mobility with Water Exercises, by Miriam Study Giles. Despite age, obesity or physical handicaps, anyone can improve their fitness with this instructive illustrated handbook. $9.95

60-Second Shiatzu: How to Energize, Erase Pain, and Conquer Tension in One Minute, by Eva Shaw. A helpfully illustrated, quick-results introduction to do-it-yourself acupressure. $7.95

Your Astrological Guide to Fitness by Eva Shaw. Ideal exercises, sports, menus, and related gifts for those born under each sign of the zodiac. $9.95

Bachelor in the Kitchen: Beyond Bologna and Cheese, by Gordon Haskett with Wendy Haskett. Fast and easy ways to make delectable meals, snacks, drinks from easily obtainable ingredients. $7.95

Order Form

If you are unable to find our books in your local bookstore, you may order them directly from us. Please enclose check or money order for amount of purchase and add $1.00 per book handling charge.

( ) Levi / *The Alaska Traveler* $9.95 _____
( ) Rogers / *The Portugal Traveler* $9.95 _____
( ) Herring / *The Cruise Answer Book - 1989* $9.95 _____
( ) Bonville / *Sicilian Walks* $9.95 _____
( ) Ludvigson / *Bedtime Teaching Tales for Kids* $9.95 _____
( ) Meizel / *Your Food-Allergic Child* $9.95 _____
( ) Nasr / *The World Up Close* $9.95 _____
( ) Adamec / *There ARE Babies to Adopt* $16.95 (cloth) _____
( ) Cardoza/Sutton / *Winning Tactics for Women* $9.95 _____
( ) Brandt/Corwen / *Fifty and Fired* $16.95 (cloth) _____
( ) Brandt/Corwen / *Fifty and Fired* $9.95 (paper) _____
( ) Giles / *Aquacises* $9.95 _____
( ) Shaw / *60-Second Shiatzu* $7.95 _____
( ) Shaw / *Your Astrological Guide to Fitness* $9.95 _____
( ) Haskett / *Bachelor in the Kitchen* $7.95 _____

$1.00 per book handling charge _____
5% sales tax for MA residents _____

Total amount enclosed _____

Name: _____

Address: _____

City: _____ State: _____ Zip code: _____

Mail to: Mills & Sanderson, Publishers
442 Marrett Road, Suite 6
Lexington, MA 02173
617-861-0992

Our Toll-Free Order # is 1-800-441-6224